ROMAN CHESTER

City of the Eagles

DAVID J.P. MASON

TEMPUS

First published 2001

PUBLISHED IN THE UNITED KINGDOM BY:

Tempus Publishing Ltd
The Mill, Brimscombe Port
Stroud, Gloucestershire GL5 2QG
www.tempus-publishing.com

PUBLISHED IN THE UNITED STATES OF AMERICA BY:

Arcadia Publishing Inc.
A division of Tempus Publishing Inc.
2 Cumberland Street
Charleston, SC 29401
1-888-313-2665
www.arcadiapublishing.com

Tempus books are available in France and Germany
from the following addresses:

Tempus Publishing Group
21 Avenue de la République
37300 Joué-lès-Tours
FRANCE

Tempus Publishing Group
Gustav-Adolf-Straße 3
99084 Erfurt
GERMANY

British Library Cataloguing in Publication Data.
A catalogue record for this book is available from the British Library.

ISBN 0 7524 1922 6

Typesetting and origination by Tempus Publishing.
PRINTED AND BOUND IN GREAT BRITAIN

Contents

List of illustrations

Text figures

Colour plates

Tables

Acknowledgements

The author is extremely grateful to a number of institutions and individuals for agreeing to supply illustrations for this book; all retain copyright to their images unless otherwise stated.

Cheshire County Council (**17**).

Chester Archaeological Society (**3, 4, 5, 6, 7, 35, 36, 37, 38, 67, 114, 131 & 132**).

Chester City Council (**9, 15, 18, 19, 21, 23, 25, 27, 28, 30, 31, 34, 42, 43, 45, 51, 52, 55, 60, 61, 62, 66, 75, 78, 81, 83, 84, 86, 87, 97, 99, 101, 102, 103, 104, 105, 106, 107, 110, 111, 113, 116, 118, 119, 120, 121, 122, 123, 124, 125, 128, 129, 133, 134, 135, 136, 139, 140, 142, 143, 144 & 145; colour plates 7, 8, 9, 10, 11, 12, 13, 15, 19, 25, 27, 32, 33, 34, 35, 36 & 37**).

David Heke (**95**).

National Museum of Wales (**12**).

Society of Antiquaries of London (**91 & 92**).

The British Museum (**65**).

The photograph of the *retiarius* relief (**94**) is reproduced by kind permission of Saffron Walden Museum.

Building reconstructions:

Julian Baum (**colour plates 22 & 23**).

Julian Baum/David Mason (**colour plates 14, 16, 17, 18, 21, 28, 29, 30 & 31**).

S. Hurst (**colour plate 20**).

Timothy Morgan (**22, 50, 53, 64, 69, 77, 82, 88, 90, 127 & 138**).

David Swarbrick (**colour plate 27**; copyright Chester City Council)

Figural reconstruction paintings:

Clive Constable (**colour plates 1, 2 & 24** — reproduced by courtesy of Tim Strickland and the Deva Roman Centre Ltd. — **colour plates 3, 4, 5, 6 & 26** — reproduced by courtesy of Chester City Council).

Graham Sumner (**colour plate 9**; copyright Chester City Council).

All the other illustrations were drawn by the author or taken from his photographs.

*'Deva, Deva gaudeamus, vocibus et mentibus...'**

*The opening lines of the school song of Chester City Grammar School.
'*Deva*, *Deva* let us praise thee, with our voices and our thoughts . . . '

Preface

Growing up in a city so rich in historic buildings and ancient monuments as Chester, it was perhaps inevitable that I should develop a strong interest in the past at an early stage in my life. Furthermore, as that city stands on the site of the once great Roman legionary fortress of *Deva Victrix* it may have been equally inevitable that, having become an archaeologist, my specialisation should be Roman Archaeology. My choice of subject was also undoubtedly influenced by my earliest experiences of archaeological excavation in the late 1960s when I had the extreme good fortune to be allowed to participate not only in the exposure of the northern half of the amphitheatre but also in the investigation of major buildings at the heart of the legionary fortress on the Old Market Hall Site. The largest excavation ever to take place in Chester and with a multitude of exciting and fascinating discoveries, the latter was a heady and inspiring experience. Little could I know then that years later I would inherit the responsibility for writing the definitive reports on some of those buildings including the most puzzling structure of Roman Chester — the so-called Elliptical Building. The end of that first stage of my archaeological education was, however, tinged with considerable sadness as I witnessed the destruction of the imposing remains of more than one Roman building to make way for underground car-parks. At the time the grief and resentment I felt was largely personal, in the sense of having lost something I considered precious and very special, but later it came to encompass the loss suffered by the people of Chester and the visitors who came to the city in the hope of seeing something of its Roman heritage. The resolve to see more of Chester's Roman monuments not merely preserved but also displayed is something I feel just as strongly today as I did 30 years ago.

Despite their physical remains having long since been removed, information about the many buildings and structures destroyed in the 1960s and earlier has been preserved in the excavation archives of the city council's archaeology service 'Chester Archaeology'. Along with the results of the numerous excavations carried out since then, and the vast collection of artefacts they produced, these are being researched and the results published in a series of academic reports. The task is huge and progress slower than all concerned would like but Chester is achieving as much, if not more, in this direction than many other historic towns and cities with similar 'backlogs'; this despite the many other calls on the available resources. Its achievements in this direction would also have been severely curtailed if it had not been for the financial and other assistance of English Heritage.

Although much of the detailed research on the evidence has still to be completed, now seems an appropriate moment to take stock of advances in the knowledge and understanding of Roman Chester. These have been made as a consequence of the vast amount of new information which has accrued during the period of 40 years since the last overview of the subject appeared in print. An account which is intended to stimulate the interest of the knowledgeable lay reader as well as informing fellow professionals is not the place for detailed arguments and masses of data, and those who desire such are referred to the reports in the Chester Archaeology monograph series. The purpose of this work is to give an overall account of *Deva* during the three and a half centuries when she was home to one of the elite units of the Roman Army. It is the story not just of a place but also of the thousands of individual men — both soldiers and civilians — and their families who were the earliest generations of Cestrians.

An account such as this by its very nature draws heavily upon the work, thoughts, interpretations and theories of various individuals to whom the author is much indebted, especially in those cases where the results of excavations have been made available in advance of final publication. Responsibility for the ideas and suggestions herein proposed however, and for any factual inaccuracies, rests with the author. Individuals to whom I owe a particular debt of thanks in this regard are John Eames, Glenys Lloyd-Morgan, Dennis Petch, and Tim Strickland along with Peter Carrington, Keith Matthews and Simon Ward of Chester Archaeology and Dan Robinson of the Grosvenor Museum. I would also like to thank Mike Morris, Chester City Archaeologist, and Sharn Matthews, Museums Officer, for facilitating access to records in their care and also to Gill Dunn and Alison Jones of Chester Archaeology and to Moya O'Mullane of the Grosvenor Museum for their assistance in selecting suitable illustrations. I am also extremely grateful to Chester City Council, the Chester Archaeological Society, the British Museum, the National Museum of Wales, Saffron Walden Museum and the Society of Antiquaries of London for permission to reproduce images from their collections. The aerial photograph of the city shown here as (**17**) is reproduced by kind permission of Cheshire County Council. Imagining what Roman Chester actually looked like has been made far easier for the reader by the excellent reconstructions prepared by Clive Constable, S. Hurst, Tim Morgan, Cheryl Quinn, David Swarbrick (conventional) and by Julian Baum (computer-generated) to all of whom the author is much indebted. Additional thanks are owed to the last-named for the enormous help he has given the author with the preparation and reproduction of illustrations for this book. I am grateful to my wife Anne-Marie both for proof-reading the text and for her patience and tolerance while I have been absorbed in the preparation of this book. I also wish to express my sincere gratitude to Miss Elizabeth Hassall without whose encouragement and persistence I might never have embarked upon a career in Archaeology.

Last, but of course by no means least, I should like to convey my deepest thanks to Peter Kemmis Betty for commissioning this book and for giving me the opportunity to compile the account I have long wished to write.

1 The quest for Roman Chester

Roman Chester was essentially a military fortress, home for more than 300 years to an imperial legion, one of 30 such elite units in the Roman Army which, led by their eagle standards, won and held Rome's great empire. Chester, or *Deva* as it was then known, lay at the extreme north-west limit of the Empire with only *Hivernia* between it and the Northern Ocean. Thus, in the Roman imagination, it stood at the edge of the World. Then, as now, commerce also played an important part in the life of the community. A garrison town soon grew up beside the fortress, along with other substantial settlements in the hinterland, and economic activity was stimulated further by Chester's possession of a natural harbour. Five hundred years after Britain ceased to be a part of the Roman Empire in AD 410, the ruins of *Deva* were still impressive. Four centuries later still, however, there was little of Roman Chester left above ground apart from sections of the fortress defences which, on the north and east sides, had been incorporated into the walls of the medieval town. Much of the fabric of *Deva* had either collapsed or been deliberately dismantled in order to extract the ready-cut blocks of stone for reuse in new buildings and constructions. Thenceforth, the grandeur of Roman Chester was revealed solely by the chance discovery of buried remains or artefacts.

Although the area enclosed by the medieval town walls was nearly twice that of the fortress, it was the position of the surviving Roman defences that dictated the line they took. The enlargement of the defended area was achieved by the simple expedient of building extension walls down to the river from the south-east and north-west angles of the *castrum* and linking the two (**1**). Roman Chester also exerted an influence upon the development of its successor in other ways. Of these, the most obvious is the location of the main thoroughfares (**2**). Thus Bridge Street directly overlies the *via praetoria* of the fortress while Eastgate Street and Upper Watergate Street perpetuate the line of the eastern and western halves of the *via principalis* respectively. Similarly, Upper Northgate Street sits over the *via decumana* and the fact that its southern continuation does not meet Eastgate Street directly opposite Bridge Street reflects the arrangement of Roman buildings in the centre of the fortress. In addition, the outward continuations of all four of these streets overlie roads emanating from the fortress: Lower Watergate Street that running down to the harbour; Northgate Street that heading north up the Wirral; Foregate Street that heading towards Northwich; and Lower Bridge Street that running down to the Dee crossing and on ultimately to Whitchurch. Lesser streets also mark the positions of Roman precursors. Goss Street, for example, overlies the minor street which ran along the west side of the headquarters building while Godstall Lane perpetuates that which separated the legate's palace from a group of barracks to the east. Hamilton Place, Pierpoint Lane, Whitefriars, Weaver Street and Trinity Street are just a few of the others.

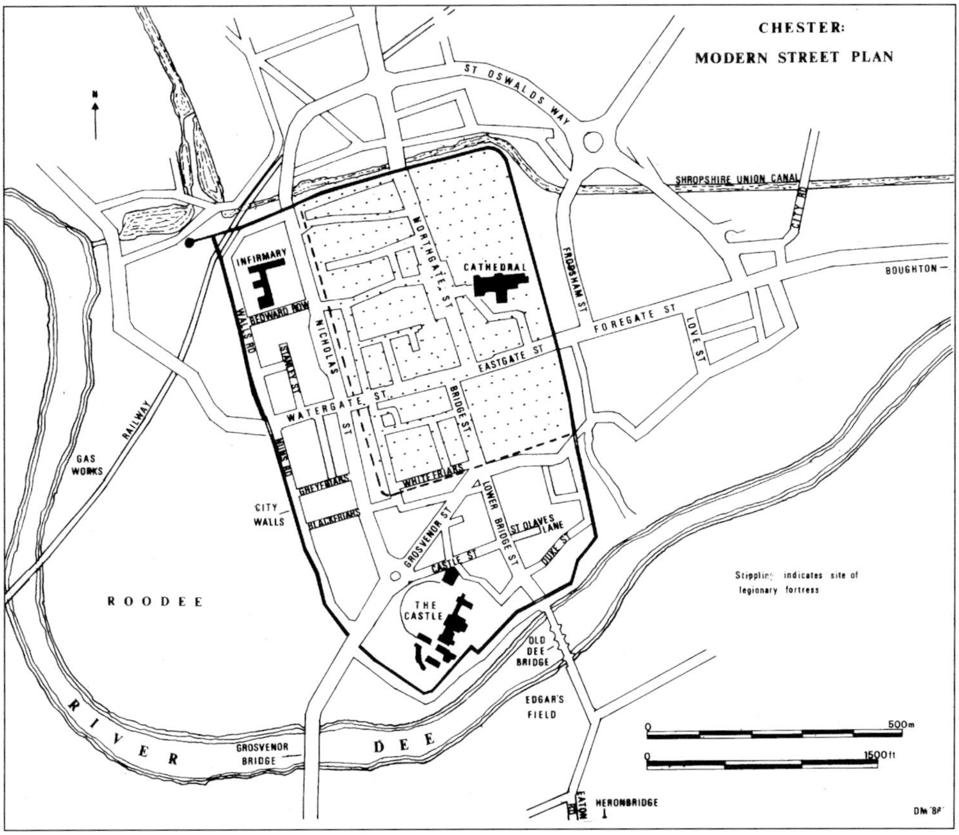

1 *Map of Chester and environs*

The ruins of *Deva* were also responsible, at least in part, for what is arguably Chester's most distinctive feature — the 'Rows' — a continuous covered walkway at first-floor level linking properties along the frontages of the main streets and which has resulted in the development of two tiers of shops.

The precise date and origins of the Rows have still to be elucidated but it is clear the system was already under development by the early thirteenth century. The ground behind Row properties is the same level as the first floor walkway and is thus generally 9ft (3.3m) higher than at the street frontage. This has come about because of the differential clearance of the ruins of Roman buildings. These were removed along the frontages of the main streets because such areas were the most sought after as building plots in the medieval town where the majority of the inhabitants made their living through commerce. To the rear, however, the debris resultant from the collapse and/or robbing of Roman structures, which could be up to 5ft (1.5m) thick, was left untouched and was in fact supplemented over the centuries by rubbish and building materials discarded by the residents of the street frontage properties. In certain areas, this process was accentuated by the fact that the Roman buildings were themselves higher than the streets beside them,

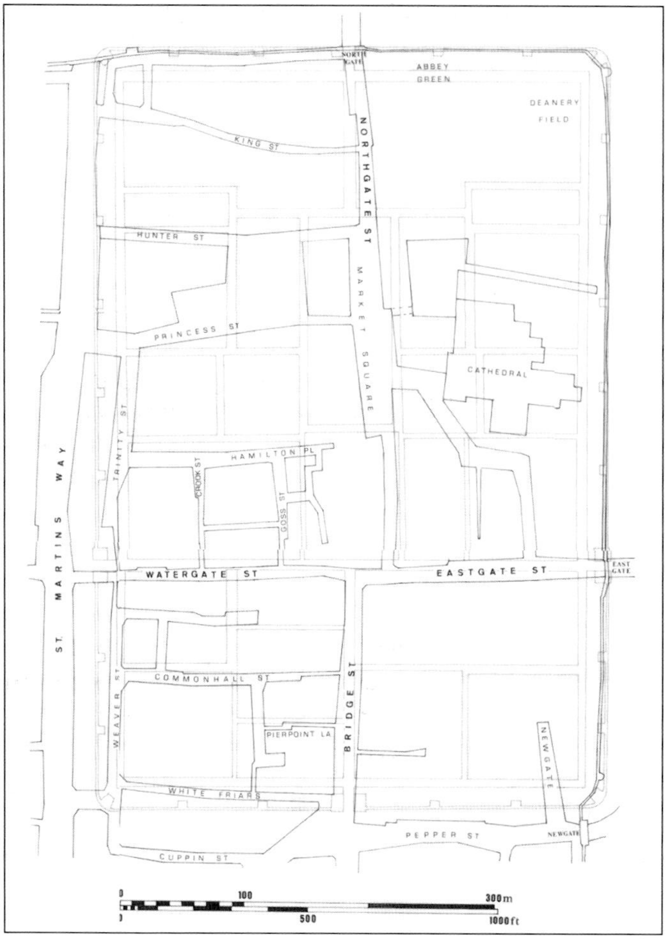

2 Plan showing outline of legionary fortress in relation to modern city

partly because the sloping ground required them to be terraced and partly because their internal floor levels tended to rise as a consequence of successive rebuildings. This is demonstrated by comparing floor levels in Roman buildings on opposite sides of Bridge Street. Thus, in the baths on the east side Roman floor level was approximately 1ft (30cm) lower than the present pavement whereas in the building on the west side the surface of its internal courtyard was more than 3ft (90cm) higher than the modern pavement. The accumulation of deposits behind the Row properties had a benign effect upon the remains of Roman buildings as, despite robbing-out of walls for reusable stone, much was sealed and protected. This continued to be true even when these 'backland' areas came to be built over for the first time in the nineteenth century as the foundations of the Victorian buildings were generally restricted in width and depth.

An early commentator on the discovery of Roman remains was Ranulph Higden, a monk of St Werburgh's abbey in the city (later the cathedral) writing in the mid-fourteenth century, who describes underground passages (sewers), vaulted dining-rooms (perhaps parts of the main bath-building) and huge stones inscribed with the names of men of antiquity (tombstones). Antiquarian accounts of discoveries begin in the

3 *Nineteenth-century engraving of the 'Roman Bath' beneath the Feathers Inn (now No. 39) Bridge Street*

seventeenth century and increase considerably in the next century. An altar dedicated to Jupiter Tanarus found in Foregate Street in 1653 and subsequently donated to Oxford University is among the earliest. The 1720s witnessed two important milestones in the appreciation of Chester's Roman past. The first concerned the discovery next door to the Feathers Inn on the east side of Bridge Street of part of a hypocaust belonging to the main bath-building of the fortress. In contrast with many Roman remains discovered subsequently, this was not destroyed but was preserved *in situ* and people were allowed to inspect it (**3**). Access was much improved when the premises above it were rebuilt in 1853. As a contemporary guidebook to Chester puts it: 'Messrs Royle, the proprietors, with that antiquarian zeal, and true public spirit, which have ever distinguished them, took especial precautions to preserve, both from injury and molestation, this curious relic of proud old Rome'. Sadly and shamefully, their magnanimous example was followed by very few property developers in later years. The hypocaust, or 'Roman Bath' as it has long and erroneously been known, is still open for inspection today. The second milestone was the visit to the city in August 1725 by Dr William Stukeley, the most eminent antiquarian of his age. He records his joy and astonishment on riding beneath the Eastgate and seeing the previously unrecognised arches of the Roman gate still standing, hidden behind the facade of the medieval gatehouse. The combined evidence of the sketches he made and those drawn in 1768 when the gate was demolished show it to have been a double portalled affair with a statue, possibly of the war-god Mars, set high up on the external face between the two arches (**4**).

The late eighteenth century saw the start of large-scale housing developments in Chester. The groundworks for one such scheme, the construction of terraces of large houses in the Linenhall Field next to the Watergate in 1778/9, led to the unearthing of large parts of a very extensive extramural baths complex. Several writers give accounts of the hypocausts and mosaics then revealed although, regrettably, no drawings of plans were

4 *Antiquarian sketches of the Roman east gate. William Stukeley 1725 (top), George Wilkinson c.1760 (centre), and Ogden & J Calveley 1774*

made. As the new houses were equipped with cellars much was destroyed. Some artefacts from this and other sites were preserved by the activities of private collectors. On occasion this resulted in their being relocated far from their place of discovery. A fine altar dedicated to 'Fortune the Home-bringer' found in the baths was donated, in the absence of a suitable local repository, to the British Museum 47 years after its discovery. Closer to home, Philip Egerton had a number of stone hypocaust pillars from the same building taken to his country house at Oulton Park along with a collection of Roman tiles destined to form the floor of a 'Druid's Temple' he was having built on the estate. Some of these *pilae* didn't make it as far as Egerton's country residence and instead ended up in the surrounds of Oakmere Lake.

The first half of the nineteenth century witnessed profound changes in society, the economy and the countryside, involving industrialisation, urban growth, social reform, and, more gradually, improvements in education. One spin-off from this was the emergence of 'learned societies' founded by individuals sharing a common interest in the study of one or more areas of the arts and sciences. Those concerned with archaeological and historical matters were amongst the forerunners. Folklore was being overtaken by research conducted along structured and systematic lines and at the same time there were many who were appalled both at the loss of historic buildings and remains and the unsympathetic quality of new developments springing up in historic centres. The Chester Archaeological Society — or to give it its unabridged title 'The Chester Architectural, Archaeological and Historical Society' — came into being in 1849, its principal founder being the Reverend William Massie, Rector of St Mary's on the Hill. Like comparable societies of the period, the membership was inevitably drawn from the higher social strata and meetings were attended by men and women of position and status. Socially unrepresentative perhaps, but their influence often secured the acquisition of antiquities which would otherwise have been permanently lost to all and, if not the preservation of remains *in situ*, then at least sufficient time for some record to be made.

An excellent example of the latter is the work done by Dr Thomas Brushfield, whose professional appointment was Medical Superintendent of the County Lunatic Asylum. He recorded the remains of the aisled exercise hall and adjoining hypocausted chambers belonging to the fortress baths exposed in 1863 when the Feathers Inn was demolished. He prepared a lengthy report on his findings, published in Volume III of the Society's *Journal* and running to 106 pages, which was to prove invaluable in interpreting other parts of the same building exposed a century later. The interest and usefulness of his account is greatly enhanced by the inclusion of photographs; this must rank amongst the earliest applications of this emergent technology in archaeological recording (**5-7**). A considerable proportion of the portable structural remains on the site, such as fragments of columns along with their bases and capitals as well as hypocaust *pilae,* which were secured for the Society and eventually placed on public display in the Water Tower Gardens. These were later transferred to the Roman Gardens established beside the Newgate in 1950 which have recently been reorganised and refurbished (**8**).

The 1880s saw a number of milestones in the history of archaeological endeavour in Chester. The rapid growth of the Society's collections of both artefacts and publications

5 The Fortress Baths; hypocaust in the westernmost chamber of the suite of sudatoria *attached to the south side of the exercise-hall as revealed in1863*

6 *Remains of exercise-hall of fortress baths revealed 1863 looking west towards Bridge Street; note wooden construction in distance erected as temporary bridge for the Rows*

led to the need to find a permanent home for them and so, in collaboration with the Chester Society of Natural Science, Literature and Art, fundraising was begun in 1883. Due in no small part to the Duke of Westminster, this yielded a sum sufficient to build the premises which were to become known as the Grosvenor Museum, opened to the public in August 1886. Ironically, the year that the museum campaign commenced also witnessed an incident that set in motion a train of events that would lead to it having to expand its premises within a decade of its opening. In 1883, a considerable section of the inner face of the City Walls west of the Northgate collapsed and, when carrying out repairs, the city authorities decided to insert a small gateway through to the exterior. Society members naturally kept a close watch on this work, not least because previous research indicated that Roman sculptured stones were present in the fabric of certain sections of the North Wall east of the Northgate. In the event the works produced not only pieces of architectural decoration from Roman buildings but also fragments of inscribed Roman tombstones and funerary monuments. As a consequence, when further repair work, this time to the section bordering the Deanery Field east of the Northgate, was started in 1887 the Society was fully prepared for the recovery, recording and storage of further material. In the intervening period, interest in Roman Chester and its hinterland had been stimulated further by the publication in 1886 of William Thompson Watkin's book *Roman Cheshire*. This included much material from the Society's collections. The work on the North Wall in 1887 produced many additional sculptures and inscriptions and in the following January a public meeting was held. Various speakers gave their opinions on the age of the walling in which this material had been incorporated, these being published in Volume 2 of the new series of the Society's *Journal*. The debates continued for several years thereafter but nearly another century was to pass before some of the more fundamental questions could be answered. The Society raised funds for further investigations west of the Northgate in the years 1890-2. By the time that the campaign finally came to an end, over 200 pieces of stonework had been retrieved and Chester found itself the proud possessor of one of the most important collections of Roman inscriptions and sculptures in north-west Europe. A catalogue of these was prepared by Professor Francis Haverfield and published by the Society in 1900, with a revised edition, compiled by Richard Wright and Ian Richmond, issued in 1955.

7 *Fallen column in fortress baths exercise-hall seen 1863*

In addition to the opening of the Museum and the publication of Watkin's *Roman Cheshire* there was yet another event in 1886 which was to prove of major import for the study of *Deva*, namely the appointment of Robert Newstead as curator of the collections of the Chester Society of Natural Sciences. As well as his main duties he assisted the honorary curator of the Archaeological Society George Shrubsole, whom he succeeded in 1903. Newstead held the position of curator, and later chairman, of the Archaeological Society throughout most of the rest of his life (even during the period from 1905 to 1924 when he was a lecturer in, and subsequently professor of, entomology in the School of Tropical Medicine at Liverpool University). For a period of more than half a century he was the leading figure in the investigation of Chester's archaeology. He brought a new, more scientific approach to the description and display of the archaeological collections, making sure that objects were properly labelled and their provenance recorded. Eventually ownership of the Society's and Newstead's personal collections was transferred to the City Corporation which had taken over the running of the Museum in 1915. His work went far beyond this, however, for he applied the same methodical approach to discoveries in the field. He managed to gain widespread acceptance among developers and builders of the principle of access to their site works to carry out archaeological recording and 'rescue' investigations. Furthermore, he mounted a number of major research excavations in the city, including those of the barracks in the Deanery Field in the north-east corner of the fortress which he carried out in collaboration with Professor John Droop of the Department of Classical Archaeology, University of Liverpool, in the 1920s. He was commendably prompt and methodical in writing up his discoveries and observations. They often appeared in the volume of the Society's *Journal* for the same year in which they occurred, grouped together under the general heading of 'Records of Archaeological Finds'; by so doing he compiled what was in effect an early version of the much vaunted 'Urban Archaeological Databases' of today.

Newstead, and other active members of the Society, kept a watch on building works throughout Chester not just within the confines of the fortress but beyond the defences.

8 The 'Roman Garden' next the Newgate prior to recent re-display scheme

As a consequence much valuable information about the extramural settlement was retrieved. A major advance in knowledge about the latter occurred in 1929 when works for the installation of a new boiler-house behind the Ursuline Convent, situated beyond the south-east angle of the fortress, exposed a section of a massive Roman wall following a gently curving course. This was immediately identified by Mr W.J. Williams of the Society (known as 'Walrus Williams' because of his large moustache) as the outer wall of the amphitheatre. Robert Newstead undertook trial-trenching during the next two years which defined the approximate extent of the structure and its degree of preservation. The Society as a whole put pressure on the City Corporation to alter a new road scheme planned to run right across the northern half of the amphitheatre site. In 1932 the City agreed to alter the course of the road, provided the Society could raise funds to cover the extra cost involved. A national publicity campaign was launched, which attracted the support of the Prime Minister of the day Ramsay MacDonald, and even went international with a successful appeal for funds in America. The authorities eventually capitulated and the Society purchased the strategically located St John's House overlying part of the northern half of the monument. It also opened negotiations with the Office of Works for the eventual excavation and display of the accessible part of the amphitheatre. Plans for this had to be shelved because of the Second World War. The project was eventually implemented in the 1960s when the Society not only donated the site to the nation but also made a very substantial financial contribution to the work.

The recognition of the amphitheatre was not Walrus Williams' only success in 1929 for he also discovered the Roman civil settlement at Heronbridge 1 mile (1.6km) south of Chester. Its investigation was to take up much of his spare time in later years, culminating in excavations carried out in the late 1940s with the assistance of Brian Hartley who was later to become Britain's leading expert on samian ware.

With the death of Robert Newstead in 1947 the City Council decided to employ a full-time, salaried curator, whose duties were still to include directing excavations in the city; Chester was extremely fortunate that the person appointed was Graham Webster. This was also his first archaeological post — he had previously been an assistant in the City Engineer's office at Lincoln where he had acquired archaeological experience. Recognising the desirability of having professional advice from someone with greater expertise than his own, he invited Ian Richmond to work on excavations proposed in Goss Street on the site of the legionary headquarters building. These took place in 1948/9 and saw a major advance in the understanding of the history of the fortress with the recognition for the very first time that the remains of timber buildings lay beneath the stone structures of the mature fortress. Richmond was subsequently commissioned by the Archaeological Society to advise on priorities for a 3-4-year programme of excavation. Instead of reacting to sites as they were threatened, this would seek answers to specific research questions. Thus the limited resources would be targeted more effectively, especially with regard to the elucidation of the exact alignment and structural development of the western fortress defences. At the same time, Webster planned and implemented a refurbishment of the Roman Stones Gallery and the creation of an entirely new display telling the story of Roman Chester — the Newstead Gallery.

Webster left in 1955 and was succeeded by Hugh Thompson, formerly keeper of the City and County Museum at Lincoln. In addition to further work on the western defences and a number of sites in the extramural settlement, Thompson completed an excavation at the west end of Commonhall Street. Begun by Dennis Petch, his replacement at Lincoln and later too at the Grosvenor, this revealed the presence of three massive granaries. The project for which he is best remembered in the city, however, is the excavation of the northern half of the amphitheatre. He began this in 1957 when curator, continuing to lead the project when a lecturer at Manchester University from 1962 to 1966 and subsequently when he became General Secretary of the Society of Antiquaries of London. The site was opened to the public in 1972. One of the most fascinating aspects of this excavation was the discovery of a system of ground-beams which had carried the superstructure of the first, timber, amphitheatre. Thompson gave much of the credit for this discovery to the skilled trowelling techniques of one of his Site Assistants — a certain David Morgan Evans. His father was secretary of the Chester Archaeological Society and he himself was to become General Secretary of the Society of Antiquaries of London many years later.

Dennis Petch took over as curator in 1962 just at the time when plans were being finalised for the redevelopment of vast areas of the city, many of which had lain as open ground since being cleared in the 1930s, alongside the provision of a new Inner Ring Road. Initially, the resources to cope with the amount of rescue archaeology all this engendered were totally inadequate. The museum curator was expected to direct excavations with the aid of an assistant in charge of a workforce consisting of a couple of labourers seconded from the City Engineer's Department together with volunteers, usually from the Archaeological Society. To maximise benefit from the latter's contribution, work often continued into the evenings and throughout weekends. The redevelopment schemes of this period were far more destructive than those of earlier times because they usually incorporated underground car parks and/or service bays, which entailed the destruction of all archaeological remains. The policy of the day was to improve access for motor vehicles into city centres whereas of course 20 years later everything possible was being done to reverse this situation with pedestrianization schemes to the fore. Sadly, this policy reversal came too late for a large proportion of Chester's archaeological heritage; what makes the situation even more regrettable is the fact that it was the most impressive remains of all that were lost.

While little could be achieved for the preservation of Roman structures *in situ,* a turning point as regards the provision for rescue archaeology came with the destruction of the great internal bath-building of the fortress in 1964 to make way for the Grosvenor Shopping Precinct. This was one of the few instances where the site was still covered by standing buildings and unfortunately the developer would not agree to any delay between their demolition and the commencement of building works to allow formal excavation to take place. Trial excavations and earlier discoveries hinted that the site might conceal the ruins of a bath-building and so it proved. They extended for more than 230ft (70m) from Pepper Street to St Michael's Arcade with intact mosaic floors and hypocausts and with walls preserved to a height of more than 13ft (4m) (**9**). The exposure of the imposing remains of this building was my first acquaintance with Roman Archaeology and although I can't recall the fact registering at the time, it must have done so subconsciously in view of my subsequent career. The demolition and site clearance works involved the temporary closing-off of the exit at the rear of St Michael's Arcade by means of the usual wooden hoarding. In this case, however, the contractors had thoughtfully incorporated a window through which members of the public could watch the building work proceeding and of course, although they might not have realised it, their precious Roman heritage being smashed up and carted away on the backs of lorries. As a 10-year-old at the time, I was a frequent visitor to St Michael's Arcade because of the excellent toyshop it contained. Peering through that hoarding window one day I was both fascinated by the frenzied activity of the earthmoving machinery in front of me and astonished by the speed with which the appearance of this part of the city had changed.

Even after the quality of the bath-building's remains had been amply demonstrated and protests against their impending destruction made at both local and national level, commercial considerations prevailed and the recovery of information was restricted to piecemeal observation and limited excavation when and where it suited the contractor.

9 Remains of main suite of fortress baths exposed by building works in 1964 and destroyed soon afterwards. Newgate/Pepper Street Site. Viewed from south

Nonetheless, Dennis Petch and his small band of helpers managed to retrieve much valuable information. The situation was much the same during the contemporary early stages of the Central Redevelopment Area scheme, where limited resources and time meant that only a few trenches could be excavated on the site of the so-called Elliptical Building. To this day, this structure is without parallel at any other site in the entire Roman Empire. To relieve the burden on the Museum staff, the investigation of this building was carried out by John Eames, Lecturer in Classical Archaeology at Liverpool University.

The destruction of the baths meant that Chester lost one of its greatest potential tourism and educational assets. Yet it did have the beneficial consequence, because of the great public outcry it stimulated, of ensuring that the investigation of archaeological sites henceforth was, for the most part, better-planned and resourced. Threats to archaeological sites were defined earlier, programmes of excavation agreed, and grants from central government were increased and matched pound-for-pound by the City Council. The Grosvenor Museum continued to carry out the excavation and post-excavation work and the Archaeological Society had a continued involvement both through managing the funds from the above sources and contributing volunteers. The number of sites to be investigated and the amount of work to be done, however, were vast and when judged in today's terms the resources, particularly for the post-excavation analysis of artefacts, were grossly inadequate. Yet by the latter stages of the Central Redevelopment Scheme — designated as the Old Market Hall Site (1967-70) — matters had improved to the extent that large-scale area excavation was possible. Sadly, the inclusion of underground car-parking beneath the new Gateway Theatre, Market Hall and the ironically and misleadingly named Forum Council Offices still meant that all archaeological remains were destroyed, including the Elliptical Building and an associated bath-house as well preserved as that encountered on the Grosvenor Precinct site. The late 1960s were an exciting time in the story of archaeological endeavour in Chester. This was when the largest excavations ever seen in the city took place, most particularly the amphitheatre and the Old Market Hall Sites, and I feel privileged to have been allowed to participate in those and many others as a schoolboy volunteer.

By 1972 it had become evident that running the museum and directing a continuing succession of excavations was beyond the capabilities of any one person. Thus the post of Field Officer was created to head up what soon evolved into a permanent team of archaeological staff designated the Excavations Section. The initial incumbent, Peter Davey, was succeeded by Tim Strickland in 1973 who, following an 'interregnum' from 1989 to 1990, was himself succeeded by Mike Morris. By the early '70s an excellent working relationship had been established between the city's planning department and the archaeologists working out of the museum whereby the latter received early notice of development schemes and planning applications. Thus the archaeological implications could be determined at an early stage, negotiations opened with landowners and developers, and applications for grant-aid made to central government (and later to their agent English Heritage). As a consequence, there were very few sites thereafter where the degree of investigation thought appropriate was not undertaken, directed usually either by Tim himself, Simon Ward or (up to late 1976 and again in the late 1980s) the writer, with post-excavation and publication under the charge of Peter Carrington.

The '70s and '80s witnessed numerous excavations, both inside the fortress and in the extramural area, some of considerable extent and complexity. In more than a few cases this involved the investigation of areas contiguous with or partly overlapping sites excavated during the first wave of redevelopment in the '60s. Most of the latter were still unpublished; indeed the stratigraphic information and finds from them had not even reached the first stage of analysis for publication. To remedy this situation English Heritage set up the 'Pre-'73 Backlog Project' with the initial aim of getting all the materials and data from unpublished sites excavated between 1946 and 1973 analysed and formed into archives ready for the preparation of publishable reports. This scheme, to which I was appointed as Project Manager, lasted from 1983 to 1986. At the culmination of the initial process it was decided to adopt a 'synoptic' approach to the publication of pre- and post-'73 sites. Excavations of sites of a specific period, parts of a single building (such as the fortress baths), or of buildings of identical type (e.g. legionary barracks), or of a similar character (such as civilian dwellings in the extramural settlement) were placed together in single volumes. This approach has necessarily increased the delay in the appearance of reports on the earlier sites but, in compensation, will allow the information to be presented in a more coherent and intelligible form.

The formal incorporation of Archaeology into the planning system and development control processes took a major step forward in 1984 when Chester was designated as one of only five Areas of Archaeological Importance in the country under the terms of the Ancient Monuments and Archaeological Areas Act of 1979. This meant that access to development sites for the purposes of archaeological investigation, over a maximum period of six months, was safeguarded by law. The advent of Planning Policy Guidance Note No.16 in 1990 concluded the integration of archaeology into the planning system nationally. It also, along with the decline in central government funding of rescue archaeology and constraints on local authority spending, led to the present system of local authority curatorial archaeologists setting planning conditions with the work being carried out by commercial archaeological contractors. Fortunately, although much of the development-engendered excavation is undertaken by such external contractors, Chester has retained its Archaeology Service and thus the irreplaceable and invaluable expertise in Chester's archaeology it possesses. Chester Archaeology (as the service is currently known) now has more time to devote to promoting public understanding, enjoyment and appreciation of archaeology, as well as carrying out much-needed and valuable research. Collaborative projects involving institutions from the local government, educational, commercial and charitable sectors have been a feature of recent archaeological endeavours and the Chester Archaeological Society continues its long tradition of promoting the cause of archaeology through lectures, publications and fieldwork. PPG 16 also enshrined the principle of minimising the disturbance of archaeological deposits as a consequence of development. This has prevented much needless destruction by forcing the adoption of more carefully and more sympathetically designed schemes. While it has also frequently resulted in archaeological investigation being confined to a few small foundation pits, with the concomitant difficulties of interpretation, it has at least afforded a 'breathing space' so that the mountain of information retrieved from excavations conducted over the previous 40 years can be analysed and published.

2 The advent of Rome

Before describing the circumstances of the Roman Army's arrival in the area now known as Cheshire, and the reasons for the choice of Chester as the site for a legionary fortress, it is necessary to outline the geography and geology of the region along with the character of late Iron Age society. The modern county of Cheshire lies at the north-western extremity of the so-called Midland Gap. It forms an extension reaching to the Irish Sea of the comparatively flat land of the Lowland Zone in the south and east and separates the two mountainous areas of the Pennines and North Wales belonging to the Highland Zone lying to the north and west. Then, as now, the shallow bowl of the Cheshire Plain provided a natural corridor for interchange between Lowland and Upland regions. Two principal routeways were involved. One from the Midlands, along the North Wales coast to Anglesey and thence to Ireland; the other from the Midlands to the crossing of the Mersey, on to the coastlands of the north-west and ultimately southern Scotland. The geology of this saucer-like depression area is characterised by glacial deposits of sand and clay through which several ridges of much older sedimentary sandstone rocks protrude. Even away from the latter the Cheshire Plain is rarely completely flat, its gently undulating terrain of varying slopes and wooded hollows affording constantly changing vistas. A number of rivers flow across the county, making their way to the Liverpool Bay section of the Irish Sea. In the west lies the Dee which flows from south to north, eventually broadening out into its tidal estuary which defines the west side of the Wirral peninsula. The latter forms an extension of a low ridge originating some 6 miles (10km) south-east of Chester and intervening between the valley of the Dee and the next river to the east, the Gowy. Next comes the most prominent feature of the Cheshire landscape — the sandstone outcrop of the Central Ridge that in places rises to a height of 705ft (215m). A major interruption of this north-south feature occurs at the Beeston Gap, utilised in more recent times by the Chester-Crewe railway line and overlooked by the dramatic outcrop of Beeston Crag with its ruined medieval castle. The sand and gravel eastern slopes of the Central Ridge lead down to the valley of the River Weaver with its important brine-springs. Beyond the latter the landscape begins to change as the western foothills of the Pennines are approached. A number of rivers flow down its slopes to the west, most notably the Bollin, which eventually discharges into the Mersey.

Marking the historic boundary between Lancashire and Cheshire, this river would have been a very significant feature of the landscape in our period. Its tidal estuary, which defined the east side of the Wirral, ran far inland and its valley was wide, flat and marshy. The landscape which characterises Cheshire continues deep into Shropshire. The two counties can be seen to form a geographical entity surrounded by areas of higher terrain where, once past the immediate foothills, easy communication was restricted to river

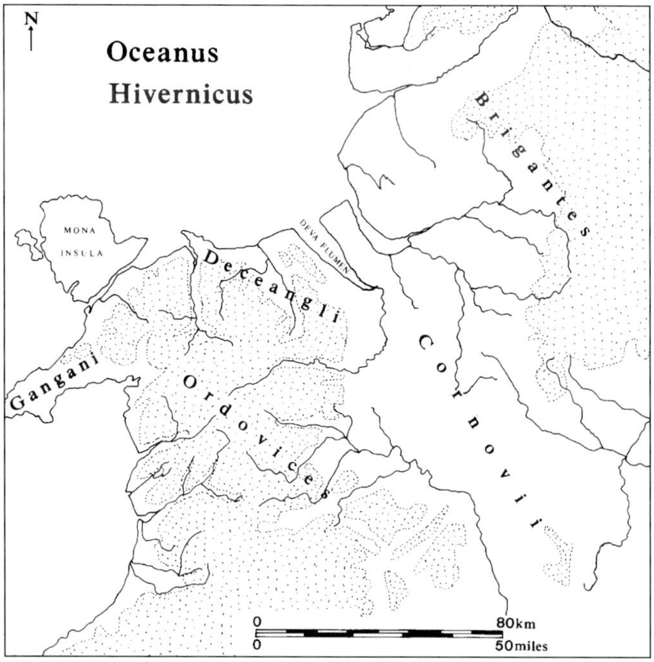

10 Map of Iron Age tribal areas in the region

valleys and, where appropriate, coastal routes.

Most if not all of what is now Cheshire belonged to the territory of the tribe known as the Cornovii whose administrative centre during the Roman period lay at Wroxeter — *Viroconium Cornoviorum* (**10**). To the north and east lay the lands of the Brigantes, the River Mersey (whose name means 'boundary river') most probably marking the boundary between the tribal territories, while to the west, occupying the lands between the Dee and the Clwyd, lay the Deceangli. The second-century geographer Ptolemy actually refers to *Deva* as a '*polis*' of the Cornovii, although why he should call it a town and assign it to the *civitas Cornoviorum* when he must have known the site was a legionary fortress standing on military land is unclear. Possibly he was referring to the *canabae* beside the fortress or, more likely, the civil settlement at Heronbridge one mile away.

The Wirral too probably belonged to the Cornovii; it has been suggested that the projecting shape of this peninsula provided the 'horn' (*Cornu*) element in the tribal name. The southern half of Cornovian territory is characterised by a large number of hillforts with a smaller number in Cheshire along the Central Ridge (**11**). Aerial photography in Shropshire during the last 20 years, coupled with even more recent intensive field survey, has redressed the imbalance in our knowledge of settlement by revealing a wealth of enclosure sites in the lowland areas. Many are single farmsteads with attached field systems and others seem to be stock compounds. Research in Cheshire is beginning to reveal a similar picture, though the even greater predominance here of moisture-retentive soils and pastoral farming renders the identification of sites rather more difficult.

Similarly, palaeoenvironmental evidence, especially pollen sampling, has demonstrated that considerable forest clearance was being undertaken as early as the middle of the first millennium BC and continued right through till the end of the Roman period. The

KEY:

solid dots indicate hillforts

Other major sites denoted by open stars

1 = Meols

2 = Northwich

3 = Middlewich

4 = Nantwich

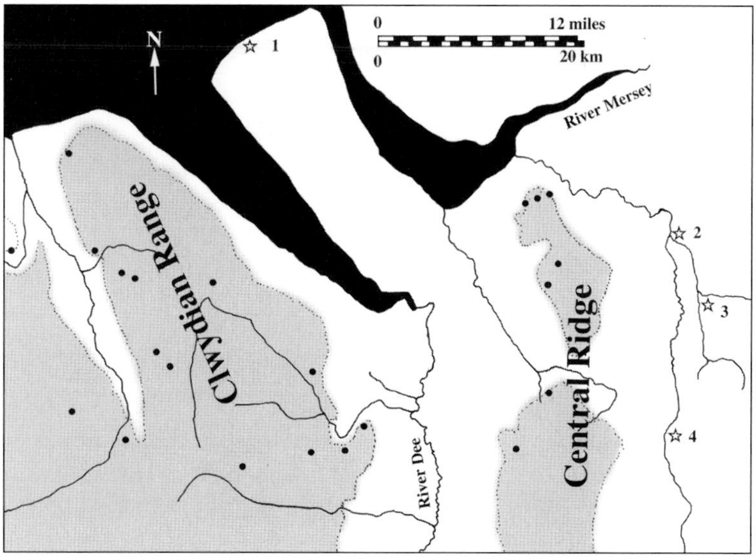

11 Map of principal Late Iron Age sites in Cheshire and North Wales

notion widely held some decades ago that northern Cornovia was a heavily forested and thinly populated backwater in later prehistory is certainly no longer tenable. Similarly, the discovery of the first villa to be found in Cheshire, at Eaton by Tarporley some 10 miles (16km) east-south-east of Chester, shows the view of Roman Cheshire as an area under military control lacking the forms of settlement common in the civil zone to be equally misplaced.

In many cases where excavation has occurred, occupation of the lowland farmsteads began in the Iron Age and continued into the Roman period. Many of those examined have also yielded plentiful evidence for the cultivation of cereals. Lying behind their protective single or double ditch system and presumably accompanying palisade, most probably represent the homes of what, for the want of a better term, might be called the 'Middle Class' of Celtic Britain. These were freeborn men who tended the flocks and crops of, and owed allegiance to, the local chieftains dwelling in their hillforts.

Hillforts probably served a variety of functions quite apart from being the strongholds of the aristocracy. Those in the more exposed locations were perhaps used purely on a seasonal basis in connection with the movement of flocks to upland summer pastures. The large lowland examples, with their massive defences and extensive level interiors such as Old Oswestry, may have been well on the way to becoming urban settlements like those known in Southern England. These are regularly referred to as *oppida*, the term Caesar employed to describe them and their counterparts in Gaul. The proposition that the Cornovii could have been as culturally advanced as the tribes much farther to the south may seem surprising. They lacked the high quality metalwork and pottery so common among their southern neighbours and, in the later Iron Age, coinage, facts often used to class them as unsophisticated. Yet the Cornovii clearly did not lack wealth. Their tribal area included much rich agricultural land and there were extensive copper deposits at Llanymynech, along the Central Cheshire Ridge, and at Alderley Edge in the east of Cheshire. Equally if not more important was the fact that they controlled three of the four inland brine springs of Britain, at Nantwich, Middlewich and Northwich in the Weaver valley (**11**). This major source of one of the most important commodities in the ancient world was one which the Roman authorities were later to exploit to the full; the Roman name for Middlewich for example — *Salinae* — means 'salt-works'. Evidence of its exploitation in the pre-Roman period comes in the form of fragments of the large, crudely-fashioned pottery jars used for its storage and distribution.

Similar vessels of 'Very Coarse Pottery', or VCP as it has become known, were also used by those producing salt from the fourth inland brine spring at Droitwich in the lands of the Cornovii's southern neighbour the Dobunni. Differences between the two variants of VCP have enabled the distribution of the output of the two centres to be plotted. It is quite clear that by the end of the Iron Age Cheshire had taken over as the main supplier of salt throughout Wales and the Welsh borders, even as far as the Severn estuary. While much of this trade would have been overland some was probably maritime in nature. The Cornovii possessed direct access to trade along the Irish Sea coasts via the Dee and Mersey estuaries. A major beach-trading site existed at Meols at the tip of the Wirral, which finds of Carthaginian, Armorican and other Gaulish coins show functioned as an emporium from at least the late third century BC. Salt may well have been the principal specialist commodity traded. This commercial settlement continued in existence throughout the Roman period and for many centuries thereafter, finally being destroyed by coastal erosion some time after the Viking settlement of the Wirral. While clearly not lacking in valuable natural resources, the Cornovian aristocracy may have preferred to display their wealth in the form of impressive hillforts, extensive land ownership and large herds, rather than by elaborate metalwork, fine pottery and coinage; a form of investment less flamboyant but perhaps more durable.

Perceptions of Iron Age settlement in the Chester hinterland were dominated for a long time by the well-known hillforts along the Central Ridge. Sites such as Eddisbury, Helsby Hill, Kelsborough Castle and Maiden Castle and, as revealed by excavations in and around its medieval castle in the 1970s, Beeston Crag, were preserved and recognised because of the less intensive agricultural regimes along the Ridge. Aerial survey during the last 15 years has begun to redress this rather one-sided picture by locating cropmark sites in the lower-lying areas of the county. Most consist of single or double ditched enclosures, generally less than 3.6 acres (1.5ha) in area, of a type widespread in southern Britain during the first millennium BC. An example of this type of site, in this particular case found as a result of investigating a findspot of Roman pottery, has recently been excavated at Irby close to the tip of the Wirral some 15 miles (25km) from Chester. The sequence uncovered is similar to that found at other such sites in the region such as Great Woolden Hall, Mellor and Tatton Park. Permanent occupation commenced in the second or third century BC and continued through the Roman period, during which there was a change in building styles and techniques from circular timber huts to stone, or at least stone-founded, rectilinear buildings. At Chester itself, proof of actual settlement has still to be found although the area later to be occupied by the legionary parade-ground beyond the east defences yielded evidence of ploughing apparently dating to the late pre-Roman Iron Age. An excavation across the line of the Roman road to Whitchurch about 3 miles south of the fortress has also shown that there had already been considerable woodland clearance before the road was built. Settlers were undoubtedly attracted to the fertile and productive Dee valley centuries before the advent of Rome, but on present evidence the settlement pattern in the Chester area consisted of individual farmsteads and was devoid of any form of nucleated community. The fact that the fortress took the Celtic name of the river it lay beside — Dee = *Deva* ('the goddess') — is perhaps itself proof that there was no pre-existing native settlement whose name could be appropriated.

Soon after the initial phase of the invasion in AD 43 the Emperor Claudius came to Britain in person, and at Colchester he received the submission of 11 British kings. Given the apparently largely peaceful incorporation of Cornovia into the Roman province subsequently, it seems quite possible that the chief of the Cornovii, in whose territory the legionary fortress at Chester was eventually established, was among those who paid homage to Claudius and entered into a treaty relationship with Rome. Aulus Plautius, commander of the invasion force, spent the following four years subduing those tribes of southern England and the Midlands, with the exception of the Iceni and the Regni who were already allies of Rome, and laying the foundations of the province. Events during the period when his successor, Ostorius Scapula, took over as governor of Britain in the late summer of 47 provided the context for the first appearance of the Roman Army in the vicinity of Chester. Roused by Caratacus, the fugitive and sole surviving heir to the kingdom of the Catuvellauni, and thinking to take advantage of the handover of command, the Welsh tribes began making aggressive moves against the Roman province. They attacked one of the tribes allied to Rome, either the Dobunni or their northerly neighbours the Cornovii. Scapula repulsed the aggressors and began to plan a more forceful response for the next campaigning season, which included the occupation of all the lands as far as the Severn and the Trent. Among the forts established to hold the newly annexed territory were those at Wroxeter, Stretton Mill and Red Hill. The storming of the Wrekin hillfort, taken to be the principal centre of the Cornovii, presumably occurred at this moment. Possibly certain elements of the tribe had also been stirred to revolt by Caratacus. Scapula led an expeditionary force beyond the frontier of the province into the Cheshire Gap with the intention of taking the fight to the homelands of the Ordovices, the main troublemakers in North Wales, and chose this route so as to cut off a possible line of retreat into Brigantia. Tacitus tells us that the territory of the Deceangli in north-east Wales had already been overrun, with much booty collected, and that Scapula 'had almost reached the sea facing Ireland' when an uprising amongst the Brigantes forced him to break off the attack. Although Cartimandua, Queen of the Brigantes, had some form of treaty arrangement with Rome, the large and federal character of her realm made close control of dissident elements difficult. Not wishing to provoke more widespread hostility Scapula broke off the campaign, despatched forces to assist Cartimandua in quelling the revolt, which would probably have traversed the Cheshire Plain, and turned his attention instead to the Silures of South Wales. Although not mentioned in the sources, it is extremely likely that the preparations for the assault on the Deceangli included detailed naval reconnaissance of the North Wales coast, with potential anchorages in the Dee estuary being noted if not actually used by the Roman fleet. In this they would have been assisted by information gleaned from the seaborne traders operating in the Irish Sea, the sort of men who later provided Agricola with valuable intelligence about the harbours of Ireland itself.

In AD 49 Scapula moved *legio XX* forward from its initial base at Colchester to assist in the Welsh campaigns. Part of it was installed in a new fortress at Kingsholm near Gloucester, with the remainder perhaps placed in several large forts along the Wye valley. *Legio XIV*, the other legion operating along the Marches, was at this time based in a fortress at Mancetter with possibly a vexillation stationed at Wall. Despite the capture of Caratacus in AD 51, handed over to the Roman authorities by Cartimandua when he tried to seek refuge in Brigantia following his last stand at Llanymynech hillfort, Welsh resistance did not falter and Roman forces experienced a number of serious reverses. Campaigning continued throughout the 50s during the governorships of Didius Gallus and Quintus Veranius, chiefly against the Silures of South Wales. This period saw *legio XIV* advancing to a new fortress at Wroxeter while part of *legio XX* was installed in another new base at Usk. The arrival of the Fourteenth at *Viroconium* was accompanied by the construction of a screen of new forts in front of it, which included Whitchurch and Trent Vale. The placing of a fort at Holt/Farndon to guard the natural crossing-point of the Dee is a possibility although the earliest Roman activity known in the area at present belongs to the later Flavian period. While there is no evidence of military activity at Chester in this period, the whole of Cheshire and the neighbouring portion of north-east Wales was undoubtedly in the firm grip of the Roman Army by the mid-50s. On the other side of the country, the network of forts by now stretched as far north as the Humber estuary. No doubt incensed by what they saw as the betrayal of Caratacus, the anti-Roman elements amongst the Brigantes, led by Cartimandua's husband Venutius, tried to take control. Initially successful against the dissidents, the assistance of Roman forces was eventually needed to enable Cartimandua to retain control of her realm.

By the third year of his governorship in AD 60, Suetonius Paullinus had broken the resistance of both the Silures and the Ordovices and was ready to launch an assault against the Isle of Anglesey. This was a prime objective because of its dual importance as a centre of Celtic religion and a major source of grain for the Ordovices. Flat-bottomed transports were built to carry the infantry across the Menai Straits and although it has been suggested these were prepared at a base somewhere along the Dee estuary, perhaps even at Chester itself, it is equally likely that they were built on the spot. The enemy had been defeated, the horrific Druidical groves destroyed, and the island captured, when Paullinus received news of the rebellion led by Boudicca, queen of the Iceni. Although the revolt was quelled comparatively quickly, the extent of the devastation meant that for much of the next decade the military's energies were devoted to restoration and police work in the south-east rather than full occupation of the recently won territory in Wales. As far as northern Cornovia was concerned this was probably a period of consolidation, with the army engaged on infrastructure projects such as extending and improving the road network across Cheshire as far as the Mersey and also perhaps into north-east Wales. The nearest forts, however, lay a little farther back at places like Whitchurch and Trent Vale. Increased exploitation of the mineral wealth of the area was probably another feature of this phase.

12 Lead ingot, possibly of the AD 60s, bearing the moulded stamp of the private lessee Caius Nipius Ascanius found at Carmel, near Holywell, Flintshire in 1950

Production of salt at the brine springs in the Weaver valley may have been stepped up some time earlier in response to the extra demand created by the arrival of *legio XIV* at Wroxeter. In north-east Wales, the appropriation of the Flintshire lead-field and its conversion into an imperial estate under the control of a *procurator metallorum* is suggested by a lead ingot found at Carmel, near Holywell. This bears the stamp of a man named Caius Nipius Ascanius who appears to have been one of the independent individuals to whom mining rights had been leased (**12**). A few years later, the working of these deposits was carried out directly by the state and the scale of extraction drastically increased to supply the amount of lead needed for the construction of the Chester fortress.

Events elsewhere in the Empire also had an impact on the situation in post-Boudiccan Britain. Relations with Parthia deteriorated in the 60s and in AD 66 Nero withdrew *legio XIV* from Britain, together with eight cohorts of Batavians, in preparation for a campaign in the Caucasus. This caused a redeployment of the remaining legions in the province with *legio XX* taking the Fourteenth's place at Wroxeter, its former bases at Kingsholm and Usk being abandoned, and *II Augusta* moving up from Exeter to build a new fortress at Gloucester. The remaining legion, *IX Hispana*, now if not before, was installed at Lincoln (**13**). Nero's suicide two years later set in motion a chain of events with repercussions that ultimately included the establishment of a legionary fortress at Chester. Nero's death plunged the Empire into a year of civil war — the infamous 'Year of the Four Emperors' — almost exactly 100 years after the previous, and far longer, period of internal strife had ended with the victory of Augustus. The eventual winner this time was Vespasian, the first of the Flavian emperors, a man who had seen service in Britain where he had commanded *II Augusta* during the invasion period. His son Titus had also served in Britain, as a tribune under Suetonius Paullinus. Shortly before Vespasian's accession there was a major emergency in Britain. Venutius, who presumably had not been strong enough to make his move during the Boudiccan Revolt, seized his chance as the Roman World dissolved into political chaos. Cartimandua had divorced him and taken his squire Vellocatus as her consort. Rather than weakening the anti-Roman faction as she may have hoped, this act probably drove many to side with Venutius. He declared war on his former wife and, as Tacitus tells us, with the aid of tribes to the north of the Brigantes he took control of the kingdom. Cartimandua had to be rescued by a force of auxiliary troops sent in by the governor Vettius Bolanus and Rome was now faced with a major hostile power on the northern frontier of the province. This was a pivotal moment in the history of Roman

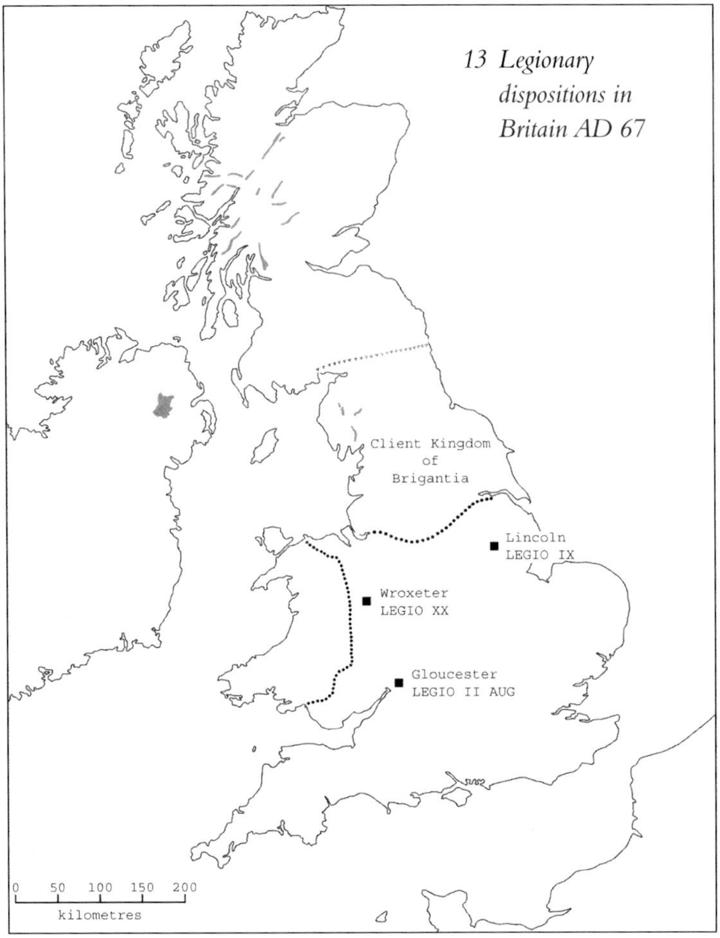

13 Legionary dispositions in Britain AD 67

Britain. Had it been possible to maintain the treaty relationship with the Brigantes, who acted as a buffer between the province and the more hostile tribes beyond them, then further warfare would have been unnecessary. Now, however, the only workable solution from Rome's point of view was the occupation and annexation of Brigantia and the punishment of Venutius' northern allies, the logical development of this policy being the conquest of the entire island attempted by Agricola. It might be thought with the benefit of hindsight that the breakdown of relations with the Brigantes would have happened sooner or later anyway so a continuation of the alliance would only have postponed the inevitable. Whatever, Bolanus undertook some campaigning against Venutius and certainly managed to contain the problem by preventing any major incursions into the province. This is likely to have involved the moving up of additional forces to the borders of Brigantia. The main attack had to wait until the Imperial accession had been finally settled. To do this, Vespasian sent his ally and relative Petilius Cerialis, an able if somewhat impetuous commander, who was already experienced in British affairs, having been legate of *IX Hispana* at the time of the Boudiccan Revolt.

Cerialis took up his appointment as Governor in AD 71 and brought with him *legio II*

Adiutrix pia fidelis, which thus restored the number of legions in the province to four. Initially stationed in the fortress at Lincoln, recently vacated by *IX Hispana* which moved forward to a new base at York, this was shortly to be the first garrison of the Chester fortress. Cerialis used his old legion the Ninth to spearhead the campaign while the Twentieth advanced up the west coast from its base at Wroxeter under its legate Gnaeus Julius Agricola. The latter's route was probably that taken by the main coastal road laid down soon afterwards which crossed the Mersey near Warrington and proceeded via Wigan and Walton-le-Dale to Lancaster and on ultimately to Carlisle. The earliest fort at the last site can be dated to 72/3, representing the initial consolidation of the newly-won territory following the defeat of Venutius. That Cerialis also mounted far-reaching punitive expeditions against the northern tribes who had supported Venutius is indicated by recent examination of the coin evidence. This strongly suggests that Roman forces penetrated deep into Scotland at this time. A feature of Agricola's conquest of Scotland in the early AD 80s was the extensive use of naval forces both to make surprise landings behind enemy lines and to keep the main force supplied with provisions. Given that the majority of forts established during his advance through western Brigantia a decade earlier were sited on navigable rivers (Wilderspool on the Mersey, Walton le Dale on the Ribble, Lancaster on the Lune, Carlisle on the Solway), combined land and sea operations are likely to have been employed on this occasion also. This may provide the context for the first major Roman presence at Chester.

Roman forces had been operating in Cheshire for more than 20 years before the fortress was founded and, with its potential as a harbour, there is a strong possibility of an earlier military base at or near Chester. This is not a new idea for the notion that it may have been the scene of pre-fortress military activity actually goes back to the beginnings of its archaeological investigation. The noted local antiquary W. Thompson Watkin first proposed that the known Roman *castrum* had once been smaller as long ago as 1886. His contention was based on the discovery in the mid-nineteenth century of three or more cremation burials within the eastern section of the fortress *retentura*. Because Roman Law forbade burials within the boundaries of a settlement, these must have belonged to an earlier and smaller, or at least differently aligned, military encampment. In later years, the sole surviving cremation urn (known as the Stevens' Urn) was pronounced to be Neronian in date. Therefore these burials came to be seen as originating from a cemetery belonging to a pre-Flavian fort, considered by some to lie in the area to the south-west of the legionary fortress occupying the spur of ground now enclosed by the medieval castle. Despite the extensive amount of excavation which has taken place both within the fortress and in its immediate vicinity, supporting evidence has proved extremely elusive. Two lead ingots found in the city datable by their cast inscriptions to AD 74 have been seen as indicating pre-fortress occupation. However, improved understanding of the chronology of the fortress-building programme in recent years suggests that these should instead be associated with the stockpiling of materials at the beginning of its construction. Some readers will be aware of the claimed discovery of the remains of pre-Flavian buildings on two sites excavated in the 1970s. One of these, 'Goss Street', lay at the east end of the barracks of the first cohort and the other, 'Abbey Green', encompassed an area beside the eastern half of the northern fortress defences where the structural remains in question were thought to represent a pre-Flavian 'box-rampart'. Subsequent and more detailed analysis of the data from both sites has overturned these preliminary interpretations and the features are now seen to represent buildings and structures contemporary with the primary legionary fortress. Also, as with the rest of Chester, the amount of pre-Flavian pottery is quite modest and in keeping with a site established in the early Flavian period. The results of the Abbey Green excavation complicated matters further as a number of cremation burials were found which had been deposited during the long period in the mid-second century when much of the legion was absent and large areas of the fortress were more or less derelict. This has cast doubt on the supposedly early date of the cremations found in the nineteenth century. The Stevens' Urn is undoubtedly Neronian but could have been deposited after *c.*120 as a long-term survival.

While some of the supposed evidence for pre-fortress occupation has now been discounted as a result of reinterpretation and most of the remainder is at best ambiguous, recent analysis of the archive of an unpublished excavation carried out in the 1960s has, paradoxically, identified a number of features which definitely do belong to pre-fortress Roman military activity. The site in question lies at the heart of the fortress and concerns the *insula* containing the so-called Elliptical Building, of which more in a moment. Beneath the courtyard of the latter, whose construction is securely dated by an inscribed lead water-pipe manufactured early in AD 79, was found an isolated 50ft (15.25m) length of steep-sided and flat-bottomed ditch just over 13ft (4m) wide and 4ft (1.20m) deep following an east-west alignment (**14**). In its form and dimensions it most closely resembles the short length of ditch with accompanying earth bank, known as a traverse, often employed as a defensive measure in front of the entrances to Roman marching-camps and temporary forts. The main rampart and ditch of this earlier base were not found (hardly surprising given the 'rescue' nature of much of the work on this site) and so it is not known whether the interior lay to the north or south. The filling of the ditch suggested it had been open for a comparatively brief period and then deliberately backfilled.

No pottery or other artefacts were found in the small proportion of fill that it was possible to excavate carefully, while the site clearance works associated with construction of the fortress had removed any deposits which could have indicated if there had been an interval between the demise of the ditch and the start of work on the Elliptical Building. Thus the date of this pre-fortress base cannot be ascertained, at least not until further evidence is forthcoming. The ditch was not the only feature found to underlie the Elliptical Building. Beneath its south-west corner lay traces of a substantial timber structure, the most obvious component of which was a rock-cut bedding-trench designed to hold a sill-beam 1ft 3in (38cm) wide. Most importantly, the alignment of this feature was very different from both that of the fortress buildings and the ditch just described, being approximately north-west/south-east. It is most unlikely therefore that bedding-trench and traverse are contemporary and parts of the same installation and so they would appear to represent two entirely separate phases of pre-fortress military activity. Once again, the section examined had a very clean fill devoid of finds and any supervening deposits had been removed by preparatory work for the erection of the fortress buildings.

While there is clear evidence for two separate military bases pre-dating the legionary

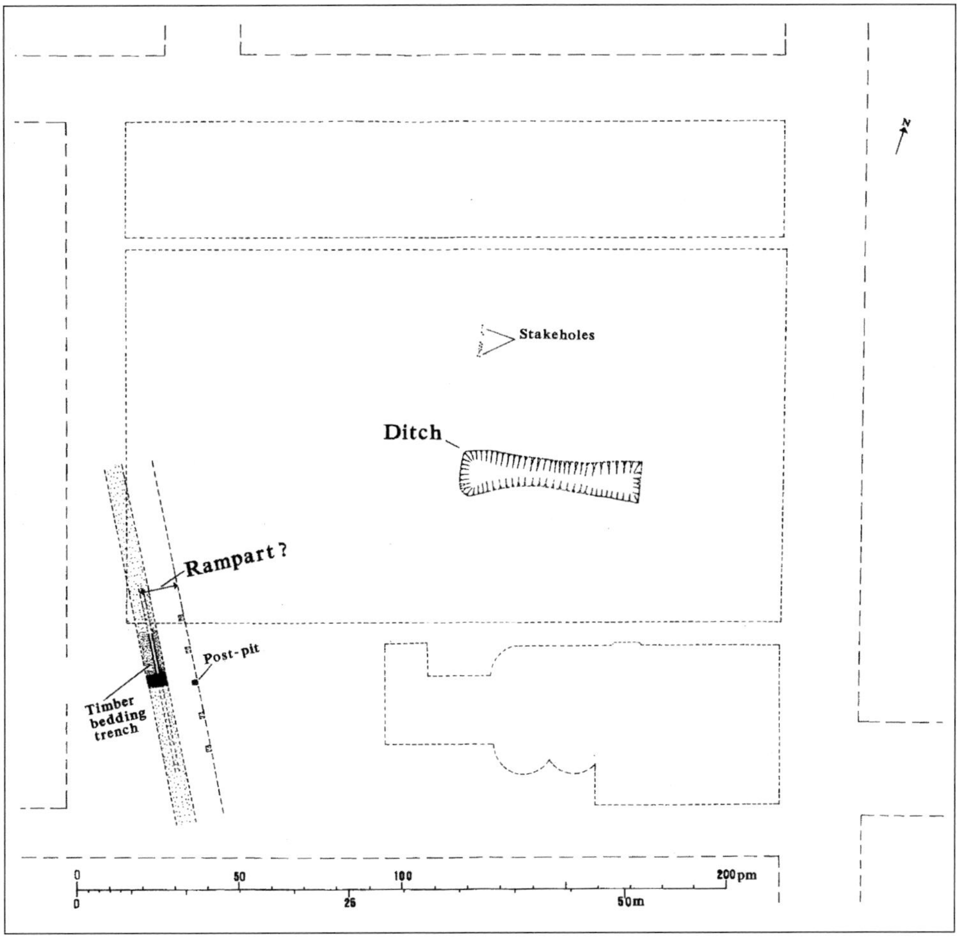

14 Plan of pre-fortress features beneath the Elliptical Building

fortress we do not as yet know the period to which they belong, the duration of their occupation, their size, nor which came first. The traverse is perhaps more likely to be associated with the first Roman presence, probably consisting of a campaign base or small fort occupying the highest part of the ridge on which Chester sits. The structural remains to the south-west of the traverse imply a more substantial and permanent installation. Ephemeral features following a similar alignment to the bedding-trench, or one at right-angles to it, have in fact been noted on a number of sites underlying the primary buildings of the fortress. If these represent slighter structures contemporary with it then a base larger than a normal auxiliary fort would seem to be indicated. There is a small collection of pre-Flavian pottery and coins from Chester as a whole but it is of little assistance in trying to date these pre-fortress phases. The primary fort might belong to Paullinus' campaigns in the late AD 50s/early 60s, while an obvious context for the later, and seemingly larger base, would be Cerialis' operations against Brigantia in the early AD 70s.

3 The imperial Roman legion

A brief description of the strength and organisation of the Roman legion as it had evolved by the Imperial period is desirable at this point so as to aid understanding of the design of a fortress. The organisation of the legions was regularised with the creation of a full-time professional army by the Emperor Augustus around 30 BC. The legion was made up of ten cohorts each with a complement of 480 men divided into six centuries of 80. Each century was further divided into ten sections of eight men. The term for a section — *contubernium* — meant tent-party and was derived from the group which shared a tent when the army was on campaign. This same division was applied in permanent barracks, which were subdivided so as to provide each *contubernium* with a pair of rooms. In Republican times centuries were usually deployed in pairs forming a unit known as a maniple. This pairing of centuries continued into the Imperial period and can be seen in the planning of fortresses where barracks are usually arranged in pairs facing one another across a minor street. The first cohort, the most senior, differed from the other nine in that its number was increased to 800 men, organised into five centuries of double strength, at the beginning of the Flavian period. This development is reflected in the greater amount of space allocated to the first cohort in fortresses of this period such as Caerleon, York, Inchtuthil and Chester compared with their Neronian or earlier predecessors at Lincoln, Gloucester and Wroxeter. Every legion also had a 120-strong force of cavalry, the *equites legionis*, whose function was largely concerned with scouting and the carrying of despatches. This apparent deficiency in mounted troops was made good by the units of specialised cavalry (*alae*) among the auxiliary units attached to every legion. In some cases, and this may have been true at Chester, an *ala* was actually brigaded with the legion in its fortress.

All legionaries were Roman citizens, for citizenship was a qualification for entry into the legion. By the end of the first century the normal period of service for the ordinary *miles* was 25 years. This may seem an extraordinary commitment to make today but acceptance into the legions was much prized. It offered regular and quite generous pay, adequate if not exactly lavish accommodation and food, comradeship, status, a clear career path with excellent chances of social advancement, a chance 'to see the world', the possibility of sharing in booty, and a substantial gratuity on retirement in the form of land, cash, or both (for uniform and equipment of legionaries *see* **colour plates 1 & 2**). The ordinary legionary however was not allowed to marry. This was only permitted after he had completed his service and retired as a veteran. Unofficial liaisons were commonplace though and the population of the civil settlement which developed rapidly beside every legionary base, the *canabae legionis*, included substantial numbers of 'common-law' wives and their children. This prohibition on marriage was lifted early in the third century and serving soldiers were officially allowed to maintain a family home in the adjacent civil settlement. By the fourth century soldiers' families were classed as part and parcel of an army unit and were included in the rations distribution as well as having transport to any new posting provided at the state's expense.

Each century was commanded by a centurion, of which there were 60 of graded seniority (**colour plate 3**). Even the lowest ranked received pay at least five times that of the ordinary legionary together with a far more generous retirement gratuity, while the salary of the most senior, the *primus pilus*, was four times this again. The *primus pilus* was commander of the first century of the first cohort but also had far wider responsibilities encompassing the entire legion. The next most senior centurion was the *princeps* who had charge of the headquarters staff and below him were the other three centurions of the first cohort, the *hastatus*, the *princeps posterior* and the *hastatus posterior*. The six centurions in the other cohorts were ranked as *pilus prior*, *pilus posterior*, *princeps prior*, *princeps posterior*, *hastatus prior* and *hastatus posterior*, but were apparently of equal status. Above the *primus pilus* was the *praefectus castrorum*, usually a man in the latter stages of his career who had risen through the centurionate to become principal centurion. In command of the legion when the legate and senior tribune were absent, his function was that of senior quartermaster responsible for all engineering and construction works, including the building of a fortress, and maintenance of munitions and equipment. He organised the baggage-train when the army was on the march and commanded the artillery during combat. From the middle of the third century, the camp prefect became the senior officer of the legion with the abolition of the positions of legate and laticlavian tribune. Forming the next tier in the military hierarchy were the six *tribunes*, men who held this short-term commission as a step in their career progression. The senior tribune was a senator designate and was known as the *tribunus laticlavius*; a term derived from the broad purple stripe he was allowed on his toga in recognition of his senatorial rank. His was a one-year post held before the age of 25 and prior to his entering the senate as a *quaestor*. Such men were gaining experience in readiness for command of their own legion in a few years' time. Their role was largely advisory but they did take control of the legion in the legate's absence. The other five tribunes were usually men of equestrian rank and were termed *tribuni angusticlavii* after the narrow purple stripe appropriate to their status. In peacetime their duties centred on camp security, physical training and overseeing of the stores and medical facilities as well as attending to judicial matters. Some of these men had graduated from the command of auxiliary cohorts and went on to attain the higher rank of prefects of auxiliary cavalry units (*alae*). Others attained high positions in the civil service as procurators. Finally, there was the *legatus legionis* himself, normally a senator in his thirties or forties who had held junior magistracies in Rome and to whom, as with the senior tribune, the position was merely a rung on the career ladder. His tenure would usually be three or four years, after which he would return to Rome hoping to be appointed to the consulship and ultimately a provincial governorship.

It might appear from the foregoing that Rome's legions were led by senior officers who were in reality merely politicians playing at being soldiers for the sake of career advancement. Although they would have been heavily reliant on the experience and professionalism of the junior officers and the men they commanded, and some individuals were undoubtedly more interested and more knowledgeable in military matters than others, this would be a gross distortion of the reality. The sons of the wealthy families from which these men came were instructed in military history and the art of war as part of their education. Theory was backed up by practical experience as they frequently participated in military exercises. Furthermore, as advancement was dependent upon success, or at the very least competence, in both civil and military spheres it was in their own interests to acquire a degree of proficiency in matters military.

Every centurion had an adjutant known as an *optio*, so called because originally he was selected by the centurion, and each century had a small administrative staff. Another position in the century was the *tessarius* whose duties included passing on the watchword of the day. The maintenance of proper records was an essential part of military life and considerable manpower was involved in record-keeping, as the discoveries at *Vindolanda* in recent years have so graphically illustrated. The chief records office (*tabularium principis*) housed in the headquarters building (*principia*) had a sizeable staff of clerks and orderlies headed by a *cornicularius*. There were those who dealt with the financial records of pay and deductions, the *actuarii, librarii* and *exactores*, as well as those who maintained records of particular supplies and provisions such as the *librariii horreorum* who looked after the granaries. Each of the senior officers also had their own administration (*officium*) which was organised under a *cornicularius* and included aides or *beneficiarii* as well as stenographers (*notarii*) to make written records of orders. In the majority of cases the men who performed these special duties, and those shortly to be mentioned, were not additional to the legion's usual manpower but were ordinary legionaries who developed extra skills for which they received consideration in the form of special allowances or privileges. Many were excused fatigues and routine duties on account of their expertise and were thus classed as *immunes* in this regard. They were still soldiers however and were expected to fight alongside their comrades when circumstances demanded.

One of the most important duties a soldier could undertake was looking after the legion's standards. These symbols acted as reference points on the battlefield where orders for the movement of formations were given in relation to them. They were devices which the soldiers could easily watch and follow, as well as affording the means by which they could locate their own units should they become separated in the confusion of battle. They also functioned as a rallying point and just like the regimental colours of later times their loss was the ultimate disgrace for the legion. The most important standard of course was the eagle or *aquila*, a symbol chosen because of its association with the principal Roman god Jupiter (**colour plate 4**). Made of gold, the eagle was depicted clasping one of his thunderbolts in its talons. Another important standard was the *imago* which bore the image of the emperor (for the tombstone of an *imaginifer* from Chester, *see* **27**). These two standards were the responsibility of the first cohort and were looked after by the *aquilifer* and *imaginifer*. Each century also had its own standard, the *signum*, which was carried by the *signifer*. In addition, each legion also had several symbols of its own. These were often associated with the anniversary of the legion's creation or the birthday of its founder and usually took the form of signs of the Zodiac. All the standards were kept in an open-fronted chamber protected by iron grills located at the centre of a range of rooms along the back wall of the *principia* cross-hall. Guarded day and night, this was the most sacred chamber in the entire fortress (**colour plate 24**).

While the standards functioned as the visible point of reference for executing commands on the battlefield, the commands themselves were communicated by means of musical instruments. These were principally the *tuba* and the *cornu*, capable of emitting clear piercing notes audible above the din of the battlefield. The first, played by the *tubicines*, was a straight trumpet used to signal advance and retreat. It was also sounded to mark the times for changing the guard in camp. The second, played by the *cornicines*, was a large circular instrument akin to a large version of the French horn and was sounded to draw the soldiers' attention to the position of the standards on the battlefield and also to sound the order to march (**colour plate 5**). These two instruments along with others were also employed on ceremonial occasions presided over by the legion's religious officials such as the *haruspex*. Weapons instruction and practice as well as the rehearsal of battlefield manoeuvres obviously featured prominently in everyday life in the legion. Training brought not only efficiency and effectiveness but also discipline and confidence. The success of the Roman Army was achieved by each and every soldier being proficient in arms, knowing how to operate with his fellows as a cohesive unit, and obeying orders to the letter. Drill and some types of weapons training took place on the parade-ground (*campus*) under the overall direction of the senior officers or, where there was one available, a distinguished veteran. In this they were assisted by the *campidoctor*, his assistant the *doctor cohortis* and an *optio campi*. The cavalry were trained by the *magister campi* and an *exercitator*, while sword instruction was given by a *doctor armorum*. Some training, especially in the use of weapons, probably took place in the amphitheatre. Large-scale manoeuvres were conducted at suitable locations in the hinterland of the fortress, as was practice in the construction of overnight camps.

There were many other specialists in the legion of which space allows mention of only a few more examples. Each legion was equipped with batteries of artillery weapons of two principal types. The first and largest were the siege catapults or *onagri* used mainly to destroy an enemy's defences, which were capable of hurling projectiles, usually large boulders weighing upwards of 50lb (22kg), over distances of 650ft (200m) or more. Weighing somewhere between 2 and 4 tons apiece, there were 10 of these massive machines per legion. The second was the bolt-firing catapult, a much larger and torsion-powered version of the crossbow from which it originated, allocated on the basis of one per century. Firing a bolt about 1ft (30cm) long with an iron head, this form of catapult was mounted on a cart — hence its name of *carro-ballista* — and had a maximum range of around 1,500ft (450m). There were probably considerable numbers of smaller *ballistae* housed in the upper chambers of the towers along the fortress wall and especially in the upper levels of the gatehouses. The artillerymen were known as *ballistarii* and their instructors as *doctores ballistarum*. In a permanent fortress the artillery would have been kept in a special storage building, possibly the same building as the armoury of spare weapons, under the watchful eye of the quartermaster. The manufacture and repair of weapons took place in the fortress workshops or *fabricae* managed by the *magister fabrum*. The medical service of the Roman Army was the most advanced in the ancient world and the level of care it provided for the sick and injured was not reached again until the twentieth century. The doctors or *medici* were of various ranks including that of centurion. There were various categories of orderly including the *capsarius*, though it is uncertain if the box that gave him his name contained medical records, drugs and preparations, or merely bandages. The health of the legion's animals was also accorded proper attention. In addition to the large numbers of sheep and cattle purchased and maintained until needed for consumption, there were also hundreds of draught and baggage animals to be looked after as well as the 300-plus horses (allowing for both mounts and remounts) required by the cavalry troop and the steeds of the senior officers. Each *contubernium* was provided with a mule to carry its tent and other equipment and every century possessed two carts, each drawn by two horses or oxen, one for the *carro-ballista* and the other for all the equipment not carried by the legionaries themselves and probably including the centurion's tent. Thus we know of various officials with veterinary duties including the *medicus veterinarius*, the *medicus pecuarius* and the *mulomedicus*.

The complement of the legion as described so far was thus around 5,500 men. This was not however the total number of individuals accommodated within the fortress. It has been estimated that there would have been somewhere in the region of 1,000-1,250 servants and slaves also present. In contrast to the slaves and servants of the senior officers who were employed and/or owned by their masters and who would have accompanied them to their next posting, these *lixae* and *calones* were professional military servants employed by the army itself. Their duties would have been many and various but probably centred on looking after the baggage animals and, for those assigned to a *contubernium*, domestic duties like gathering fuel and assisting in the cleaning and maintenance of equipment. If ordinary soldiers had personal servants — although this may in fact have been something that was prohibited — they would have lived in the *canabae* beside the fortress with all the other non-military personnel. In the case of the legate and his senior officers, wives and families were permitted to live with them in their large courtyard residences which afforded comfortable and well-appointed accommodation. This privilege was also probably extended to centurions.

Even the legions of the Republican era, recruited largely on an annual basis and laid off at the end of the year's campaigning season, were shadowed by considerable trains of civilians. These included people who made their living by supplying the soldiers with all sorts of comestibles, luxuries and entertainments as well as those who hoped to set up business enterprises in the wake of the conquering legions. The numbers of such a group would have been swelled as the campaign progressed, presuming it was successful, by others including those who had formed personal attachments to individual legionaries. To those in command, these civilian appendages could be a nuisance and a number of generals of the period are on record as complaining about their distracting the troops, upsetting discipline, and getting in the way of military operations. Scipio Africanus for example ordered the expulsion of merchants and traders from his main camp as did Metellus during the war against the Numidian king Jugurtha. The rapid expansion of the Empire in the late Republican period, the creation of a standing army by Augustus, and the installation of permanent garrisons in many provinces combined to create the perfect conditions to promote the growth and development of this phenomenon. What had begun as collections of tents and flimsy shacks rapidly developed into sizeable settlements of substantial buildings. This was especially true of the examples outside legionary fortresses, which were bound to attract larger numbers of civilians because of the greater market the size and pay of a legion provided. At Mainz, the extramural settlement already covered a large area by AD 25 and that beside the double legionary fortress at Xanten had grown so large by AD 69 that Tacitus described it as 'having the appearance of a town'. Despite their greater substance, however, these settlements continued to be known by the term originally used to describe the simple 'booths' which appeared beside camps of the Republican period — *canabae legionis*.

As army units were now stationed in one place for periods of years the need for goods, supplies and services over and above those provided by the military authorities grew. The merchants (*mercatores*), traders (*negotiatores*), sutlers (*lixae* of a different sort) and others who had once been such a pain to army commanders were now welcomed. They were positively encouraged to set up business near the camp, both to provide the soldiers with the luxuries and entertainments they needed to occupy their off-duty hours and to assist the military in obtaining its ordinary supplies on a contractual basis. Common-law wives of legionaries and the offspring of such unofficial unions became an increasingly significant element of the extramural population as did legionary veterans and their families. The illegitimate, usually peregrine sons of these liaisons were given Roman citizenship upon enlistment (a strong motivation for signing on and an arrangement which guaranteed the army a steady stream of recruits), giving their *origo* or place of family origin as *castris* 'the camp'. Ultimately, this process led to the emergence of hereditary military families; the sons of soldiers and veterans raised in the *canabae* being recruited into the legion and they in their turn marrying and repeating the cycle.

Already by the middle of the first century the existence of these communities as part and parcel of military units had been given *de facto* recognition by the army command although it was some time before the legal situation was clarified. As one would expect, the growth of these settlements was closely regulated. The legion could not afford to have the effectiveness of its defences impaired by agglomerations of civilian buildings. Indeed, by the time that Chester was founded it appears that the development of an extramural settlement beside fortresses was not merely anticipated but actively planned for. Included were the zoning of areas for particular types of building and activity, and the provision of certain essential facilities for the civilian population such as a bath-building. Such planning was essential given the wide range of structures and facilities that the legion itself needed to construct outside the defences. The proportion of Roman citizens in these communities was very high and they quickly organised, presumably under the overall aegis of the legate or the *praefectus castrorum*, councils to look after the everyday regulation and administration of their communities. The inscriptions these bodies erected to record their decisions and public works refer to the magistrates and other officials they appointed while the community as a whole is usually referred to as the '*veterani et cives Romani consistentes in canabis...*', that is 'the veterans and (other) Roman citizens settled in the *canabae* of' such and such a fortress.

At most legionary fortresses founded before the middle of the second century a second civil settlement rapidly grew up a short distance beyond, and entirely separate from, the *canabae*. Generally located 1-2km out from the *canabae* and with an open space interposed between the latter's cemetery and its own, these outer civil settlements could be very substantial and in some cases grew to a greater size than the fortress suburbs. In a few cases, such as *Carnuntum, Aquincum* and *Viminacium* they were elevated to the status of self-governing towns or *municipia*. This phenomenon of '*siedlungsdualität*' as it has been termed by German scholars also occurred at some of the legionary fortresses in Britain, including Chester. It is thought to have been the result of people wishing to settle as close as possible to the fortress but outside the area under the direct control of the legion known as its *prata* or *territorium*.

The Roman legion is thought of first and foremost as an efficient fighting-machine and the instrument of conquest. Once the enemy was defeated it imposed and maintained a peace which facilitated social, political and above all economic development by which new peoples were assimilated into and shared in the prosperity of the Roman commonwealth and became Roman. It not only defended the Empire from incursions from outside which would disturb that prosperity and disrupt civilised life but also contributed directly to the development of the provinces by assisting in the building of their infrastructure — roads, bridges, aqueducts and major public buildings — which enabled society to function on the Roman model. A permanent and mature legionary fortress like Chester was far more than just an army camp. With its attendant civil settlements and close ties with the indigenous population such places were microcosms of Roman society in general where soldier and civilian, immigrant and native gradually blended into a single community.

4 The foundation of the fortress

15 Denarius *of the Emperor Vespasian issued by the Rome mint in AD 74*

Strategic and political background

The collapse of the treaty relationship with Brigantia was a pivotal moment in the history of Roman Britain. Rather than reinstating Cartimandua or a successor client-ruler it was decided that lasting peace could only be achieved by the annexation of Brigantia and, as a natural corollary of that decision, the completion of the subjugation of the Welsh tribes. The second of these objectives was largely achieved by Cerialis' immediate successor Sextus Julius Frontinus (AD 74-7) leaving only the final reduction of Anglesey to be carried out by Gnaeus Julius Agricola (AD 77-84) in the first year of his governorship. This was the overall context for the placing of a legion at Chester. The near-doubling of the size of the territory under direct Roman control during the AD 70s necessitated a thoroughgoing and permanent redeployment of the military forces in Britain. This redeployment consisted essentially of the removal of the remaining garrisons from Southern England and their transfer to new bases in Wales and the North. In the wake of this 'demilitarisation' a policy of Romanisation and urbanisation was vigorously promoted in the South. Events in Britain during this period were of more than mere local concern; they were also of great interest to the new Emperor Vespasian (**15**). The Brigantian situation in fact afforded Vespasian something that every emperor desired at the start of his reign: the opportunity to achieve a great military victory and thus enhance his reputation and fitness to rule in the eyes of his subjects, not least the army. This was particularly important in Vespasian's case because of the violent circumstances in which he became emperor and as the founder of a new dynasty — the Flavians. As already mentioned, both Vespasian and his elder son Titus had experienced military service in Britain; it can be seen that the decision to adopt a policy of advance and conquest in the province had as much to do with political propaganda back at Rome as it did with local exigencies. Having commanded *legio II Augusta* back in AD 43, Vespasian would have seen at first hand how Claudius used the invasion of Britain to strengthen his grip on power during the first faltering years of his reign, especially as the latter was able to claim that he had been victorious where even the great Caesar himself had failed. Its importance to Vespasian is illustrated by the fact that he sent his best generals here. By further conquests in Britain he not only continued the policies of

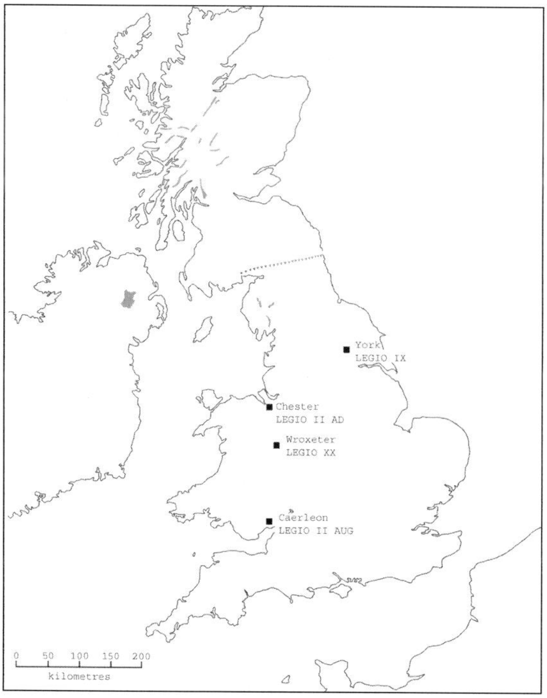

16 Legionary dispositions in Britain AD 75

Claudius but also established in the mind of the populace a link between himself and the last of the popular Julio-Claudians, thereby imbuing the new dynasty with an air of prestige and legitimacy. In the first half of AD 75, propaganda concerning the victories in Britain culminated in the ceremonial extending of the sacred boundary of the city of Rome (the *pomerium*), an event symbolising the extension of the Empire itself and a demonstration to the capital's citizens that Rome had not deviated from its divine mission to rule the world.

The redeployment of military forces in the opening years of the Flavian era included the advance of the Second *Augusta* to a new base at Caerleon in South Wales and the moving across of the Second *Adiutrix* from Lincoln to build another new fortress at Chester. As we have seen, elements of the latter may in fact have been at Chester for some time. The Ninth *Hispana* had moved forward to York from Lincoln a few years earlier, while the fourth legion in Britain, the Twentieth, remained at Wroxeter where it had taken over from the Fourteenth *Gemina* *c.*AD 65 (**16**). Although of limited strategic importance during the initial phases of Roman penetration into the region, Chester came into its own with the expansion of the province in the AD 70s. The occupation of the Cheshire Plain as a means of driving a wedge between the Ordovices and the Brigantes had long been recognised and in the period of consolidation following their subjugation it made sense to exploit this natural advantage by installing a legion in the area. The deciding factor in the selection of Chester as the site for the new fortress was undoubtedly its accessibility by sea via the estuary of the River Dee. In that period, the Dee was navigable right up to the sandstone ridge on which the fortress was built. Also, because of the conditions prevailing at the end of the last Ice Age, the river had gouged out a large bowl-shaped area immediately west of the ridge, which afforded ample space for harbour facilities. This was a vital asset because a legion required a vast amount of food and other supplies and it was far easier to transport large quantities of goods by water than land. Thus fortresses were sited next to navigable rivers wherever possible. The possession of a harbour was also important for the shipping of men and materials to the forts dotted along the coasts of North Wales and north-west England as well as for the mounting of combined land and sea operations. Also, contingency plans had already been laid for the conquest of Ireland if Tacitus' remarks about Agricola's ambitions are to be believed, an enterprise in which Chester would have played a key role had it ever taken place. The site was also the lowest point on the Dee where a bridge could easily be constructed and this crossing now became an important link in the principal line of military communication in the province running from Caerleon to York. Indeed, located at an equal distance from these other two fortresses and with a direct line of communication back to the South-East and the Channel ports, as well as facing out into the *Oceanus Hivernicus*, Chester in many ways was now the nodal point of the 'frontier' zone of Britain.

Given that *legio* XX was at Wroxeter, only 40 miles (64km) from Chester, it would have been in keeping with the general pattern of fortress building in Britain if it and not *II Adiutrix* had constructed the new base at *Deva* with the latter replacing it at *Viroconium*. However, the origins of the Second may have made it particularly eligible for this role given the coastal position of the new fortress and the location and nature of the campaigning that had to be undertaken in the AD 70s. This legion was raised initially from marines belonging to the section of the Mediterranean fleet based at Ravenna who in the autumn of AD 69 joined the forces of Vespasian in their assault on the army of Vitellius which held Italy. By March of the following year Vespasian had rewarded their support by enrolling them in a new legion — *legio II Adiutrix pia fidelis* (the 'Second Support Legion Loyal and Faithful') — which meant they gained the increased pay and privileges that went with legionary status. Shortly afterwards, the legion was despatched to help put down the Revolt of Civilis in Germany which was followed by its posting to Britain in AD 71. The subjugation of North Wales and the North of England involved combined land and sea operations on a considerable scale as did Agricola's invasion and occupation of Scotland in the period AD 78-84. Thus it made the best use of the individual expertise of these two legions for the Twentieth to take the lead on land with *II Adiutrix* spearheading the amphibious landings. The Second was also the only legion in the province whose loyalty to the Flavian cause was absolutely unquestionable and, as is explained below, this may have been another reason for its installation at Chester

Siting of the fortress

Because the local topography and the surrounding landscape have changed so much in recent centuries it is difficult now to appreciate many of the factors which caused the Roman Army to select Chester as the location for a legionary fortress. The course of the Dee was undoubtedly the most influential. As it approaches Chester from the south the Dee swings sharply to the west to cut through the low ridge of sandstone, forming a narrow gorge before opening out again into the bowl-shaped area now occupied by the Roodee racecourse (**17**). The narrowness of the gorge and its rock banks facilitated the bridging of the river while the broad expanse of the Roodee afforded a natural harbour. The fortress was sited on the north side of the river some distance back from the steep drop down to the latter but still able to command the crossing. In addition to a gentle downward slope to the south the portion of the ridge occupied by the fortress also had something of a 'hog's back' profile, sloping away both to the east and to the west. Thus,

17 *Aerial photograph of Chester showing outline of fortress and position of major approach roads. North at top of picture*

from the highest point within the defences at +95ft (29m) OD (Ordnance Datum) near the north gate the ground fell away to *c.* +72ft (22m) OD and *c.* +80ft (24.2m) OD at the north-west and north-east angles respectively. A more level site was available to the east, and a more elevated one to the north, but this spot was preferred because of its commanding view of the bridge, the protection afforded by the river on the south and the west, and its proximity to the harbour. The southern defences were sited close to the head of a deep defile lying to the south-west and a similar but lesser feature to the south-east. This enhanced the effectiveness of the defences and also made it easier to defend the extramural areas to the west and south should the situation arise. Also, as is described below, the terrain of this part of the ridge facilitated the design of an efficient drainage system for the fortress. An additional advantage of the site, though not one relevant to the precise positioning of the fortress, was the availability of a permanent water supply in the form of copious natural springs located a little over only a mile (2km) to the east.

Date of construction

The precise date of the beginning of work on the fortress has long been a subject of debate. This has centred largely on two pieces of inscriptional evidence from the site: lead ingots cast in AD 74 (**18**) and lead water pipes manufactured during the first half of AD 79 (**19** & **colour plate 15**). Some have associated the latter with the early stages of the construction process and the former with a pre-fortress base. Others, however, have regarded the ingots as actually marking the start of building work, though perhaps

18 Lead ingot found with the remains of a timber jetty at the Roodee 1886. Expanded, the inscription translates as: '(Cast) while the Emperor Vespasian Augustus was consul for the fifth time and Titus, acclaimed imperator, *consul for the third time' i.e. AD 74. On the side is the word Deceangl meaning 'mined in the land of the Deceangli'*

19 Inscribed lead water main found c.*50m north of Eastgate Street on the site of the* praetorium *in 1899. Expanded, the inscription translates as: '(Made) when the Emperor Vespasian and Titus, acclaimed* imperator, *were consuls for the ninth and seventh times respectively and when Gnaeus Julius Agricola was Governor of Britain' i.e. AD 79 (before 24 June)*

produced and stockpiled in advance. The ingots are the earliest known to have been produced during the period of direct Imperial working of the Flintshire lead-fields. It is tempting to assume the impetus for this was the decision to erect a legionary fortress at Chester and the very significant quantities of lead this would require. A consideration of the time required to complete the construction of certain fortress buildings also favours the earlier date. For example, we know from a fragmentary commemorative inscription dating to the reign of Vespasian (but after AD 71) that the baths (*thermae*) were already operational by the middle of AD 79 at the very latest and could well have been finished several years earlier (**34**). The massiveness and technical sophistication of the bath-building, with its complex vaulted superstructure and intricate heating and water distribution systems, made its construction a complicated process. Furthermore, the extensive use of concrete, which had to be allowed to set properly, also meant that certain stages of the process could not be hurried. Consequently, a minimum period of two years would seem appropriate for its construction. Furthermore, at Inchtuthil, where work on the *thermae* had not even begun when the fortress was abandoned after three or four years occupation, it seems it did not feature in the primary wave of construction activity. Finally, it now seems likely that the two lead water pipes bearing cast inscriptions which date their manufacture to the first half of AD 79 belong to a single water main supplying the strange Elliptical Building, an extravagant, non-utilitarian structure which is most unlikely to have been given priority in the construction schedule. Consequently, on present evidence a date of either AD 74 or 75 for the beginning of work on the fortress seems the most probable, although AD 73 or even 72 cannot be totally discounted.

Construction process, logistics and plan

Whatever military installation had previously existed at Chester was completely demolished and its site cleared ready for the laying-out of the new legionary fortress. The majority of the initial buildings were built of timber for the sake of expediency although it was clearly the intention to replace them in stone as and when circumstances allowed. A few however were constructed in stone from the beginning. The baths for example had to be of masonry construction because of the fire risk from the extensive hypocaust systems and there were a number of other buildings which were built of stone from the beginning, in some cases perhaps for reasons of prestige. The construction process was a major undertaking. It would have required careful planning and scheduling of the operations involved including the acquisition and transportation to the site of the vast quantities of raw materials needed, as well as the preparation of detailed designs for individual buildings, facilities and the supporting infrastructure. A legion was capable of all these tasks and needed no outside expertise. It was organised and functioned as a fully self-supporting unit containing within its ranks all the specialists needed to design and build an entire fortress; it was a combat unit and engineering corps combined.

We do not know what proportion of the legion was actively engaged in the construction but this would presumably have been at least half its strength. Temporary accommodation would have been required for the workforce and stockpiled materials. The fortress at Inchtuthil, unencumbered by modern settlement, demonstrates the extensive nature of such temporary works. There was a labour camp about the same size as the fortress itself, a stores-compound, and a defended enclosure which contained comfortable accommodation for the officers in charge of the construction programme. Chief amongst these of course would have been the *praefectus castrorum*. As is usual in such circumstances, the commandant and the other senior officers probably did not take up

Table 1: estimated fortress construction statistics
Flavian — timber requirements

FORTRESS **Building**	**Worked timber** (cubic feet)	**Uncut timber** (cubic feet)	**Weight** (tons)	**Wagonloads** (1,763lb load)
Barracks	511,520	682,014	12,348	15,682
Rampart buildings	38,163	50,883	921	1,170
Senior officers houses	42,403	56,537	1,023	1,300
Auxiliary barracks	48,233	64,311	1,163	1,479
Principia	30,035	40,035	725	921
Hospital	35,336	47,102	852	1,083
Praetorium	14,134	18,834	341	433
Others in *latera praetorii*	47,703	63,604	1,152	1,462
Store	10,600	14,134	255	325
Workshops	17,668	23,534	426	542
Tabernae	50,353	67,138	1,215	1,543
Rampart	153,710	204,947	3,711	4,712
Gates & towers	22,085	29,435	532	677
Totals	**1,021,943**	**1,362,508**	**24,664**	**31,329**
EXTRAMURAL FACILITIES				
Construction camp/annexe	176,678	235,512	4,264	5,415
Amphitheatre	13,357	17,809	323	410
Mansio	17,668	23,569	427	542
Harbour works	42,403	56,537	1,024	1,300
Bridge	14,134	18,834	341	433
Scaffolding	3,534	4,700	85	108
Grand totals	**1,289,717**	**1,719,469**	**31,128**	**39,537**

Woodland felled to provide 31,128 tons of timber:-
@ yield of 40 tons per acre = 778 acres
@ yield of 80 tons per acre = 389 acres
@ yield of 120 tons per acre = 256 acres

residence until the fortress was well on the way to completion. Little is known of the equivalent works at Chester. Lengths of an early military-style ditch following an east-west alignment were found beneath later civilian buildings east of the fortress during excavations in the 1930s and might conceivably belong to one of the construction compounds. Alternatively, they might belong to an annexe attached to the fortress. This

Table 2: estimated fortress construction statistics
Flavian Thermae

Material	**Quantity** (tons)	**Weight** (tons)	**Wagonloads** (1,763lbs load)
Rock excavated	247,350	17,224	21,884
Wall facing-stones	418,000	7,382	9,379
Mortar	77,738	4,330	5,501
Concrete	47,703	2,657	3,376
Brick & tile:			
i) Roofing			
— tegulae	33,176	371	471
— imbrices	40,001	125	159
ii) Hypocaust			
— pedales	70,000	334	424
— sesquipedales	2,800	63.8	81
— bipedales	2,200	64	81
iii) Wall/vault lining			
— double tubuli	54,736	635	807
iv) Flooring			
— spicata	200,000	60	75
Tesserae	3,057,175	9.8	12
Lead:			
i) Distribution pipes		39	50
ii) Reservoir lining		34	43
Totals	—	**33,328**	**42,343**

appears to have been the function of a turf rampart found just outside the south-west angle during the Cuppin Street excavations of the late 1980s. Running along the southern edge of the deep gulley which once crossed this area, this seems to have defined an annexe attached to the western half of the southern defences in the Flavian period.

That the construction of the legionary fortress and its ancillary structures required large quantities of raw materials and manufactured items is obvious but it is only when detailed calculations are made — set out in the accompanying **Tables 1 & 2** — that the true scale of the logistics involved becomes clear. Timber was undoubtedly the material required in the greatest bulk, perhaps as much as 1,750,000cu ft (49,525m^3) in its unworked state. This equates to something in the region of 31,500 tons (32,000 metric tonnes) which, on the basis of a generally agreed average carrying capacity of wagons in the ancient world of 1,750lb (800kg), would have to be transported in the form of 40,000 wagonloads. If one assumes 200 days in the year when conditions were suitable for transport and building operations, then this translates into 200 wagonloads on each and every one of those days, or 100 wagonloads on each working day over two years. The situation would of course have been complicated by many other factors such as the number of wagons and draught animals available for work, the order and speed of the building operations, the time it took to fell and prepare the timber and the distance that the timber had to be transported. The impact on the surrounding landscape must have been quite dramatic with acre after acre of woodland disappearing week after week for months on end. The brushwood and smaller branches not needed for building would have been used as fuel for the dozens of furnaces and kilns in the construction camp producing the thousands of metal items, especially nails, needed for the building process. Ingots of copper, iron and lead had to be brought to the site, by sea wherever possible. The lead from the Flintshire mines for example would have been loaded on to ships on the coast somewhere near either Prestatyn and/or Flint, as happened later, and brought to the fortress up the Dee estuary, as evidenced by the discovery of an ingot of AD 74 in association with the remains of a jetty in the harbour area. Lime would have been needed both for the plaster wall-rendering in the timber buildings and also for the restricted number of stone structures in the fortress and was probably obtained from the same area. Although stone buildings were small in number, the quantities of additional materials required for their construction were considerable. The *thermae* alone would have needed over 6-7,000 tons of mortar and concrete, nearly 1,700 tons of brick and tile (including 70,000 bricks each 1pM square, used to form the hypocaust pilae), and more than 400,000 blocks of stone for the wall-facings. Fortunately, the stone did not have to be transported very far, as sandstone of reasonable building quality was widely available on the site. However, the 7,500 tons of rock this figure represents still had to be quarried, and all those blocks dressed, by hand. This was also true of the 3 million *tesserae* needed for the floor mosaics in this complex.

An overall plan for the fortress and designs for the individual buildings, including dimensions, would have been prepared by the legionary *architectus* and his assistants under the overall supervision of the *praefectus castrorum*. The plans (*formae*) themselves were presumably executed on papyrus or some similar material although a copy of the fortress ground plan may have been prepared on a more durable material such as a slab of stone or marble or a sheet of bronze. We know from Vitruvius that the drawings might also include elevations (*orthographia*) and artist's impressions (*scaenographia*). All of these would have been lodged in the fortress archive in the headquarters building (*principia*) and it is clear from the case of the Elliptical Building (see chapter 11) that such records could be kept for a very long time indeed; in this instance for something approaching 150 years. The defences and the accommodation for the men would obviously have had priority in the construction programme closely followed by food stores, the hospital and probably the *principia*. At what point building of the senior officers' houses was fitted into the schedule is unclear but could well have depended on the whims of the individual legate. Given the time needed to build the *thermae*, a start was probably made soon after the first wave of construction activity but completion would have taken at least a year.

Selection of the site was followed by the detailed surveying of the fortress and its subdivision into plots by the *agrimensores* and the marking out of the lines of the individual buildings by the *mensores*. Like the other fortresses in Britain, Chester was laid out using

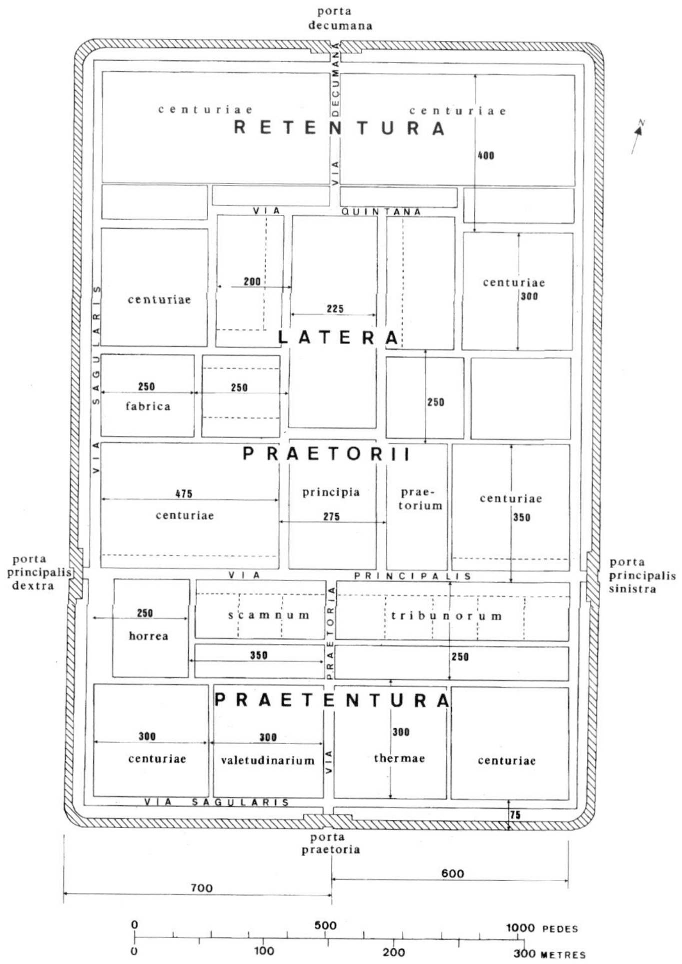

20aPlan of the primary fortress of c.AD 75 showing principal streets, major zones and lesser divisions, location of main buildings, and dimensions illustrating the employment of units based on multiples of the Roman foot or pes. *KEY:* centuriae = *barracks;* principia = *headquarters building;* praetorium = *legionary commander's residence;* fabrica = *workshops;* horrea = *granaries;* thermae = *baths;* scamnum tribunorum = *tribunes' houses;* valetudinarium = *hospital*

units based on multiples of the Roman foot or *pes Monetalis* — 1pM being the equivalent of 295mm or just over 11½in. The actual surveying was carried out using an instrument known as the *groma* which consisted essentially of an iron or bronze cross with four arms set at 90 degrees to one another, from the ends of which plumb lines were suspended. It was supported on a staff which was located off-centre so that the instrument could be positioned over a precise point using another plumb line hung from the centre. This arrangement also enabled the surveyor to take sightings through opposing plumb lines and, by employing markers, to set out straight lines and right-angles. Discrepancies did occur, as will be seen in the case of the Elliptical Building, but the overall level of accuracy was impressive. By the time that Chester was founded a more or less standard shape for the legionary fortress had evolved from the arrangements of the marching-camp. This took the form of a rectangle with rounded corners often referred to in modern literature as the 'playing card' shape. The position of certain of the principal buildings was common to all fortresses as was the placing, for obvious reasons, of the barracks in the plots closest to the defences. Beyond these conformities, there was considerable variation in the

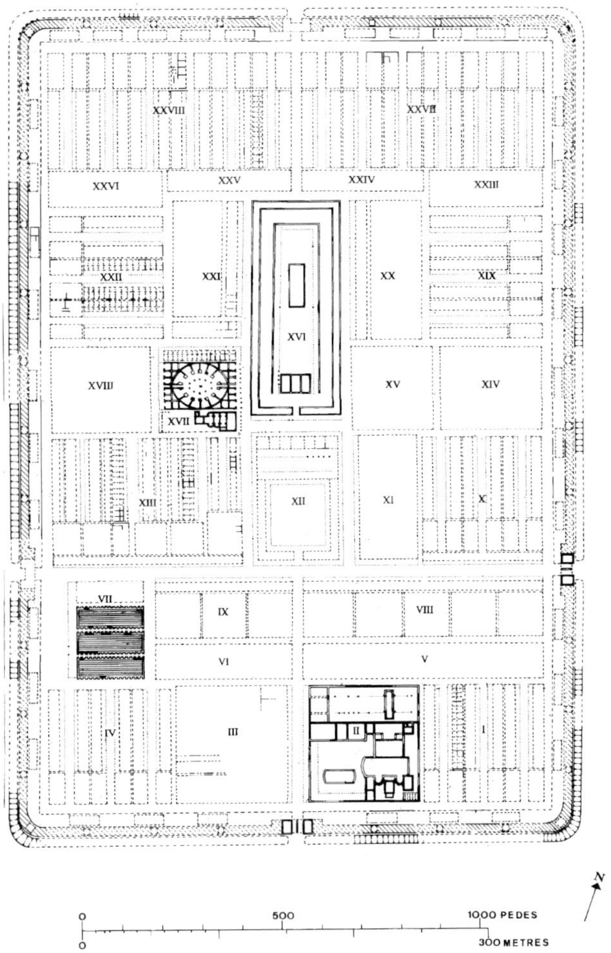

20b Plan of the primary fortress of AD 75 showing known (solid lines) and restored (brokenlines) buildings. A numbering system using Roman numerals has been employed for the individual blocks or insulae *for ease of reference*

disposition of the remaining buildings from one fortress to another and there certainly was not a standard fortress plan. Having said that, the internal arrangements of the Chester fortress exceed the parameters of normal variation to such a degree that they can be called extraordinary.

The primary step in the laying-out of the fortress was choosing the position and orientation of the *principia*, which determined the alignment of the entire fortress. At Chester it faced south overlooking the river crossing. With the site of the *principia* established, the line of the two principal streets of the fortress could be fixed (**20a**). Running across its frontage was the *via principalis* and at right angles to this, running away southwards on the alignment of the centre-line of the *principia*, was the *via praetoria*; all other streets were laid out on a grid respecting their alignment. The lines of the main streets are still evident today. Eastgate Street and Watergate Street follow the line of the *via principalis* and Bridge Street that of the *via praetoria*. The rearmost portion of the fortress was divided by another major street — the *via decumana* — whose line is perpetuated by the northern stretch of Northgate Street. This continued the alignment of the *via praetoria* but did not link up with it for it ran into a second transverse street — the *via quintana* (the 'fifth' street) — which separated the rear and central divisions of the fortress interior. Separating the area to be occupied by buildings from the defences was a perimeter road, which ran all the way round the enclosure. This was the *via sagularis*, so named because this was where the centuries assembled in full uniform including the military cloak or *sagum*. The *via principalis* and the *via praetoria* were bordered on both sides by covered walkways, either verandas supported by timber posts or porticoes carried by stone columns attached to the frontages of individual buildings. Long stretches of the two main streets connecting the *via principalis* with the *via decumana* were similarly equipped. Along most of these thoroughfares the verandas/porticoes fronted long narrow buildings known as *tabernae* which appear to have been used for a variety of purposes but chiefly storage. The four main gates of the fortress lay at the points where the first four of these roads crossed the line of the defences. The sites of the east and north gates — the *porta principalis sinistra* (main gate, left hand) and the *porta decumana* — are overlain by gate structures of recent times while the positions of the south gate and the west gate — the *porta praetoria* and the *porta principalis dextra* (main gate, right hand) — have disappeared from the townscape owing to the extension of the defences in the early medieval period. The interior was thus divided into three zones. The forward portion between the *via principalis* and the southern defences was the *praetentura*, the central zone defined by the *via principalis* and the *via quintana* formed the *latera praetorii*, and the rear zone between the *via quintana* and the northern defences was termed the *retentura*. Each of these zones was itself divided into a varying number of lateral strips or *scamna* containing individual plots or *insulae*. For ease of reference a numerical sequence has been devised for the plots (**20b**).

As measured over the ramparts the dimensions of the primary fortress were 1,945ft (592.8m) north/south by 1,351ft (411.7m) east/west, giving an area of 60.28 acres (24.40ha). This is very close to the presumably intended dimensions of 2,000 by 1,400pM. The stone curtain wall subsequently added to the face of the rampart increased these dimensions to 1,953 and 1,359ft (595.25 and 414.1m) respectively, taking the overall size of the fortress to 60.9 acres (24.65ha). The area of the Chester fortress is fully 20% greater than its close contemporaries at York and Caerleon, whose overall sizes were 50.17 acres (20.3ha) and 50.64 acres (20.50ha) respectively. The extra space was provided by increasing the relative length of the fortress, making its length to width ratio close to 3:2. At York and Caerleon it approximates to 5:4. Chester's greater size has been the subject of much debate and various explanations have been put forward. These are examined in the next chapter together with a new theory, which, if correct, would change perceptions of Chester's status in late first-century Britain.

A perimeter zone 80pM deep accommodated the defences and a strip of ground behind them known as the *intervallum* which contained cookhouses and bread-ovens as well as the *via sagularis*. The building space defined by the latter street thus measured 1,847 by 1,224pM (545 by 361m) giving a usable building area of 48.58 acres or 19.67ha. The principal streets, such as the *via principalis* and the *via praetoria*, were 30pM wide while many of the minor ones were either 20 or 15pM in width. The *praetentura* was divided into two *scamna*. The forward one was 280pM deep and its sinistral (east) half was divided into two *insulae*. That bordering the *via praetoria* (*II*) contained the principal bathing complex or *thermae* and that beside it (*I*) the barracks of one cohort laid out *per strigas*, that is with their long axis at 90 degrees to the *scamnum*.

Both *insulae* were 300pM wide if the measurement of that containing the baths also includes the minor street down its east side. The outer *insula* in the south-west corner (*IV*) has not been explored but is assumed from comparison with the arrangements in other fortresses to have held barracks for another cohort. Traces of primary timber buildings have been found in the *insula* opposite the baths (*III*) but insufficient is known to enable their function to be determined. Given the frequent pairing of baths and hospital on adjacent plots in fortresses it is possible that this *insula* housed the legionary *valetudinarium*. The area between the front *scamnum* and the *via principalis* also has a depth of 280pM, if one includes space for the street separating it from the former. It has only been explored to any significant extent at the west end where there was a group of certainly three and more probably four granaries (*horrea*) in *insula* VII. Much of the rest of this area, to both sides of the *via praetoria* (*V*, *VI*, *VIII*, *IX*), would have been taken up by the residences of the tribunes and the *praefectus castrorum*. Fragments of mosaic flooring and hypocausts certainly confirm the presence of well-appointed residential type buildings in later periods. Part of the equivalent area at Caerleon was occupied by accommodation for an *ala* of auxiliary cavalry and the same may have been true at Chester.

It was mentioned above that most fortresses have a length to width ratio of 5:4. In the majority also, the distribution of the internal area between the front and rear halves of the fortress is of the order of either 2:3 or 9:11. At Chester the length to width ratio is 3:2 and the forward/rear split approaches 30/70. Chester has two *scamna* in its *praetentura* of more or less equal depth while both Caerleon and York, and others, have an extra *scamnum* of about half size. They also have three *scamna* of approximately equal size in the rear division of the interior. To compensate for this one might expect Chester to have a half-sized *scamnum* added to either the *latera praetorii* or the *retentura*. In fact, the *latera praetorii* was provided with an extra *scamnum* of full-size while the *retentura* in addition received another *scamnum* of about one third the normal depth. Two other fortresses, *Novae* and *Novaesium*, have unusually long rear halves but each has only one extra *scamnum* of less than full size. Both also lack the extra 'half-size' *scamnum* in the *praetentura* like Chester. With the vast amount of excavation during recent decades it can now be seen that it is the arrangement of the central zone — the *latera praetorii* — that sets Chester apart from its fellows. The *scamnum* bordering the *via principalis* was the largest, with a depth 325pM. The *principia*, occupying the central plot overlooking the junction with the *via praetoria* (*XII*), did in fact project a little further back than this, resulting in two double right-angled turns in the course of the 15pM wide street at its rear. West of the *principia*, occupying all of the space between it and the defences, lay the barracks of the first cohort (*XIII*) while to the east stood first the legionary commandant's residence or *praetorium* (*XI*) and then another group of barracks sufficient for a cohort (*X*). In both cases the barracks were laid out *per strigas*. The distribution of buildings described thus far is quite conventional but this ceases with the next *scamnum* to the north where both the layout of plots and the type of buildings contained in them differ markedly from the standard. In the centre was an enormous building of courtyard plan, which occupied not just the *insula* immediately behind the *principia* but also the one behind that again (*XVI*). Measuring 540pM or 160m, another unusual feature of this building was the fact that it was built in stone from the very beginning. The nature of the buildings intended to occupy the two *insulae* in the eastern half of this *scamnum* (XIV & XV) is not known as, owing to the presence of the cathedral, there has been little excavation in this area. The *insula* west of the southern half of the enormous building just mentioned contained four buildings, the largest of which was the Elliptical Building, so called because of its ovoid shape. Here too the primary version of this building was constructed of stone. The standard of construction was in fact of a very high quality with foundations of hard concrete set in pits and trenches cut deep into solid rock and supporting neatly coursed masonry. Its superior construction was equalled by its exotic and unique architectural form, so far unparalleled not merely in the context of legionary fortresses but indeed in both civil and military branches of Roman architecture anywhere in the Empire. Beside the Elliptical Building, to the south, was a small bath-building while the remaining portions of this *insula*, consisting of the south-west corner and a strip along the northern edge, were occupied by linear store buildings (*tabernae*) of timber construction. The westernmost *insula* in this *scamnum* (*XVIII*) was occupied by one or more timber buildings. In later periods this was the site of the main workshops or *fabrica*. Whether the primary structure performed the same function is uncertain, as only fragments have been investigated. One part had a timber floor raised on joists but this could have been an office rather than a working area.

North of the possible *fabrica*, in the next *scamnum*, lay the barracks of another cohort (*XXII*) this time aligned *per scamna*, that is parallel with the *scamnum*. Although unproven another cohort was very probably accommodated in the *insula* (*XIX*) at the opposite end of this *scamnum*. As just described, the central plot in this range was occupied by the rear half of the gigantic building behind the *principia*. The *insula* immediately to its east (*XX*) has not been explored to any extent. That on the west side (*XXI*) was bounded on the east and south sides by long, narrow storage buildings. The remainder was left as open ground for many decades and it appears that whatever was intended to stand here was not even begun when the plan was abandoned.

The *scamnum* behind the one just described was very shallow being about one third the usual depth. Furthermore, the inner plots (*XXIV & XXV*) were shallower than the outer ones (*XXIII & XXVI*), owing to the fact that the central three plots in the *scamnum* immediately to the south projected around 10m farther north than those bordering the *via sagularis*. This caused the *via quintana* to 'dog-leg' at two points along its course. Minor explorations have taken place in the western half of this *scamnum* but the nature of the primary buildings, assuming any were actually constructed, is unknown.

The *retentura* contained a single *scamnum* 280pM deep which was completely occupied by barrack accommodation for four cohorts, laid out *per strigas* (*XXVII & XXVIII*).

The men

Although the identities of the senior officers in *legio II* during its time at Chester are unknown, the names of a number of centurions and lower ranks are preserved on inscriptions. As for the centurions, only their names are known as they are mentioned on

21 *Tombstone of Gaius Iuventius Capito, soldier in* legio II Adiutrix, *in the century of Julius Clemens, who died aged 40. Recovered from North Wall (west), 1891*

the tombstones of soldiers who served under them. Such men include Julius Clemens, Vibius Clemens, Mettius Ferox and Petronius Fidus. Another centurion, Julius Secundus, is mentioned on the tombstone of an ordinary legionary found at Bath. The man in question, Caius Murrius Modestus, had presumably been sent to Bath to see if the hot springs could help cure an injury or affliction. Sadly, they proved ineffective for he died at the age of 25. Interestingly, the name Julius Secundus also occurs as one of the one joint dedicators of an altar found in the civil settlement at Heronbridge, 1½ miles south of Chester. It might just be the same man although his is a fairly common name. Other legionaries whose identities are known from their tombstones include Gaius Calventius Celer, Lucius Terentius Fuscus and Gaius Iuventius Capito (**21**), all of whom had been recruited from the Claudian colony of *Aprus* in Thrace. There is also Quintus Valerius Fronto from *Celeia* in Noricum and Lucius Valerius Seneca from *Savaria* in Pannonia.

5 The early fortress in detail

The defences

The primary defences of earth and timber, just like the wooden internal buildings, were provisonal structures built of impermanent materials for the sake of expediency in potentially hostile conditions. They were intended right from the beginning to be replaced by more permanent structures as and when circumstances and other demands on manpower permitted. The rampart was 20pM wide and consisted of a core composed variously of sand, clay, or rubble held in place by revetments of stacked turves 6 to 8pM thick front and rear. Its base consisted of a close-set grid of logs laid transversely, in two rows in some sectors, while further layers of timber strapping were incorporated in the main body of the rampart at regular vertical intervals of around 1pM to increase its stability and strength (**colour plate 8**). The timbers were generally less than 8in (20cm) in cross-section. The stubs of branches have been detected on some timbers and brushwood was used for some of the uppermost layers of strapping. This suggests that the timbers were the lesser boughs left over from felled trees whose trunks and main branches were to be employed as the main structural components of fortress buildings. Owing to the weight of the rampart and organic decay the timbers are usually found on excavation to have been compressed to a thickness of ½in (10mm) or less. Individual turves can often be discerned in sections taken through the rampart and are generally rectangular with a size of 1ft x 1ft 4in (30 x 40cm). The front face of the rampart was battered to form a slope of around 75 degrees while the rear face rose almost vertically to its maximum height of about 5ft (1.5m) (**colour plate 7**). The overall height of the rampart to walkway level is unknown. The maximum surviving height is around 9ft (2.70m) and it may be that the original full height was 10pM or 2.95m. It is not impossible however that it was as much as 15pM or 4.42m. The top of the rampart would have been finished as a level surface carrying a timber walkway protected by a palisade or breastwork at the front and with a safety rail along the rear (**22**).

Timber towers (*turres*) were provided both at the corners and at regular intervals on the long stretches in beween the latter and the gates. Little is known in detail of the angle-towers as only one post-pit of that at the south-west angle has been observed. Similary, only one example of an interval tower has been investigated to date but this has provided useful information. This was found during the Abbey Green excavations of 1975-8 on the eastern sector of the north defences. Three of the four rock-cut pits for its corner timbers were found enabling its dimensions to be fixed as 15pM or 4.42m square. The impressions of the actual posts also survived and were around 1ft 2in (35cm) square in section. The pits had sloped rear faces to facilitate placement of the posts. Confirming the logical supposition that the towers were built before the rampart, the filling of the post-pits was overlain by the basal log corduroy of the latter. From its position it is clear that this tower was the first one east of the north gate and this allows the spacing of the towers belonging to the primary defences to be determined at *c.*150pM or 45m. The total number of towers was either 34 or 36. The uncertainty stems from the fact that the length of the defences between the *portae principales* and the angle-towers is greater than the spacing for two towers at the usual intervals but rather less than that needed to accommodate three. Thus if the spacing was a little longer than usual the total number of towers would have been 34 or, if slightly shorter, 36. The height of the towers is entirely speculative but on the assumption that they incorporated a roofed platform 10pM above the rampart walkway their overall height, as measured from ground level, would have been in the region of 29ft (9.5m). Nothing is known of the timber gatehouses of the original defences. They were however undoubtedly similar to those of other contemporary fortresses, with twin portals flanked by towers a little larger than the single examples elsewhere along the circuit and joined by a covered fighting-platform.

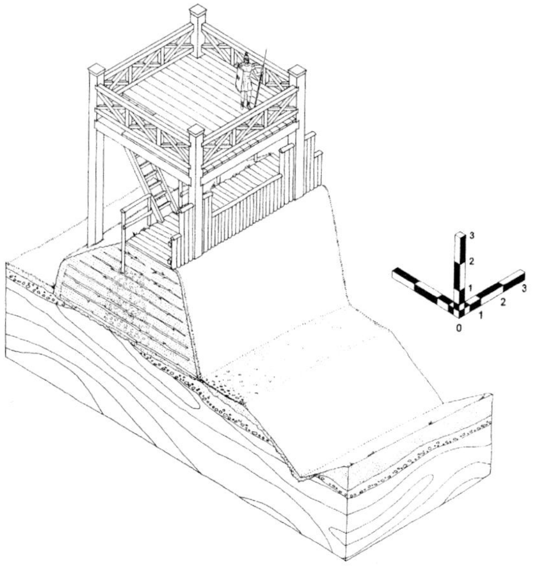

22 Reconstruction of the primary turf and timber fortress defences

In front of the rampart and separated from it by a berm about 6ft (1.8m) wide was a single ditch. Largely removed by its successors, this appears to have been a comparatively modest feature at a little over 5ft (1.5m) deep and about 10ft (3m) wide. As in later periods, there was probably a patrol-track along its outer edge.

The *intervallum* zone

Behind the defences lay a 60pM wide strip of ground known as the *intervallum*. This has been sampled on all four sides of the fortress, most extensively on the west side north of the *porta principalis dextra* and on the north east of the *porta decumana*. Occupying the inner third of this strip lay the *via sagularis*. This road ran round the entire perimeter of the interior and enabled the rapid assembly of the centuries from the neighbouring barracks and their movement to particular sections of the defences. Alongside its inner edge ran the large drain into which all the other drains of the fortress discharged, its contents eventually being conveyed to the exterior via culverts running diagonally beneath the *via sagularis* and the defences at the south-east and south-west angles. The remainder of the *intervallum* was given over to the accommodation of 'rampart buildings' and ovens placed here for easy access from the barracks and, in the latter's case, also to minimise the risk of fire. In their later form the rampart buildings were arranged in groups of three, one to each pair of barracks. They may have functioned as stores or armouries or they may have served as mess-rooms where the legionaries took certain of their meals communally in a number of 'sittings'. Some of their stone successors definitely functioned as cook-houses, with the ovens brought indoors. The later rampart buildings of stone conformed to a standard size and plan, measuring 70ft (21.3m) long and 24ft (7.3m) wide and divided internally into three rooms, with the central one being rather narrower than the other two. No complete example of their timber predecessors has been excavated, although judging by an example behind the west defences excavated in the 1960s their dimensions and internal arrangements were very similar. The ovens were sited in the spaces between the rampart buildings in batteries of three or four. A particulary well-preserved example of the Flavian period was examined during the St Martin's Fields excavation in 1964/5 opposite *insula* XXII. Built with clay-bonded walls of sandstone, this was horseshoe-shaped in plan with an internal diameter of 10ft (3m). The stoking-area in front of the oven had board-revetted sides held in place by posts set in the usual trench. These posts may also have supported a roof over the storing-area. The build-up of soot and ash around the oven, together with signs of successive repairs to the oven itself, indicated prolonged and intensive usage.

The barracks

Current understanding of the standard barrack of the Flavian period is based on the partial examination of a number of barracks in various sectors of the fortress over the last 40 years. The picture therefore is a composite one and the degree to which certain of the details applied to all barracks will only become clear if and when it becomes possible to reveal several complete examples belonging to different cohorts. The method of construction was that employed for all timber buildings of the early fortress. Narrow trenches were dug along the lines of the principal walls into which vertical posts were set at intervals varying from 3-5ft with the excavated material then put back in the trench around them and compacted (**23**). These posts were square with a section of about 6in (15cm) judging from the stumps sawn off and left in the ground to decay when the buildings were demolished. For the internal walls, the gaps between the main posts were filled in using wattle panels covered each side with a thick layer of daub. The whole was then rendered with plaster and given a lime wash finish. The exterior face of the outer walls may well have been clad with horizontal overlapping planks for better weatherproofing. It is assumed that wooden shingles would have been used to cover the roof. The floors were of compacted clay and sand.

The barracks were arranged in facing pairs separated by a minor street 20pM (5.9m) wide and with the centurion's quarters at the end adjacent to a major street (**24**), in effect either the *via sagularis* or the *via principalis*. Each pair of barracks and the intervening street

23 Example of a post-in-trench wall foundation typical of the earliest fortress buildings, Old Market Hall Site, Phase III, 1968

24 (below) Restored plan of Flavian timber barracks

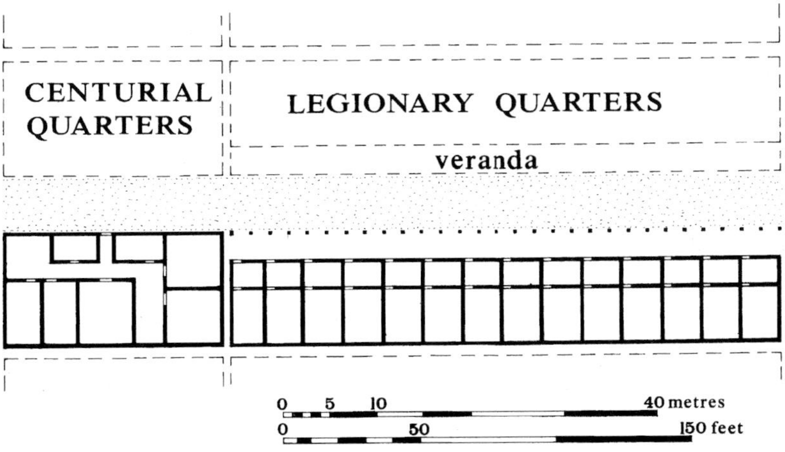

occupied a strip of ground notionally 100pM (29.5m) wide. In reality, because adjacent pairs of barracks were separated by a narrow alleyway, the space actually available for the buildings was reduced slightly. Each cohort of barracks thus occupied a plot 300pM (88.5m) wide. Each barrack block (*hemistrigium*) was 280pM (82.5m) long overall, of which 80pM (23.6m) was taken up by the centurion's quarters and the remaining 200pM (59m) by the legionaries' accommodation. The actual space allotted to the latter was slightly less as there was a narrow alley between the men's block and the centurion's quarters. Of the *c.*40pM (11.8m) width of the men's block, 30pM (8.85m) was assigned to the accommodation (20pM to the inner room and 10pM to the outer) and 10pM (2.95m) to a verandah supported by posts along its frontage. The main part of the building was subdivided into 14 pairs of rooms varying from 12-15pM in width. This is two more than in the subsequent stone barracks, but the same as the number of *contubernia* in the slightly later barracks at Inchtuthil. As a century consisted of 10 *contubernia* with 8 men apiece then on a

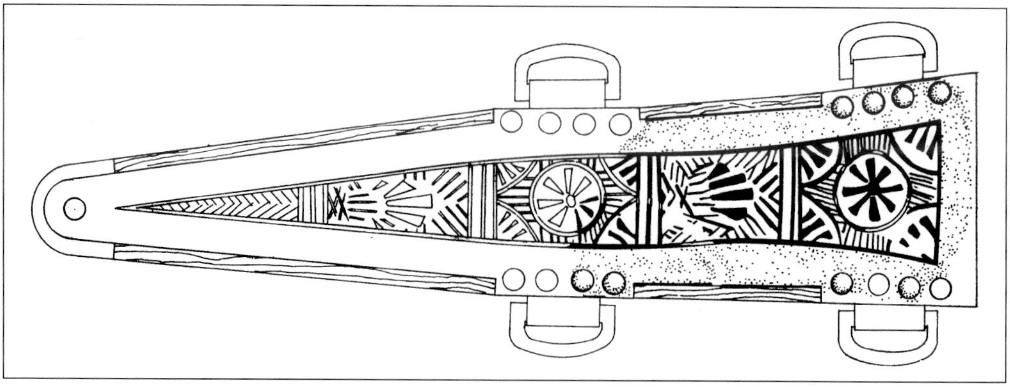

25 Drawing of inlaid silver or tin decoration on iron legionary dagger scabbard revealed by X-ray photography. First cohort barracks Crook Street Site 1974

strict definition there need only have been 10 sets of rooms. In fact extra rooms are found in the barracks of most fortresses. They were presumably used either to store surplus equipment, as separate accommodation for the non-commissioned officers such as the *optio*, *tessarius* and *signifer*, as living-quarters for the century's servants, or a combination of any or all of these. The inner and larger room, the *papilio*, was the living and sleeping area. The outer, the *arma*, was used for storage of the legionaries' everyday equipment — the large, rectangular shield (*scutum*), body armour of overlapping metal strips (*lorica segmentata*), helmet (*cassis*), javelin (*pilum*), short sword (*gladius*), dagger (*pugio*) (for decorated dagger scabbard *see* **25**), pickaxe (*dolabrum*) — along with various other acoutrements. Maintaining and cleaning arms and equipment to the standard required by the centurion must have taken up many hours of the legionary's time (**colour plates 1 & 2**).

As far as can be judged, the internal arrangements of the centurion's houses were very similar to those of their stone replacements, consisting in essence of a central narrow corridor with rooms opening off to either side. Not only was the accommodation far more spacious than that allotted to the ordinary legionary, but the standard of appointments was far higher. This was amply demonstrated by the large quantity of fine painted wall-plaster recovered from a centurion's house in the first cohort group during the Crook Street excavation of 1973. Sufficient was recovered to enable a reconstruction of the scheme of decoration (**colour plate 9**). Later centurion's houses incorporated a latrine room with a lead-lined outflow discharging directly into an external drain. The same arrangement may have existed in the primary buildings though the outflow was probably timber-lined.

The barracks of the first cohort lying west of the *principia* were arranged rather differently owing to its greater size. Wherever tested, the layout of the Flavian timber barracks has been found to be the same as the stone buildings of the second century. It consisted, as at Caerleon, of a mix of blocks of normal *contubernia* and others only one room wide: in our case, five of the former and six of the latter plus another narrow example set transversely along the north end of the three blocks at the west end of the *insula*. Precisely how the five double centuries of the first cohort were accommodated is

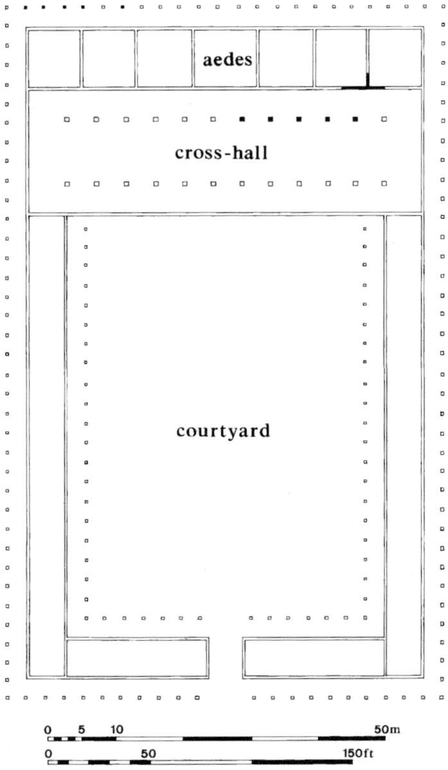

26 Plan of primary headquarters building of timber

unclear. The quarters of the five most senior centurions of the legion were, as one might expect, considerably more palatial than those of their junior colleagues. The quarters of the most senior of all the centurions, the *primus pilus*, were as usual situated closest to the *principia*. Although only a minute percentage has been explored its overall size can be estimated as about 82ft (25m) east-west by 105ft (32m) north-south. In fact, the two blocks of men's accommodation to the north were made shorter than usual to provide the required space. One other centurion's house in this group has been partially examined and this is the building exposed on the Crook Street 1973 site which yielded the collection of painted wall plaster just mentioned. This building appears to have been the same size as a normal centurial block, a situation repeated at Caerleon where the building in question occupies exactly the same position relative to the other houses with two of larger size to either side. Possibly these more modest quarters were provided for a junior centurion who took on the *primus pilus*' nominal duties as centurion of the first century.

The headquarters building — *principia*

The headquarters building, the administrative and religious focus of the fortress, was positioned centrally (*XII*) overlooking the junction of the two principal streets and facing the front gate of the fortress (**26**). Such buildings were laid out to a standardised plan with three basic components. Fronting the *via principalis* was a large open courtyard surrounded on three sides by ranges of offices and/or stores usually fronted by porticoes, access being gained via a monumental entrance centrally located in the side facing the street. The courtyard served as a meeting-place where guard details could be assembled and changed and where small parades could be held. It also probably contained a small platform and altar where religious sacrifices were made by the legate to read the omens. At the back of the courtyard and running across the entire width of the plot was an aisled cross-hall or *basilica*, the stone versions of which can be compared for size and majesty with the nave of

27 *Tombstone of Aurelius Diogenes the* imaginifer *or Bearer of the Imperial Effigy. He holds the effigy of the reigning emperor, set atop a pole and now defaced, in his right hand. Recovered from North Wall (east) 1887*

a medieval cathedral. At one end of the hall there would have been a platform or tribunal from which the legate would address officers and men, issue orders and announce imperial decrees and events, perform military ceremonies, and review disciplinary proceedings. It would also have contained altars and statues, including one of the reigning emperors.

The cross-hall was entered from the courtyard through a centrally positioned doorway and directly opposite lay the legionary shrine (*aedes* or *sacellum*) where the standards were kept. This was the central one of a range of rooms, usually five in number, on the far side of the hall which comprised the third element of the building. The legion's standards were ranged around the *aedes*, which also contained images (*imagines*) of the emperor and his family, and were guarded day and night. One of the Chester tombstones commemorates an *imaginifer*, a certain Aurelius Diogenes, and he is depicted carrying the *imago* (**27**) while an altar found in the *retentura* records a dedication to the *Genius* of the standard-bearers of the Twentieth Legion by Titus Flavius Valerianus, a member of their guild (*collegium signiferi*). An early third-century document from the archives of the *cohors XX Palmyrenorum* stationed at Dura Europos (the *Feriale Duranum*) lists many of the festivals which the army had to observe. In addition to those concerned with the rites of the principal deities, and the imperial cult (including the annual oath of allegiance to the emperor), there are also festivals associated with the cult of the *signa* (standards). These included the *Rosaliae Signorum* when the garrison, or a large part of it, was assembled in the courtyard of the *principia* to watch the standards brought out, paraded and then decorated with crowns of roses. This was followed by a thanksgiving ceremony (*supplicatio*). The *aedes* also housed the regimental treasury which contained military funds, used to purchase supplies and suchlike, the legion's pay-chests, and the savings — some mandatory and some voluntary — of the soldiers. These funds were administered by the *signiferi*. In some cases where the rest of the *principia* was of timber, the *aedes* was built of stone to protect the standards from fire. In others, the floor of the *aedes* was raised above ground level to create sufficient space beneath for a timber-revetted pit where the pay-chests would be more secure. A later development in which the Chester *principia* shared was the construction of a sunken and vaulted strongroom under the *aedes* which functioned as the treasury or *aerarium*. The rooms to one side of the aedes contained the central record office (*tabularium*) of the legion staffed by clerks (*librarii*) under the supervision of the *cornicularius* and his deputy the *actuarius*. On the other side lay the offices of the standard-bearers whose responsibilities included maintaining records of all the legion's financial transactions and the accounts of individual legionaries. One only has to survey the scope of the collection of official records found at the auxiliary fort of *Vindolanda* to get an idea of the scale of the archives of a legion which had a complement at least ten times the size, along with a far greater diversity of matters needing to be recorded.

That the first *principia* at Chester was built of timber was revealed in an excavation along its west side in 1948/9 conducted jointly by Sir Ian Richmond and Graham Webster. This was in fact the first occasion that timber buildings had been recognised at Chester. Beneath the flooring of the external colonnade of the stone *principia* they discovered a north-south linear feature which they interpreted as the post-in-trench foundation of its predecessor. This led them to re-examine the foundations for column bases of the stone period cross-hall preserved in the basement of premises on the west side of Northgate Street. Here they discerned traces of filled-in trenches belonging to the range of offices along the back of its timber precursor. This in turn enabled them to identify an east-west line of regularly spaced, square, rock-cut pits found many years earlier a short distance to the south as the posts of the north aisle of the earlier *principia* (**28**). There matters rested until 1969 when the final phase of excavations on the Old Market Hall site exposed the rear portion of the rooms along the back of the cross-hall west of the *aedes*. This disclosed a line of post-pits belonging to a veranda along the north side of timber *principia* positioned a few metres south of the back wall of the stone building. Significantly, the line of post-pits stopped *c.*13ft (4m) short of the north-west corner of the stone *principia*, at which point there was a north-south eavesdrip gully with street surfaces beyond. It is clear therefore that the feature found by Richmond and Webster, and encountered again during the Goss Street excavation of 1973, could not have been the west wall of the timber *principia*. The nature of the surfacing east of the gully suggests that there was an external

28 The rock-cut foundations of the cross-hall of the timber headquarters building preserved beneath the column bases of its stone successor, on display at 23 Northgate Street

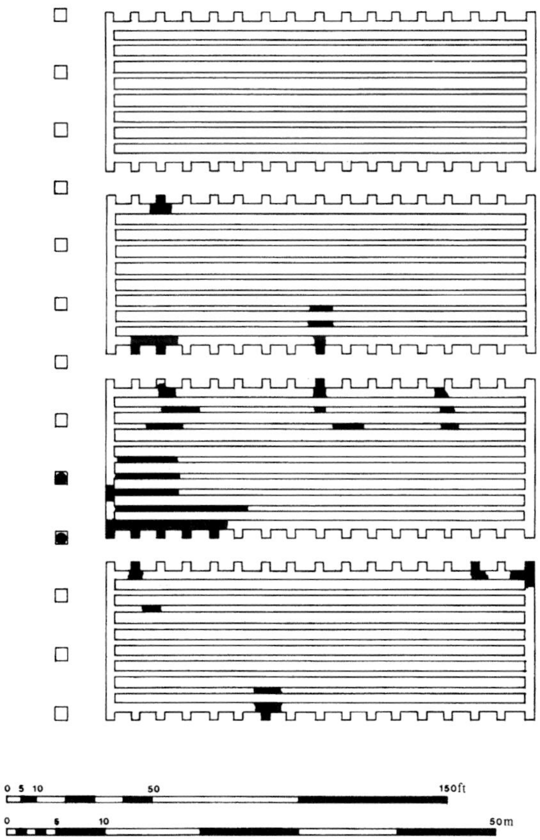

29 *Plan of the legionary granaries next to the west gate*

veranda down this side of the building also and probably therefore down all four sides. Assuming symmetry about the long axis, the timber *principia* was *c.*28ft (8.6m) shorter in the east-west dimension than its stone successor, which in turn means that the streets along its east and west sides were *c.*14ft (4.3m) wider than their later counterparts at 28ft instead of 14ft (30pM vs 15pM). The overall dimensions of the timber *principia*, an outline plan of which can be seen in **26**, were thus *c.*350pM (103.5m) north-south by *c.*220pM (65m) east-west. The cross-hall can be estimated to have had an overall width of 60pM (17.7m), divided into a nave 30pM wide and two aisles of 15pM each, with the range of rooms along its north side being 30pM (8.85m) deep.

The granaries — *horrea*

Reflecting the Roman Army's diligence in forward planning, the grain-stores in each fort were designed to hold a minimum of six months supply of this most important element of the soldier's staple diet. The *horrea* at Chester, or at least most of them, were located on the south side of the *via principalis* close to the west gate (*VII*). The choice of a site just inside the gate and beside the road leading down to the harbour reinforces the supposition that the majority of the legion's grain arrived by ship. This would have been brought not only from the south of the province but also in all probability from abroad as well, as is known to have happened at both York and Caerleon. There are particular problems associated with the storage of large quantities of grain. Germination and mildew owing to excess temperature and moisture have to be prevented, as does damage or contamination by rodents or birds. In addition, there is the very weight of the grain itself and its capacity to move in a semi-fluid manner in bulk storage. To counteract these difficulties the Roman granary was designed with a raised floor supported on sleeper walls. In the masonry examples the lower part of the outer walls was pierced by ventilators at regular

30 *Outer wall of granary showing ventilator, Commonhall Street 1956*

intervals to allow air to pass beneath the floor. Air circulation was further improved by breaks in the sleeper walls opposite the ventilators. The granaries were usually long rectangular buildings, which enabled the grain to be stored in hoppers or bins to either side of a central gangway, with a loading platform along one end. Because of their greater structural strength stone granaries could hold more grain than their timber equivalents, but even their outer walls had to be supported by closely spaced buttresses. Particular attention was paid to the soundness of the roof, including eaves which projected further than usual from the wall face in order to minimise lateral water penetration.

Excavations in 1954-6 revealed three stone-built granaries and there is space for a probable fourth to the north beside the *via principalis* (**29 & 30**). Convincing traces of underlying timber granaries were seen neither in the 1950s nor during additional explorations in 1988. Furthermore, during the more recent work it became clear that the type of concrete used for the foundations was very similar to that employed in the foundations of stone buildings of the Flavian period elsewhere in the fortress. It appears therefore that the granaries were built of stone *ab initio*,

31 *Internal sleeper walls of granary, Observer Printing Works 1987*

although at what point in the fortress construction programme is impossible to determine. It is perfectly possible, for example, that grain supplies during the early years of the fortress were stored in granaries beside the harbour. The three granaries examined conformed to a standard design with dimensions of 159ft by 45ft (48.5m x 13.7m), or 51ft (15.5m) including buttresses, and thus their length was almost four times their breadth. The outer walls were just over 3ft thick and the 3ft wide buttresses were spaced 10ft apart as measured centre to centre. The ventilators appear to have been placed between every other pair of buttresses and were just over 2ft wide. Inside, there were seven sleeper-walls supporting what had presumably been a stone slab floor (**31**).

The main baths — *thermae*

The principal bath-building or *thermae*, measuring 280 x 290pM overall (82.6 x 85.5m), occupied the whole of the *insula* immediately east of the *porta praetoria* (*II*). Legionary bath-buildings like that at Chester were among the forerunners of the great imperial baths erected in Rome during the second century. They were a proving ground for many of the constructional and other innovations subsequently introduced into urban baths. The quite rapid evolution in the design of such buildings can be seen by comparing the successive examples built by legionary craftsmen in their fortresses and veteran colonies during the Claudian (*Vindonissa*), Neronian (Exeter, Augst *'frauenthermen'*) and Flavian (Avenches, Caerleon) periods. Although the Chester baths come quite late in the sequence they nonetheless mark an important stage in the development of such buildings, as they are the earliest known example to incorporate a covered exercise hall of basilical

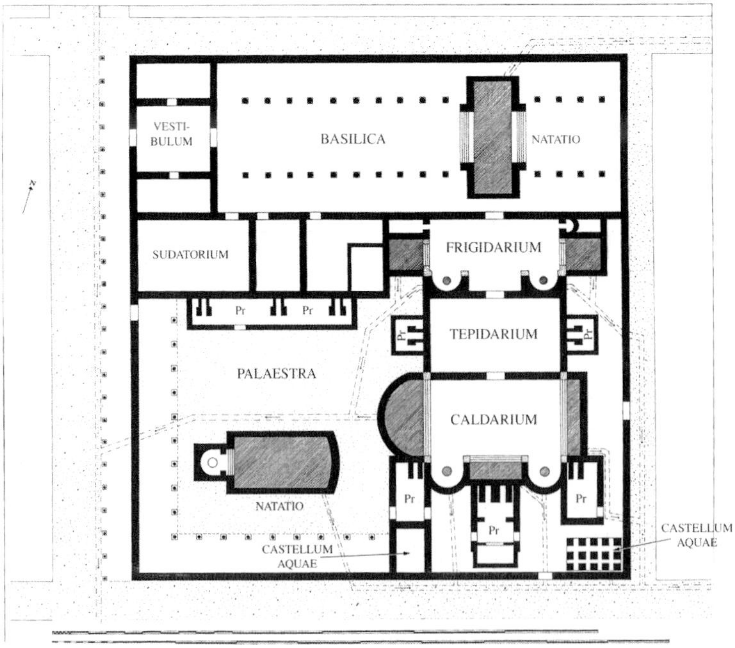

32 *Restored plan of the fortress baths —* thermae *— of c.AD 75 with plunge-baths and communal wash-basins shaded*

33 A reconstruction of the fortress baths

form (**32**). The design of legionary and civic baths was moving towards the inclusion of such a facility in any case, at least in the north-western provinces. Perhaps however its provision at Chester was due to the impact of the British climate on the men of *legio II Adiutrix* who until very recently had been stationed on the northern coast of the Adriatic. Despite the inclusion of this additional facility the architect managed to achieve an extremely compact and space-efficient design for the Chester *thermae* (**33**). The baths were provided by the authorities to ensure good hygiene among the troops and thus minimise the risk of reduced fighting capability caused by disease and infections. But they were more than simply a place to cleanse the body. They were also a sports, recreation and social centre, much like the leisure centres so common in our own time. This was where the soldiers could bathe and relax, soothe their aching limbs with oils and liniments, tone their bodies with exercise, and, most importantly, exchange gossip and criticise their superiors.

The exercise-hall or *basilica thermarum* occupied most of the north end of the *insula* and was the first significant part of the building to be explored. Its remains were exposed by the demolition of a coaching-inn, The Feathers Hotel, in 1863 and were recorded by some of the founder members of the Chester Archaeological Society, principally Dr Thomas Brushfield. The photographs taken at the time, which must be among the earliest examples of archaeological photography, show two lines of column bases with lengths of fallen columns beside them together with blocks of masonry from the upper levels of the superstructure (*see* **7**). A view taken looking back towards Bridge Street also shows the temporary wooden structure — looking very much like something one would have encountered in the Klondike — erected to maintain the walkway of the Rows (*see* **6**). Immediately west of the hall and approached via the colonnaded portico fronting the *via praetoria* was the main entrance into the baths, consisting of a central *vestibulum* flanked on either side by a changing-room or *apodyterium*. The hall itself measured 220pM long by 80pM wide (64.9 x 23.6m) and was divided by two rows of columns into a nave and two aisles 40pM and 20pM (11.8 and 5.9m) wide respectively. The columns, carved from local sandstone and about 0.75m in diameter at the base of the shaft, were spaced 12pM (3.54m) centre to centre and originally stood about 20pM (5.9m) high. Examples of these can be inspected in the 'Roman Gardens' near the Newgate. The columns would have supported arcading which in turn carried walling which rose above the sloping roofs of the adjacent aisles to a height sufficient to enable the provision of clerestory windows to light the interior of this great hall. The height of the nave ceiling is estimated at 56ft (17m). Large, tall windows would also have been incorporated in the eastern gable wall (**colour plate 14**). Although the Romans were extremely competent glassmakers, such windows would have been made up of numerous small panes of glass, probably no more than 1pM square, set in a metal framework. The *basilica*, surfaced with sand, was the indoor equivalent of the open air exercise-yard known as the *palaestra* and enabled exercise to be taken even when the weather was inclement.

Most unusual was the equipping of the *basilica* with a swimming-bath (*natatio*) duplicating that in the *palaestra*. This was located towards the east end of the *basilica* and was so large that the design of the nave colonnades had to be modified to accommodate it. In contrast with the remainder of the interior, the floor around the pool was surfaced with small bricks set in mortar and arranged in a herringbone pattern (*testacea spicata*). It is interesting to note that the only other legionary *thermae* to incorporate such a feature are those of the early second century at *Aquincum*, also built by *legio II Adiutrix*. There, a *natatio* is interposed between the *basilica* and the *frigidarium*. During clearance of the remains two conjoining fragments from an inscription were found at the foot of the south wall of the *basilica* about halfway along its length. The large size of the letters (6in on the top line), the excellent quality of the carving, and the use of Purbeck Marble all show this was an important inscription. There can be little doubt that this was the commemorative plaque dedicated at the time of the building's completion and set high up on the south wall of the *basilica* for everyone to see. Although only a handful of letters survive, originally highlighted using a red pigment, they are sufficient not only to confirm the imperial nature of the inscription but also to date it to the reign of Vespasian. Various restorations of the detailed text of the inscription are possible, one of which is shown here (**34**). Whichever version one chooses, however, this was clearly a very large inscription indeed with a length perhaps as great as 24ft (7.5m) and obviously carved on a number of component slabs.

The *thermae* contained two suites of baths, one based on dry heat like the Scandinavian sauna and the other affording a very steamy atmosphere of high humidity like Turkish baths. The first of these was attached to the western half of the south side of the *basilica* and consisted of a range 40pM (11.8m) broad divided up into three chambers (*sudatoria*) of differing sizes. The largest of these lay at the west end adjacent to Bridge Street and part of its hypocaust had in fact been exposed and placed on display as 'the Roman Bath' in the

IMP CAES VESPASIANO AVG PM TR P P P COS VIIII ET TITO CAES
ARI IMP PONT TR P COS VII ET CAESARI AVGVSTI FILIO DOMITI
ANO BASILICAM ET BALNEVM THERMARVM LEG II ADIVTRIX PI
SVB GN IVLIO AGRICOLA LEG AVG PR PR PROV BRITANN FECIT

34 A possible restoration of the fragmentary inscription recording the baths' completion during the governorship of Agricola (AD 77-84) but before Vespasian's death in 79. Text restoration by Dan Robinson, drawing by Cheryl Quinn

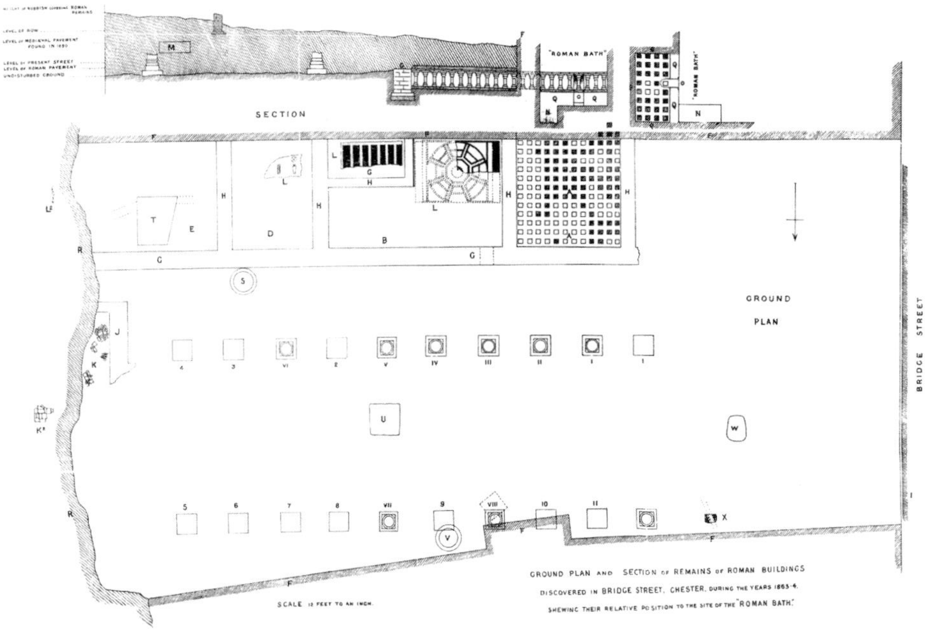

35 Fortress baths, plan of the remains discovered in 1863

eighteenth century. Indeed, it remains on display to this day in the cellar of 39 Bridge Street. All the baths were equipped with hypocaustal underfloor heating and all, at least in their latest guise, were provided with mosaic floors. These rooms were partially examined along with the *basilica* in the 1860s and the pattern of the mosaics, largely geometric, can be seen from the records then made of the surviving fragments (**35**).

The other bath-suite occupied the whole of the eastern half of the complex lying south of the *basilica*. It consisted in essence of three large bathing-halls lying side by side and arranged in a north-south progression of increasing temperature —*frigidarium*, *tepidarium* and, hottest of all, the *caldarium*. This simple design has been termed, for obvious reasons, the row-type or *reihentyp* plan. In this bathing regime the visitor passed through the chambers until reaching the *caldarium* by which time he would be perspiring freely and could remove the dirt and perspiration with an oiled, bronze blade or *strigil*. Plunge-baths of hot water were available for further cleansing and to luxuriate in. The return journey through the halls culminated with a dip in the cold plunge-bath in the *frigidarium* to close the pores of the skin. Although the overall design appears straightforward, it concealed a complex and sophisticated infrastructure of heating and water-supply as well as the application of highly advanced techniques in the use of concrete for a variety of structural purposes including roof-vaulting. All these technologies were to disappear with the collapse of the Roman Empire and were lost to the West for fifteen centuries.

While the three halls had common internal dimensions of 40x70pM (11.8 x 20.65m), the ancillary facilities appended to each varied considerably. This part of the baths was

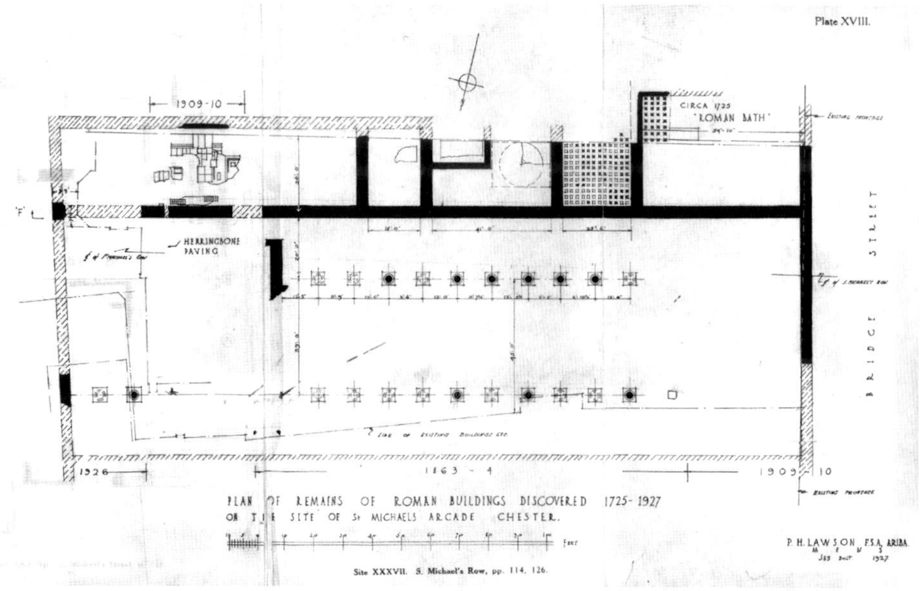

36 Fortress baths, plan showing additonal discoveries of 1909/10 and 1927

entered via a doorway 10pM (2.95m) wide, positioned in the south wall of the *basilica* opposite the *natatio* giving access to the *frigidarium*. Part of this was examined during the works of 1863 with further elements recorded during building works in 1909/10 and 1926/7 (**36**). The later investigations revealed it to have a mosaic floor executed in black and white *tesserae*. Although badly damaged in places its subject was clearly a tableau of marine creatures (**37 & 38**). Opening off the east end of the hall was a chamber with a sunken floor of *testacea spicata* and this clearly served as the cold plunge-bath or *piscina* (**colour plate 10**). Given the high degree of axial symmetry in legionary bath-suites of this type it is likely that the chamber at the opposite end of the *frigidarium*, intervening between it and the other bath-suite to the west which it subsequently became part of, began life as a second *piscina*. The south-east corner of the hall was equipped with some form of washing facility, most probably a large, raised, circular wash-basin (*labrum*) set in a recess. Again, because of the symmetrical design of these buildings, this arrangement is likely to have been repeated in the south-west corner.

The other two halls together with the various support structures around them were revealed by contractor's excavations for the construction of a new shopping precinct in 1963. The degree of preservation was quite remarkable and included walls standing to a height of 13ft (4m) or more, intact hypocaust systems extending over large areas, areas of mosaic flooring, and even large sections of collapsed roofing-vault. Sadly only the briefest and most cursory form of investigation was permitted, often only after the archaeology had already been severely truncated by the contractor's machines. The magnificent remains of this majestic building, which could have become a major cultural and tourism asset for the city, were ripped apart and carted off for use as landfill and levelling material.

37 Fortress baths, drawing of marine tableau mosaic seen in 1909/10. North is to the left

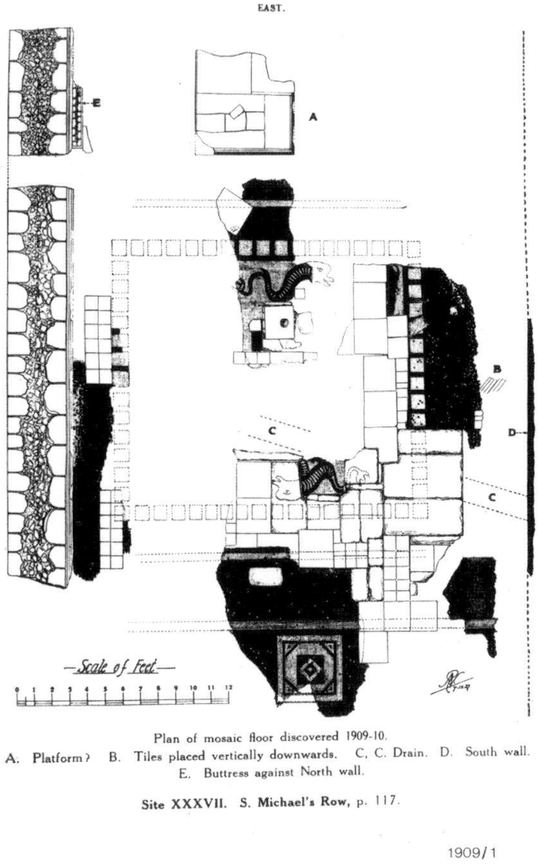

Not all was lost, however, as a considerable amount of information was recorded 'in the teeth of the bulldozers', from which it has been possible to interpret this part of the complex. While the size of the *tepidarium* was restricted to the area of the hall, the *caldarium* was lavishly equipped with extensions. Appended to the east end, running the full width of the hall, was a 7ft (2.1m) extension housing a hot plunge-bath (*alveus*). A similar but much larger bay, most probably semi-circular in plan, projected out from the west end of the hall and this too would have contained an *alveus*. Opening off the south side of the *caldarium* was a trio of arched bays. The central rectangular one housed yet another hot plunge-bath while the apsidal ones to each side probably contained a *labrum* supplied with either hot or cold water.

These three halls were of massive construction. Their main walls were of stone-faced concrete nearly 4ft (1.2m) thick while their concrete barrel-vaulted ceilings can be

38 Fortress baths, close-up of sea-creature depicted in marine tableau mosaic

estimated to have soared to a height of 53ft (16.1m) above floor level. Tall arched windows set in the end walls and probably arranged in two tiers would have illuminated their interiors which would have been resplendent with highly colourful and, to modern eyes, garish schemes of painted decoration. The entire floor area of the *tepidarium* and *caldarium*, including the projecting bays of the second, was raised upon a hypocaust set in a rock-cut 'basement' 5pM (1.5m) deep (**colour plate 13**). This consisted of a grid of close-spaced pillars (*pilae*) built of bricks 1pM (295mm) square (*pedales*) resting on a bed of concrete. They were capped with three layers of large, flat bricks, the lowest formed of 2pM (590mm) square *bipedales* with each corner resting on a pillar. This was sealed by the floor proper consisting of a layer of concrete 1pM thick and containing numerous small fragments of brick and tile. Mosaic was then laid on top of this. The interior face of the walls in the *tepidarium* and *caldarium*, and also those of the *sudatoria* in the other bathing-suite, were given a continuous lining formed of hollow, box-shaped bricks known as *tubuli*. This lining (*tubulatio*) was also continued across the vaulted ceiling. Regularly distributed flues connected the lining with chimneys venting to the exterior either at eaves level or higher up the roof structure. This system created the draught necessary to get the hot gases to spread evenly throughout the hypocaust before being drawn up into the *tubulatio* at the edges of the room. This meant that not only the floor but also the walls and even the ceiling were heated; they then radiated this heat to the interior of the room. With the high level of humidity in the *caldarium* the temperature would not have to rise very much to create the conditions for profuse perspiration. Warming all the interior surfaces in this way meant that the heat produced by the furnaces was used in the most efficient manner possible. Heat loss to the exterior was minimised and condensation on the wall surfaces was reduced, while the employment of vaulted ceilings not only did away with the need for intermediate roof supports — inconvenient in a room used by large numbers of people — but also meant that any condensation which did form did not drip onto the heads of the bathers but trickled down the curved surface to the floor.

Heat was supplied by three furnace chambers (*praefurnia*). The main *praefurnium* and its attached fuel-store were sited beyond the projecting bays along the south side of the *caldarium* and contained two furnaces. These supplied heat to the *caldarium* hypocaust, which also fed into the hypocaust of the *tepidarium* via arched flues set in the base of their party wall. In its original form, the *tepidarium* hypocaust was also heated by two much smaller furnaces of its own, one set against the middle section of each of its end walls. From the arrangements made in other bath-buildings, one can be sure that the furnaces in the main *praefurnium* would have had bronze boilers set above them to supply hot water to the nearby *labra* and also for the cleaning and total replenishment of the *alveus* each night. The water in the *alveus* was heated throughout the day both by the heat passing beneath its floor and by a device known as a *testudo*. This was a lead or bronze tank of semi-circular cross-section set lengthways above the furnace with its outer open end flush with the side of the *alveus* and its base slightly lower than the *alveus's* floor. Thus water from the latter would pass into the *testudo*, be heated and then re-circulate into the bath. In addition, each of the much larger plunge-baths at either end of the *caldarium* was served by its own *praefurnium* with similar internal arrangements.

Water for the boilers was supplied from a large cistern (*castellum aquae*) positioned at the south-east corner of the complex abutting its perimeter wall. Its foundation was a massive structure taking the form of a raft of extremely hard concrete 4ft (1.2m) thick measuring 37ft x 24ft (11.3 x 7.4m) (**colour plate 11**). Set atop this were 15 large stone blocks arranged in three rows of five on which once stood stone pillars supporting the raised water-tank, the latter presumably formed of lead sheeting attached to a timber or iron framework. The position of the pillar bases suggests a tank *c.*29 x 17ft (8.8 x 5.2m) in size and it has been estimated, based on the levels of the facilities to which water had to be supplied, that its floor was raised a minimum of 12ft (3.65m) off the ground. Assuming that the depth of water in the tank was 5ft (1.5m) it would have held approximately 13,638 gallons (62,000 litres) of water. This was supplied by a 8in (20cm) diameter lead water-main linked directly to the aqueduct reception tank (*castellum divisorium*) located near the east gate.

A second reservoir was positioned behind the *praefurnium* which served the *alveus* at the west end of the *caldarium*. This took the form of a rectangular chamber measuring 23 x 15ft (7 x 4.6m) internally. It had a flooring of massive blocks of sandstone 1½ft (45cm) thick and up to 5 x 3ft (1.5 x 0.9m) in size which, like the walls, would originally have been covered with lead sheeting (**colour plate 12**). An extension of this flooring ran through the west wall of the chamber close to its north end on a diagonal alignment. It marked the course of the feeder pipe to an open-sir swimming-bath situated in the centre of the fourth and final component of the baths complex, the *palaestra*. Occupying roughly 25% of the ground area of the *thermae* this was the open-air exercise area surfaced with sand and most probably lined on its south and west sides by a colonnaded portico. Only the south-east corner of the swimming-bath was seen in 1964 so its overall size is unknown but probably measured in the region of 30 x 50ft (9 x 14m). Like the other cold pools it was equipped with a floor of *testacea spicata*.

Some statistics concerning the volume and weight of materials required for the baths' construction were mentioned in the previous chapter and a full table is included here (**Table 3**, p83). Obviously with its various pools, plunge-baths and fountains, such a building consumed vast quantities of water, and over the course of each 24-hour cycle somewhere in the region of 187,000 gallons (850,000 litres) may have been required. The amount of fuel needed is the most difficult figure to calculate. Experiments involving the reconstruction of much smaller bath-buildings have been undertaken but the resultant computations of fuel requirements have varied wildly. The most recent experiments have taken place at the full-scale simulation of a bath-building outside the fort at Wallsend where the results suggest a higher degree of fuel efficiency in hypocaust systems than previously imagined, with a consequently much reduced rate of consumption. Be that as it may, to keep the nine large furnaces of the Chester *thermae* supplied must have needed several tonnes of wood each day.

The building behind the *principia* (39)

Nothing was known about the nature of the building or buildings occupying the *insula* (*XVI*) immediately behind the *principia* until the Old Market Hall excavations of 1967-9,

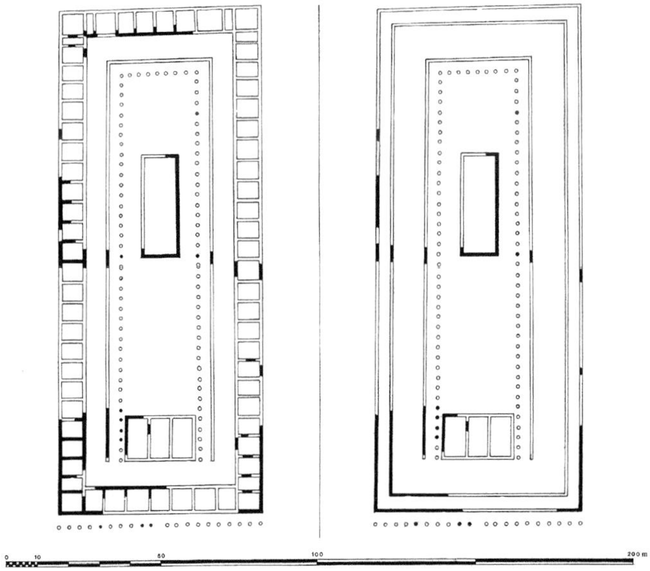

39 Plan of enormous building to the rear of headquarters building: right — plan of original and unfinished Flavian building; left — modified plan of building actually constructed c.AD 100

although it was assumed, on the analogy of the arrangements in many other fortresses, that this was the site of the legionary commander's residence. Thus when Phase I of those excavations revealed the south-west quadrant of a courtyard building it was initially thought to be the *praetorium*, an interpretation which subsequent discoveries were to render improbable. The plan of this stone building consisted of outer ranges 30pM (8.8m) wide overall on the south and west divided into rooms consistently 16pM wide in the former and varying from 18-24pM (5.8-7m) wide in the latter. The south range incorporated a centrally located entrance passageway and a 4m-deep colonnaded portico along the exterior. The rooms were notable for their doorways which all faced inwards and were as much as 10ft (3.3m) wide. Further in, another colonnaded portico ran parallel with the west range. It is unclear if the intervening space was roofed over or left open as a narrow yard. Immediately beside the portico and opposite the entrance through the south range was a free-standing structure 29½ x 46ft (9 x 14m) in size, containing three large chambers. The rooms in the outer ranges were clearly designed for storage purposes and it was suggested that the residential quarters of the legate lay in the northern half of the building (at that time it was thought the *insula* was of a normal size, in this case about 220pM north-south). Although the structures just described had been completed in the early second century, many of them reused the foundations of an earlier unfinished building. These foundations were of the cobble-concrete variety typical of Flavian masonry buildings at Chester, a date confirmed by the absence of any traces of a preceding timber phase. In the original scheme the outer ranges were rather narrower at 20pM (5.9m) and there was no sign of internal partitions, although work may have terminated before these were started.

In the late 1970s and early 1980s a new campaign of excavation was undertaken 200ft (61m) farther north which encompassed the area immediately east of Hunter's Walk. Here a range on the same alignment and with identical dimensions as the outer range on the Old Market Hall site was discovered, which in addition was divided into rooms of similar size and regularity. The foundation of an earlier front wall for a much narrower range was also encountered. Furthermore, to the east of this was a colonnaded portico which again was on precisely the same alignment as that found to the south. The suspicion began to grow that rather than the two *insulae* anticipated there had in fact been a single enormous building. This idea was reinforced by discoveries made subsequently during observation of pedestrianisation and utility operations in Hunter Street and the Market Square. An east-west range of similar character was found beneath Hunter Street and elements of another running north-south were noted along the whole length of the Market Square. The dimensions and internal divisions of the latter were identical to that on the west side of the building and traces of a corresponding internal colonnaded portico were also found. Set centrally in the northern half of the central courtyard area was a long narrow building measuring 45 x 110pM (13.2 x 32.4m). Linking all these structural elements together results in a building 220pM (65m) wide and 540pM (160m) long (**39**). Although that sector of the outer ranges which could prove beyond any doubt that we are dealing with a single building has not been examined, the close similarity in alignments, dimensions, constructional characteristics and chronological sequence between all the areas which have been seen makes the case well nigh proven. Furthermore, the preparation in recent years of a publishable report on the Elliptical Building and neighbouring structures occupying *insula XVII* to the west has shown that the east-west street north of these buildings lay farther to the south than previously thought. Consequently, if one were to divide the space behind the HQ into two *insulae* the southern plot would have a north-south dimension of no more than 165ft (50m) which would render it far too small to accommodate the legate's residence. The hypothesis of a single large building is thus preferred. Its plan, however, with identical ranges of utilitarian design on all four sides, makes it quite plain that it was not the *praetorium*. It now seems certain that this lay in *insula XI* east of the *principia*, the other regular location for the *praetorium*, where fragments of the features one would expect in such a palatial complex — hypocausts and mosaic floors — have been seen on various occasions in the past.

An altar dedicated 'To the Mighty Saviour Gods' by the physician Hermogenes was recovered from a site lying within the confines of the enormous building in the nineteenth century (**128**). Another, set up to Aesculapius, Hygeia and Panacea by another physician, Antiochos, was found during the 1967-9 excavations reused in the courtyard paving (**128**). It is hardly surprising that the recovery of two altars set up by doctors from the same building should give rise to the suggestion that it was the legionary hospital. Neither was found in its original position, however, and they could quite easily have been brought from some neighbouring building for reuse. The nearby *praetorium* is one such possibility as these men could have been the personal physicians of the legate and quartered in his residence. The layout of the accommodation is also at variance with that of legionary *valetudinaria* known elsewhere, which are easily recognisable by their double ranges of wards lying either side of a corridor and with the wards grouped in twos or threes separated by narrow passages. The wide doorways of the rooms in the outer ranges, up to 10ft (3m) wide and presumably closed with shutters or large doors, suggest rather that this building had a storage function, perhaps as the main armoury. It is difficult,

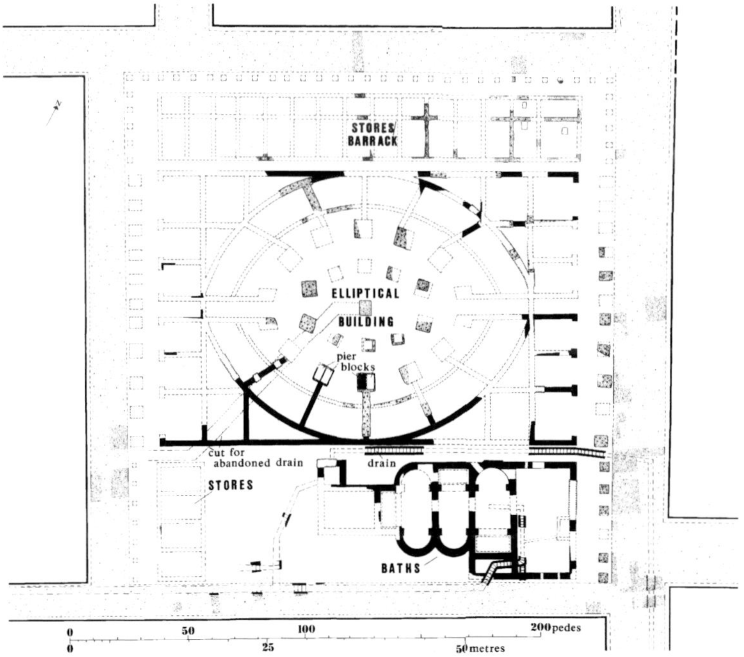

40 The Elliptical Building as excavated

however, to see why a stores building of this type should have been given priority over buildings such as the *principia* as regards construction in masonry and also, if it was accorded such priority, why it was left unfinished for two decades or more. It is also apparent that the provision of such an enormous building must be connected with the unusually large size of the *latera praetorii.* These are matters which will be addressed in the next chapter along with the broader aspects of the next building to be described the 'Elliptical Building'.

The Elliptical Building and neighbouring structures

This enigmatic structure was situated to the dextral rear of the *principia* occupying most of *insula XVII*, the latter measuring a little over 200pM (59m) square. The first hint that the building in this area was somewhat unusual came in 1939 when Professor Robert Newstead of the Chester Archaeological Society and Professor John Droop of the Department of Classical Archaeology, University of Liverpool, conducted excavations immediately west of the Town Hall in the wake of slum housing clearance. The funds were raised by means of an appeal for public donations which produced the princely sum of £481 12s 9d which was sufficient to employ a team of eight labourers for three months. As was the normal practice of the time, they cut a series of long narrow trenches across the area with the aim of detecting walls and then following them so as to determine the plan of any buildings encountered. They located a wall running east-west for at least 130ft (40m) and were surprised to find that it was joined from the north by a curving wall with which it merged for about 45ft (14m). Traces of four radial walls heading northwards were also found together with seemingly isolated areas of concrete and, at a much higher level, paving made up of large slabs of sandstone. They attributed the building to the end of the first century and the later paving to the third century. Newstead and Droop were at a loss to explain the function of the building. Its plan loosely resembled that of a theatre but they recognised that the walls were not capable of supporting the tiered seating of such a structure. For want of a better description the appellation 'theatre-like building' was henceforth applied to the structure.

No further work was done on this site until the 1960s when firm plans for its redevelopment emerged. Limited rescue work in 1963-5 was followed by more extensive 'area excavation' from 1967-9, both directed by John Eames of Liverpool University's Department of Classical Archaeology. These investigations revealed that the remains seen in 1939 were merely one half of the building which was in fact approximately oval in plan consisting of a central courtyard surrounded by a range of wedge-shaped rooms fronted by a colonnaded portico, the whole enclosed by a rectangular frame-wall to reconcile it with the surrounding orthogonal street grid (**40**). Consequently, this most unmilitary building was renamed 'The Elliptical Building'. That its construction had commenced during the earliest years of the fortress was confirmed by the discovery of a lead water-pipe running up to a fountain-monument at the centre of the courtyard which exhibited a moulded inscription dating its manufacture to the first half of 79 (**colour plate 15**). The building had not been completed, however, for work stopped before all the foundations had been inserted. The site lay derelict for a while and then part of it was levelled and some timber workshops constructed. After these were demolished, in the early second century, the site of the Elliptical Building reverted to an open space on which large amounts of industrial waste and other discarded materials were dumped. The project was resurrected in the opening decades of the third century, during the general rebuilding of the fortress, when a new Elliptical Building of a somewhat modified design was built and it was to this that the paving recorded by Newstead and Droop belonged. A further surprise was the discovery of a small bath-building immediately south of the latter; surprising because legionary fortresses normally contain only one bath-building. Other commitments prevented the excavator from preparing a publishable report and this task was eventually undertaken by the present writer in the mid-1990s. This explains why it is only very recently that the full details of this amazing building have been clarified.

As originally conceived, the plan of the Elliptical Building consisted of a central courtyard about 30 x 50pM (8.9 x 14.8m) in size around which was a 15pM (4.44m) deep portico supported by ten columns (**41**). Behind this again was a 30pM deep range of 12 wedge-shaped chambers which were notable for their monumental, arched doorways 12pM (3.55m) wide. About halfway into the chambers was a slight concentric foundation which can have carried little more than a screen of small columns or, more probably, a low balustrade. On the building's shorter sides the enclosing perimeter wall doubled as the back wall of a range of six rooms facing out onto the adjacent street giving the building overall dimensions of 200pM (59.2m) east-west by 112pM (33.2m) north-south. The wide doorways of these rooms, which may have functioned as *tabernae*, opened onto a colonnaded portico. Each of the spandrel-shaped areas in the corners between the outer wall of the curvilinear ranges and the perimeter wall was subdivided so as to form a square

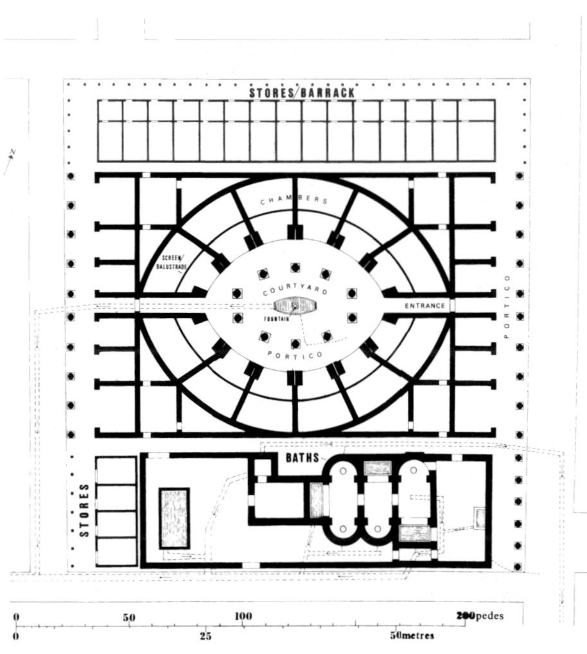

41 Restored and corrected plan of the Elliptical Building of c.AD 79

chamber which may have formed a right-angled extension of the street-frontage range. The only means of access to the centre of the Elliptical Building was via a long, narrow entrance passage 6pM (1.8m) wide set centrally in each of the street-frontage ranges.

The foundations of this building were truly impressive. Those for the chamber entrances for example took the form of 8ft (2.5m) square pads of cobble-concrete 3ft (0.9m) thick sunk in rock-cut pits. On these were laid pairs of stone pier blocks 12-15in (30-40cm) thick and 6 x 3ft (1.77 x 0.88m) in size. Although only 2-2½ft (60-75cm) thick, the walls were built of finely dressed masonry even below ground level and were set on concrete foundations laid in deep, rock-cut trenches (**42**). At the exact centre of the courtyard lay the 5ft (1.5m) square concrete foundation for a monument. Illustrating the vagaries of partial excavation, one of the 1963-4 trenches had just missed this feature and it was only spotted as it was in the process of being demolished by contractor's machinery during site clearance the following year. What form the superstructure was intended to take is unknown although the inscribed lead pipe running up to the foundation shows that it was to include a fountain and thus almost certainly a surrounding pool. The circumstances of its hurried investigation were in some ways fortunate as the mechanical section through it revealed a fascinating feature beneath the foundation which may not otherwise have been spotted. Cut into the rock floor of the foundation pit along the entire length of its east side was a narrow trench about 1½ft wide and 1ft deep (45 x 30cm) filled exclusively with clean earth (**43**). This would appear to have been the focus for some form of dedication ceremony held at the centre of the Elliptical Building at the inception of its construction and, like many other aspects of this building, points to its importance. A feature associated with the fountain-monument shows that even Roman builders were not immune from making mistakes. A structure of this sort obviously requires a drainage culvert, and to accommodate this a trench 6ft (1.8m) wide and deep was excavated into solid rock over a distance of about 100ft (30m) from the fountain to a point near to the south-west corner of the building. This had taken place at a very early stage in the building process and when the surveyors began to peg out the lines of the walls on the ground they discovered that several of them coincided with the line of the culvert trench. The whole thing had to be backfilled with rubble into which the foundations of some of the walls and the column bases of the courtyard colonnade were subsequently inserted. The comments of the men who had laboured to dig the trench can well be imagined. A replacement culvert on a new alignment, most probably running out beneath the west entrance passage, would presumably have been provided had the building been carried through to completion. Nor was this the only error. A more serious one was committed in the laying out of the northern half of the building. The main surveying point was placed too far to the north and so the chambers at the

42 *Elliptical Building, south wall of east entrance with concrete foundation of column belonging to street frontage portico in foreground*

43 *Elliptical Building, foundation of fountain monument at centre of courtyard with ritual trench or* mundus *cut in its rock floor*

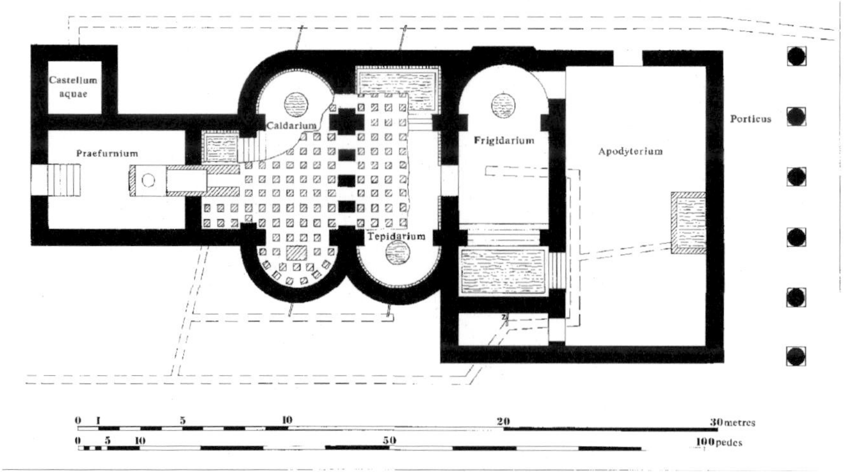

44 Plan of the Elliptical Building baths

centre were much narrower than those at the ends of the range, whereas those in the south range were of almost equal width, and the foundation pads for the columns of both the internal and external porticoes were in the wrong position with regard to the neighbouring ranges and the entrance passages. Whether these errors would have been corrected if the building had been finished is a moot point.

The portion of the *insula* lying south of the Elliptical Building was mostly occupied by a minor bath-building of the sort of size and design one might find outside an auxiliary fort (**44**). Begun at the same time as the Elliptical Building, but actually finished and used, it followed the usual *reihentyp* design with a large changing-hall at the east end which led into the suite of *frigidarium*, *tepidarium* and *caldarium* beyond which lay the *praefurnium* and water cistern. Almost the whole of this building, which measured 46 x 105ft (14 x 32m) overall, was excavated in 1969 although the releasing of the site for archaeological investigation in phases meant that there was never a point when it was revealed in its entirety. This was a great pity not only because of the practical problems this caused regarding its investigation but also because it would have enabled the building to be seen at its most impressive. Like the ruins of the *thermae* seen a few years earlier, at the time of excavation walls still stood to a height of nearly 13ft (4m) and several of the hypocausts belonging to the latest phases of the building were completely intact.

Had it been seen by the public completely revealed this might have led to the bath-building being preserved for future generations. Entry into the baths was gained via a doorway in the centre of the *apodyterium*'s north wall. This room featured a *pedilouve* or foot-bath against the centre of its east wall while doorways at opposite ends of the west wall led into the end bays of the neighbouring *frigidarium* (**45**). The northern apsidal one contained a cold water *labrum* while its rectangular counterpart to the south housed a cold plunge-bath (*piscina*). Opening off the south-west corner of the changing-hall was a small chamber which, as it was located above one of the main drainage culverts, probably served

45 *North apse of cold-room —* frigidarium *— in Elliptical Building baths*

as a latrine. The north bay of the *tepidarium* was rectangular and the south bay apsidal, probably containing a *labrum* and warm plunge-bath respectively. Finally came the *caldarium* with an apsidal bay equipped with a hot water *labrum* at both ends and a hot plunge-bath or *alveus* in a rectangular bay opening off its west side. Beyond was the combined *praefurnium* and fuel-store. Excavations in 1993 farther to the west confirmed earlier impressions that an open yard lay in this area with, beyond, a short range of timber-built *tabernae* occupying the south-west corner of the *insula*. The primary drainage system in the yard area suggests that it may have been the intention to include a swimming bath in the range of facilities but, if so, this was never installed.

The north end of the *insula* was occupied by a long narrow timber building which was excavated in 1968 during Phase III of the Old Market Hall site. It was 34ft (10.3m) wide overall and was equipped with a veranda along its northern frontage and subdivided into pairs of rooms in the same manner as a barrack block. While it could have performed this function it is equally if not more likely to have been used as stores. The positioning of the three main buildings within the *insula* suggests it was apportioned, from north to south, on a ratio of 1:3:1.5.

The Elliptical Building has been a source of puzzlement ever since it was discovered, and the recent elucidation of its detailed design and history have if anything merely added to its mystery. It is a truly unique structure. No building even remotely like it has been found in any other fortress and even an empire-wide search of the variants of building types in both military and civil branches of architecture has failed to yield a close parallel. Previous theories advanced regarding the building's function have included a palatial residence, a theatre, a market, a gladiatorial training-school, and an elaborate *palaestra* belonging to the neighbouring bath-building, all of which fail to convince, while the more frivolous suggestions have encompassed such uses as a brothel, a lighthouse, or a chariot park. Despite its impressive structural quality it was obviously not intended to support tiered seating, and the existence of a fountain and pool at the centre of the small 'stage' or 'arena' would have been rather inconvenient. The lack of closer integration between

Elliptical Building and baths rules out the residence and *palaestra* theories, as does the lack of suitable living accommodation with appropriate appointments such as hypocausts. The plan of the Elliptical Building does bear a superficial resemblance to those of certain market buildings (*macella*) which often have circular or oval courtyards with round, hexagonal or octagonal pavilions at the centre housing a fountain or cistern. However, even those in major towns are much smaller than the Elliptical Building and they are far simpler architecturally. More importantly, market buildings are essentially civil structures operated by civilians even though the activities in the larger examples were overseen by government officials with the support of soldiers. Where markets were provided at legionary fortresses they were large rectangular buildings — essentially *fora* — placed outside the defences as evidenced by the examples found at *Carnuntum* (Petronell), *Vindonissa* (Windisch) and *Noviomagus* (Nijmegen). Even if such a facility had for some reason been included among the intramural buildings it is difficult to see why it should have been the subject of such lavish structural and architectural treatment when far more important buildings such as the *principia* were built of timber.

With their massive foundations and 12 chambers accessed via monumental arched doorways the curvilinear ranges clearly constituted the most important element of the Elliptical Building. In view of the height of those doorways, estimated at nearly 20ft (6m), the range was obviously tall but almost certainly one-storeyed while the colonnaded portico and the chambers behind were probably to be covered by a common, possibly vaulted, roof-structure. Thus, in essence, the building consisted of 12 chambers purposely designed for the display of their contents which, owing to the successful isolation of the central courtyard from the hustle and bustle of fortress life beyond, could be contemplated in an environment of relative tranquillity (**colour plates 16, 17 & 18**). The screen or balustrade feature might also imply that the ordinary visitor was forced to admire the contents from a respectful distance. What the chambers were intended to contain must of course remain unknown for this building was never finished and there are no clues from its third-century successor, even assuming that the latter performed the same function which is by no means certain. However, given the location of the building in a legionary fortress the possibilities are fairly restricted and must be connected with the commemoration and celebration of some aspect of the Roman State. The fact that there were 12 chambers could be significant. This number had a special importance in the ancient world for many reasons and in a variety of ways. One thinks of the 12 Signs of the Zodiac in connection with the mapping of the heavens, the 12 months of the Augustan calendar, the 12 major points of the compass, and the Twelve Tables of Roman Law. Rather more pertinent perhaps are the 12 principal deities of the Roman pantheon — Jupiter, Juno, Mars, Minerva, Vesta, Diana, Apollo, Ceres, Neptune, Janus, Mercury, and either dea Roma or Vulcan — or a combination of certain of these with personifications of those virtues most important in military life such as *Discipulina* (Discipline), *Fortuna* (Good Luck), *Honos* (Honour), *Pietas* (Patriotism) and *Virtus* (Valour). The concept of the Elliptical Building as a temple is a little difficult to accept as temples were usually located outside the defences of military establishments. This general rule may not have applied, however, if the building concerned was for the formal and official commemoration, if not actual worship, of the protective deities of Rome in contradistinction to the private

Table 3: fortress baths' estimated daily water requirement

Facility	quantity (litres)
Basilica	
i) *natatio*	197,400
ii) fountain	55,000
Palaestra	
i) *natatio*	302,400
ii) fountain	55,000
Frigidarium	
i) *piscinae*	54,000
ii) *labra*	55,000
iii) latrine & drinking fountain	12,000
Caldarium	
i) *alveii*	66,264
ii) *labra*	55,000
Grand total:	**852,064 litres each 24-hour cycle**

Table 4: estimated military daily (24-hour) water requirement

Purpose	Facility	Quantity (litres)
Hygiene	Main baths	850,000
	Elliptical Building baths	80,000
	Watergate baths	850,000
	Amphitheatre baths	100,000
	Mansio baths	100,000
	Blackfriars baths	80,000
	Hospital	20,000
Industrial	Workshops	40,000
Refreshment & cooking	Fountains & troughs	150,000
Ornamental	*Praetorium* & Elliptical Building fountains & pools	100,000

Grand total = 2,370,000 litres or 521,337 gallons (UK)

homage by an individual to the cult of a single deity; and it has to be remembered that the ritual trench found beneath the foundation of the central monument does endow the building with something of a religious or quasi-religious character. Perhaps, therefore, it was akin to the numerous sanctuaries of the imperial cult (variously known as *Sebasteia, Caesareia,* and *Augusteia*) which appeared in increasing numbers throughout the Empire during the first century celebrating the power and wisdom of the Emperor and the majesty of Rome. And then there is the very form of our building. A shape so unusual and awkward must have been chosen for some special reason. Can it be mere coincidence that it closely resembles the shape of the inhabited world (the *oikumene* or *orbis terrarum*) as perceived by ancient geographers such as Eratosthenes of Cyrene and the Roman Strabo who thought of it as a single, vast oval landmass with the Mediterranean lying at its centre and surrounded by ocean? In this connection it is worth noting that the administrative dioceses into which the Empire was divided in the fourth century numbered 12 (perhaps a reflection of some earlier notional division?), while the large-scale pictorial map of the Empire commissioned by Augustus and set up on the back wall of the *porticus Vipsania* in Rome was probably arranged in 24 panels. If this line of reasoning is correct then the Elliptical Building was designed as a physical and symbolic representation of the Roman World — an '*imago mundi*' or '*imago orbis Romanum*' — with its chambers intended to be adorned with pictorial and sculptural representations of the lands, peoples and cities of the Empire together no doubt with propaganda images attesting Rome's 'divine destiny' to rule the world along with the wisdom and divinity of its Emperors. As such it would belong to the chain of experiments which attempted to find an architectural form to express the unity of Rome, its rulers, and its gods culminating in the Pantheon. Why such an exotic and extravagant building should have been provided in the middle of a military base on the fringes of the Empire is a question to be addressed in the next chapter.

Buildings in *insula XXI*

The history of *insula* XXI's development has much in common with those containing the Elliptical Building and the large building behind the *principia.* Measuring 175pM east-west by 350pM north-south (51.6 x 103.2m), the original layout catered for three separate buildings. Along the south side was a timber building of unknown function partially explored during Phase III of the Old Market Hall excavations of 1968. This was 40pM (11.8m) wide overall and was divided longitudinally into two equal halves by a spine wall. The eastern margin of the plot was occupied by another timber building, examined during the Hunter Street/Princess Street excavations of 1978-82. This was 30pM (8.85m) wide with a veranda facing the street and could have been yet another range of *tabernae.* The investigations just mentioned also explored most of the remainder of the *insula* revealing that, whereas the construction of the Elliptical Building and the building behind the *principia* had started and then been interrupted, the erection of whatever building had been intended here had not even commenced when this hiatus in the building programme occurred, the site remaining largely derelict for the next 150 years.

Other buildings

The positions of some of the other buildings are known or can legitimately be surmised even though they remain largely or wholly unexplored. The *praetorium* must have stood immediately east of the *principia* while the houses of the tribunes and the *praefectus castrorum* lined the south side of the *via principalis*. The *valetudinarium* might have occupied one of the *insulae* in the *latera praetorii* north-east of the *principia* or alternatively stood in *insula III* in the *praetentura* opposite the main baths. At least one of the *insulae* in the first of these areas was probably taken up by stores of one sort or another. The shallow zone lying between the *scamnum tribunorum* and *insulae I* to *III* may, as at Caerleon, have been occupied by barrack accommodation and stabling belonging to a squadron of auxiliary cavalry.

Water-supply and drainage

A reliable water-supply was obviously an important consideration in the siting of any settlement in the ancient world and it was particularly important in the case of a Roman legionary fortress not only because of the size of the garrison but also because of the Roman obsession with baths and bathing and the vast quantities of water this required. For example, it has been calculated that the *thermae* alone may have consumed as much as 187,000 gallons (850,000 litres) of water every 24 hours and the total for the fortress as a whole over the same period could have been as much as 527,936 gallons (2,400,000 litres). It also has to be borne in mind that Roman water-supply systems functioned on the basis of constant flow. Except for maintenance or repair works the supply was never shut off completely. If supply exceeded demand in any part of the system the excess was diverted to another branch and ultimately, if not required by any user, into the sewers to contribute to their regular flushing and thus preventing the build up of potentially system-threatening amounts of silt. This might seem a somewhat wasteful approach to us, as indeed it was, but under normal circumstances water conservation was not an issue, for once a supply sufficient for the needs of a settlement was in place it flowed without interruption to all customers, except when the exigencies of the normal distribution priorities came into play. As an illustration, it has been calculated that the average Roman household consumed in one day the amount of water that would last its modern equivalent two months; in other words a consumption rate 60 times that of today. As well as the underlying social and cultural attitudes towards the question of water-supply, the Roman approach was largely dictated by the very practical consideration that the fittings and control mechanisms then available — taps and stop-cocks — could not, unlike their modern counterparts, cope with the pressures resultant from shutting off a supply without some alternative outflow into which the water could immediately be channelled.

Chance discoveries rather than deliberate excavation have provided valuable information about *Deva*'s aqueduct. Although the term conjures up mental images of a tall arched structure stretching for miles across the countryside Chester's aqueduct was in fact of a different but nonetheless equally common form in the ancient world, namely the

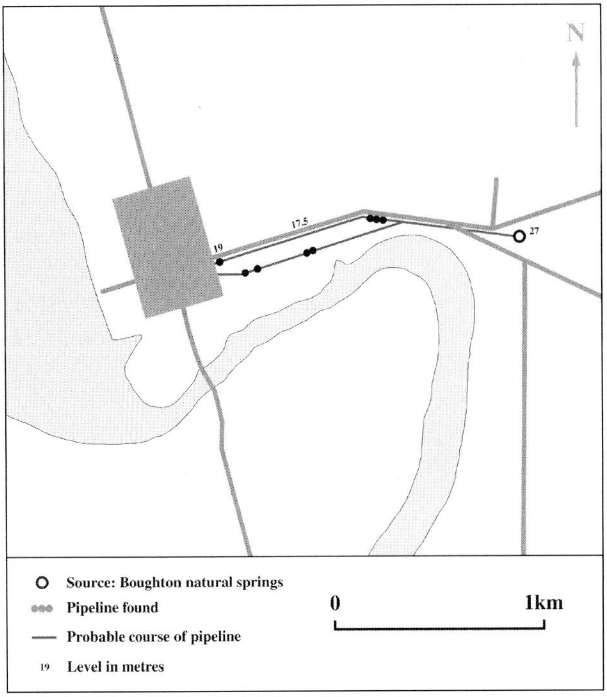

46 Map of pipeline/s of the fortress aqueduct

buried pipeline. The source of the water-supply lay 1 mile due east of the fortress in what is now the suburb of Boughton. It was at this spot that water trapped in a sand and gravel aquifer between two strata of boulder clay broke through to the surface in the form of springs (**46**). An altar dedicated to the 'Nymphs and Springs' was found here in 1821 amidst the ruins of a structure marking the aqueduct source. This had been erected by the Twentieth Legion but it is clear that the aqueduct must already have been in existence by the time it replaced the Second *Adiutrix*. The topography and hydrology of the area have changed significantly since the Roman period and it is impossible now to determine the quantity of water these springs produced. That it was considerable, however, is indicated by the fact that in the late 1880s Chester railway station was flooded to a depth of 3ft when the excavation of a new cutting intercepted the water-bearing stratum. No traces of any other form of water-supply have been found and we must assume that their output was sufficient for the garrison's needs. The water was transmitted to the fortress via two, or possibly more, underground pipelines formed of interlocking earthenware pipes. The individual pipes averaged 2ft (60cm) in length with an internal diameter which varied from 4-6in (102-152mm) and the pipelines were laid at the base of a trench nearly 6ft (1.8m) deep and packed around with clay to prevent the pipe rupturing from the internal pressure. One pipeline ran alongside the road leading to the fortress east gate with another following a parallel course about 330ft (100m) to the south. The second of these was either never finished or became redundant after a short period of use, for the pipe was missing from a length of its trench examined close to the defences in 1971 where the filling contained pottery no later than the end of the first century. Alternatively, it could of course have been rerouted. The other pipeline entered the fortress at the *porta principalis sinistra* and it was most probably here that the main reception and distribution reservoir for the entire fortress — the *castellum divisorium* — was sited. Lead offtake pipes from this carried water to various parts of the fortress and the amount each received could be regulated according to varying demand throughout the day and night; the *thermae* for example would require the greatest quantity from late evening onwards when its various pools were drained, cleaned and replenished.

The baths probably had their own dedicated pipeline while other pipelines would have supplied lesser *castella aquarum* located throughout the fortress from which smaller bore pipelines would have fed individual buildings as well as street-side troughs and drinking fountains. One such subsidiary *castellum* existed during the early second century at the south-east corner of *insula* XXI, north of the Elliptical Building, and its base consisted of a masonry platform 20ft (6m) square. Most of the lead water-mains had a bore of 2½-3in (60-90mm) although a discarded section of one found in a rubbish deposit east of the fortress had a bore of 8in (200mm) and may indicate the size of the main which supplied the *thermae*. All of the pipes found so far had been manufactured by the normal method of taking a flat, rectangular sheet of lead up to 10pM (2.95m) long and, when barely solidified and still very malleable, bending it around a wooden, bronze or copper core to form a cylinder. When the core or mandrel was withdrawn the two edges were then soldered or welded together using molten lead, a process which resulted in the formation of the prominent raised seam so characteristic of Roman lead pipes. The pipes, which were thus oval or pear-shaped in cross-section rather than truly circular, were always laid with the seam uppermost so that repairs could be effected more easily should the joint fail. The jointing of pipes was achieved by enclosing the ends of adjacent sections in a 'sleeve' or 'box' of sheet lead and the seams then soldered. Pipes of much smaller diameter than those mentioned above supplied smaller buildings or parts of buildings.

One might get the impression from the above description that providing the fortress with its water supply was a relatively easy and straightforward task. It is only when one takes into account the respective heights above Ordnance Datum of the source and destination that the subtleties of the system become apparent. The Boughton springs issued at a height of 89ft (27m) OD while water-mains have been found in parts of the fortress at a height of 92ft (28m) OD to which one has to add another 3-6ft to allow for a reasonable discharge height above ground level. Clearly therefore, as the aqueduct functioned by gravity feed the water must have been raised artificially at the source. Water mains have been found approaching the *retentura* of the fortress, the highest point of the interior at *c.*100ft (30.5m) OD, and it seems reasonable to assume that the distribution system was designed so that water could be supplied to all parts of the fortress. Taking into account the need for a head of water sufficient to ensure a reasonable velocity and volume of flow it is probable that the water at source was raised through at least 15ft (4.6m) before it entered the aqueduct. There were various methods for achieving this available to the Roman engineers. There were mechanical water-lifting devices such as the continuous bucket-chain linked to a treadmill, the windlass, and the force-pump, driven by either human, animal or water power. Water could also be forced to rise under pressure by sealing the springs under a thick raft of clay. The easiest and most common method, however, was the construction of a reservoir around the springs by means of a dam or dams, the water level rising naturally to that of the water-bearing strata in the catchment area. As the land to the north and east of the springs rises to a height in excess of 125ft (38m) OD then this arrangement seems perfectly feasible. It would of course have meant a structure of considerable proportions around the springs. Roman ground level at the east gate lay at *c.*67ft (20.5m) OD and the pipeline was buried 6ft (1.8m) below this. Thus, from source to point of arrival the pipeline fell from *c.*105ft (32m) to 61ft (18.6m) OD.

This is equivalent to a gradient of one in ten and given the pressures generated one can appreciate why the pipeline was buried beneath 6ft of clay. On arrival at the east gate the pipeline would have risen vertically to discharge into the *castellum divisorium*. The water level in this had to be maintained at *c.*103ft (31.5m) OD in order to achieve a head sufficient to supply the north end of the fortress. Thus the vertical rise would have been around 43ft (13m). As ground level here was at *c.*67ft (20.5m) OD one can be fairly sure that the *castellum* would have been raised off the ground, either on a solid platform or on a grid of columns/pillars, like the main reservoir of the *thermae*.

With hundreds of thousands of gallons of waste water being produced every day, the drainage system of the fortress had to be equally efficient and effective. Like the system of water supply, this was achieved entirely by gravity. Beneath most of the major streets ran large sewers into which the eavesdrip gullies and minor covered drains discharged. These were up to 5ft (1.5m) deep and 3ft (90cm) wide and many of the early examples were timber-lined. Others, such as those serving bath-buildings, were given linings of mortar-bonded masonry with floors of either stone slabs or large flat bricks. Drainage was aided considerably by the topography of the fortress site. As the long axis of the fortress ran along the spine of the 'hog's back' landform, the sewers beneath the lateral streets drained naturally down to the fortress perimeter where their contents disgorged into the ring-sewer beneath the *via sagularis*. This in turn passed beneath the defences at the south-east and south-west angles to exit the fortress and eventually discharge into the Dee. The sewers underlying the *via principalis* and *via praetori*a passed out of the fortress beneath the gates. Care was taken in the design of the system to ensure that the large quantities of waste water from installations such as bath-buildings were directed into the sewers in such a way as to achieve the maximum purging effect. Thus the drains serving such buildings sometimes take what at first sight appears to be rather circuitous and illogical routes but which were in fact necessary to divide the outflow and direct it to the sectors where additional flushing was required.

6 A fortress fit for a governor?

Certain peculiarities of the Chester fortress were described in the preceding chapter, most particularly its exceptionally large size among the fortresses in Britain. Various theories have been advanced in the past to account for this such as the inclusion of accommodation for a detachment of the fleet, the presence of several units of auxiliary troops, or simply that its buildings were more generously proportioned than those in other fortresses. Sufficient of the interior has now been explored to show that these earlier theories can be discounted. The extra space was required for a group of 'special' buildings belonging to some grandiose scheme for the centre of the fortress, which was halted soon after work had started (**47**). Construction of the Elliptical Building ceased just when its walling was beginning to rise above ground level and the project was abandoned for 150 years. Work on the large building behind the *principia* stopped when the foundations were still being inserted, but resumed after an interval of some years when the building was completed to a modified plan. The main building in *insula XXI* meanwhile was not even started and its site lay open and mostly unused for a century and a half. In contrast, the buildings essential for the everyday running of the fortress were completed and used. These included the barracks, granaries, the *principia*, the *thermae*, and the rampart buildings and bread-ovens along the *intervallum*. No two legionary fortresses have exactly the same internal layout, even those built successively by the same legion. One might thus conclude that the eccentricities in Chester's design were more apparent than real and were simply due to the usual variations on the basic plan, perhaps accentuated in this particular case by the fact that Chester was the first fortress constructed by *legio II Adiutrix*, a legion recently raised in Italy. Yet the fortress it erected at *Aquincum* a few decades later exhibits no such eccentricities. Also, the plan of the Chester fortress as revealed by the work of recent years, with its unusual number and arrangement of *scamna* in the *latera praetorii*, gives the strong impression of a standard design altered and distorted for some singular and unusual purpose. Before discussing what that purpose may have been there is another peculiarity of the fortress which merits attention.

The stone curtain wall subsequently added to the front of the turf rampart is an unusually impressive structure. The fine details of its construction, described in the next chapter, need not concern us here for we need merely take account of its overall style and quality. The corner and interval towers which replaced their timber predecessors were built in the normal manner with walls composed of facings of small blocks (*opus vittatum*) enclosing a mortared rubble core (*opus caementicium*). Yet the curtain wall itself was constructed of large blocks of stone laid in regular courses and without any bonding material, in a style known as *opus quadratum* (**48**). The employment of this very striking and monumental form of construction at other military sites in Britain was limited to

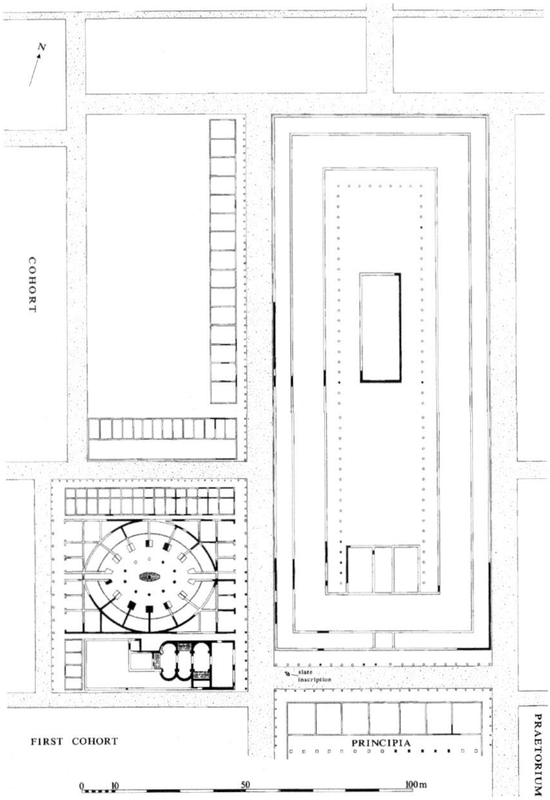

47 Plan of 'special' buildings at centre of the fortress

structures of special significance (most commonly fort gates). In Roman architecture in general its use was restricted to public constructions of major civic, political or religious significance such as city gateways, aqueducts, bridges, triumphal arches and temples. It was already something of a rarity by the late Republican period because of advances in the techniques of concrete construction. This had the advantages of being less cumbrous to use than large blocks of dressed stone and also enabled structures to be erected more quickly and cheaply because it did not require a skilled workforce. The Chester fortress wall was further distinguished by its being embellished at the base with a projecting chamfered plinth and at parapet-walk level by an unusually elaborate moulded cornice. The latter is again a feature whose use is normally restricted to gates rather than entire defensive circuits (**49 & 50**). It may also have been adorned with particularly elaborate coping-stones carved with the image of a bearded deity (**51-53**). The availability of easily worked stone could have been the determining factor in the choice of *opus quadratum* and there would presumably have been sufficient masons in the legion with a mastery of the techniques involved. Yet everything about this wall proclaims a concern not with mere practicalities but with the demonstration of power and prestige through architectural monumentality.

The date of this wall has been much discussed in recent years as a result of renewed research on the Chester defences brought about chiefly by the need for major repair and stabilisation works. Hard dating evidence is difficult to come by owing to the scarcity of undisturbed contexts associated with the wall and the small amount of finds they contain. What is clear is that the process of rebuilding the timber rampart buildings in stone had already begun by the end of the first century. Given the similarity between their masonry and that of the wall towers, the latter are probably of a similar date. A fragment of an imperial inscription carved on a slate slab with letters 7in (180mm) tall, found near the east wall and belonging to the reign of Trajan (98-117), could belong to the memorial plaque set up, perhaps over the east gate, to commemorate the completion of the defences.

48 The fortress wall east of the Northgate

49 The elaborate cornice of the fortress wall

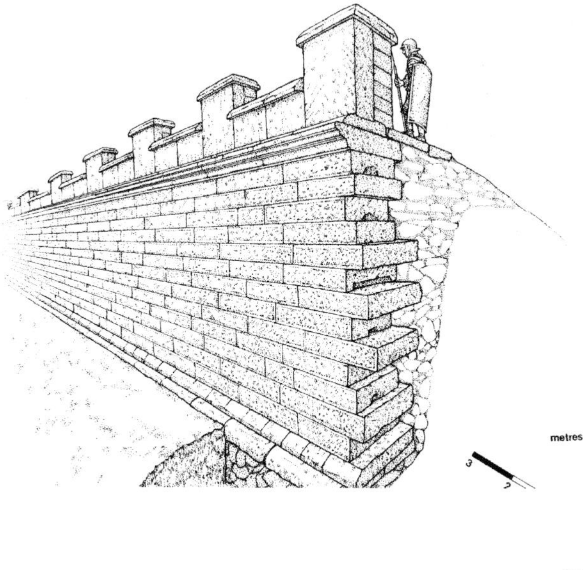

50 Reconstruction drawing of the fortress wall

51 Coping-stone decorated with bearded head possibly from parapet of fortress wall

52 Close-up of bearded head shown on ***51***

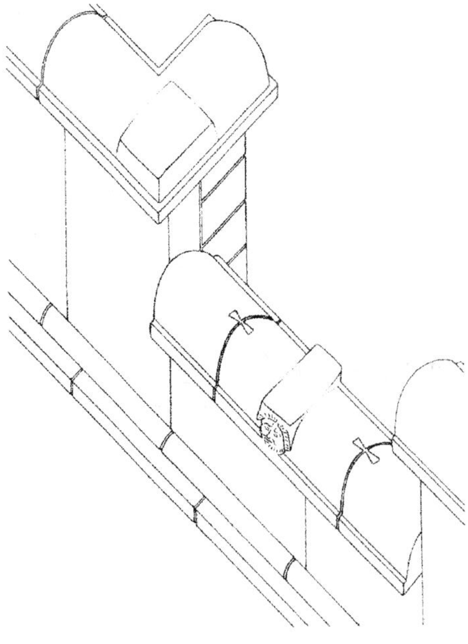

53 Reconstruction of fortress wall showing coping-stone in position

Table 5: estimated fortress construction statistics
Stone fortress defences

Element	**Volume** (cubic feet)	**Weight** (tons)	**Wagonloads** (1,763 lbs load)
Curtain wall	459,364	31,988	40,642
Towers	167,632	11,673	14,831
Gates	169,329	11,791	14,981
Totals	**796,325**	**55,452**	**70,304**

It has been suggested that the *opus quadratum* wall was in fact a third-century replacement for an earlier wall constructed, like the towers, with an *opus vittatum* facing. But no evidence of any such wall has come to light despite extensive investigations. The nature and degree of the erosion which subsequently affected the face of the curtain wall before repairs were instituted *c.*300 could not have occurred during the intervening period of 70 years if the wall had been erected during the major overhaul of the fortress of *c.*220-230. Like every other facet of the fortress design, the specification for its defensive wall was probably drawn up at the time it was being planned (i.e. in the early 70s) and there is evidence that a start on its construction was made soon after the fortress was established. This would fit with the situation at Inchuthil, where a stone wall was added to the front of the rampart within the three to four year lifespan of the fortress. Excavations for the insertion of new drains in 1886 immediately in front of St Michael's Church revealed the foundations of the eastern half of the *porta praetoria*. These were investigated by a local antiquary who reported that the concrete was so hard that it resisted the procurement of a sample. Another portion of the same foundation was exposed in 1908 a few metres to the north of the first discovery. On this occasion it was Professor Robert Newstead's turn to be impressed by the character of the concrete, which was said to be nearly as hard as the boulders used for aggregate. In the light of these comments, and other remarks by Newstead, it seems very probable that we are dealing here with the most resilient form of concrete known in Chester, that employed in the early Flavian period. It was quite usual in the process of building defensive walls for the gateways to be erected first, followed by the curtain wall and towers. That it might have taken upwards of 20 years to complete the circuit is understandable given that the curtain wall alone entailed the quarrying, dressing and transportation of approximately 40,000 of these massive blocks. Furthermore, the process was very probably subject to periodic disruption by poor weather, the absence of vexillations seconded to the campaigns in Scotland in the early 80s, and the changeover of legions *c.*90.

In attempting to find an explanation for the Elliptical Building, its excavator John Eames concluded that the order to construct such an unusual building in a legionary fortress could only have come from an authority higher than the legionary legate, in other

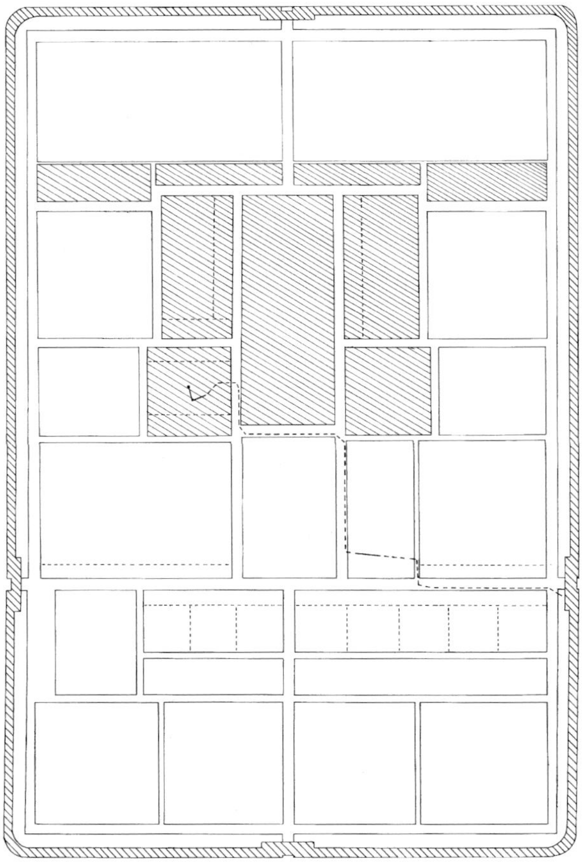

54 Plan of possible governor's enclave at centre of the fortress

words the provincial governor himself and, consequently, that it was the intention to make Chester his headquarters. Accommodating the governor and his entourage, which included not only his personal retinue but also scores of administrative and legal officials as well as a bodyguard of 1,000 auxiliaries, would certainly account for it being 20% larger than its sister fortresses. The provision of fortifications of high quality and monumental character would be an appropriate embellishment for the headquarters of the ultimate authority in the province and an impressive expression of the power, majesty and permanence of Rome (**54**). Further, the selection of *Deva* as the place from which the semi-divine power of the Emperor was exercised through his representative would have been particularly apposite; its name had very strong connotations of divinity. Although some might find the idea of Chester as the governor's headquarters difficult to accept, it makes sound strategic and operational sense given the new forward policy adopted by Vespasian in the early 70s. Brigantia and North Wales had just been subjugated, the size of the province had been increased considerably, and the scene was set for further conquests in the North and perhaps even across the Irish Sea. The governors appointed in this period were generals as opposed to mere administrators and the situation required a command base closer to the 'front' than Colchester, or wherever the governor's headquarters had been located previously. Chester was ideally located for such a purpose. It was equidistant from the fortresses at Caerleon and York and linked with both them, the south-east and the Channel ports by an excellent road system. Most importantly, it possessed the best harbour on the west coast and could thus be supplied by sea as well as having the capacity to act as a base for naval operations. Although perhaps not the best location from which to launch an invasion of Ireland (south-west Scotland would surely have best fulfilled that role), Chester was well positioned as the administrative centre of an envisaged new province of '*Britannia et Ivernia*'. Seen in this context, the decision to place *II Adiutrix* at Chester may have had as much to do with its undoubted loyalty to Vespasian and the Flavian dynasty as with its competence in maritime matters.

The term 'capital' has deliberately not been employed in this discussion because its use would be inappropriate for the system of Roman provincial administration in which the various functions of government were undertaken by separate bodies. The governor looked after military and judicial matters and the administration of recently conquered areas, the procurator supervised the financial affairs of the province, and the quasi-autonomous, self-governing cities and *civitates* took care of local government in the more settled areas. As the governor was a personal appointee of the emperor, power was exercised more on a personal than an institutional basis. Essentially, government was where the governor happened to be at any given moment. There would have been times in the pre-Flavian period when the governor was peripatetic a lot of the year, his administration, or a large part of it, moving with him from fortress to fortress or from town to town. This would also undoubtedly have been true in the Flavian period when first Cerialis, then Frontinus, and finally and most spectacularly Agricola, were busy conducting campaigns over great tracts of territory. However, the expansion of the province in the early 70s, with the increased administrative burden it brought, together with Vespasian's concern with order and efficient administration throughout the Empire, may well have resulted in the decision to establish a more permanent base for that section of the provincial administration headed by the governor.

Seen as components of the accommodation required by the governor and his entourage, it is possible to assign notional functions to some of the 'odd' buildings at the centre of the Chester fortress. The massive building behind the *principia*, for example, seems well suited as the main administrative block, with the outer ranges containing the offices of the various divisions of the *officium*. The isolated structure set imposingly in the northern half of the internal courtyard functioned perhaps as the audience-hall or *aula* where the governor would receive deputations and preside over trials. Because of its arrested development, *insula XXI* can be regarded as lying within this special enclave and, assuming a symmetrical arrangement, so too can *insulae XV* and *XX*, along with the extra and shallow strip made up by *insulae XXIII-XXVI*. These would have contained living accommodation for the administrators and bodyguard, additional storage facilities and presumably the residence of the governor himself. This might, though, have stood on the river frontage outside the fortress like the governor's *praetorium* at both *Aquincum* and *Carnuntum*. As for the Elliptical Building, its presence is more understandable in the context of an imperial enclave. A monument commemorating Rome and its Emperors, and especially the achievements of Vespasian and Titus in restoring peace and order to the

Roman World, would have been most apt at the governor's headquarters. For at this time, the incumbents were not only personally appointed by the Flavians but were also their friends and, in some cases, their relatives, with charge of a province that was selected to be the scene of military triumphs that would bolster the image of the new dynasty. There beneath the monument standing at the centre of its courtyard was an earth-filled trench symbolising the territory for which they were responsible. The building was designed not simply to be celebratory, but also to impress upon dignitaries from the British tribes visiting the governor the irresistible might of Rome and the vast extent of the commonwealth to which they now belonged. Beside it was a bathhouse where the visitors could refresh themselves before their audience with the emperor's representative and also appreciate the more obvious advantages of embracing *Romanitas*.

Such thinking would have been in keeping with the measures taken in the south and east of the province during the Flavian period to accelerate Romanization. These measures included the creation of eight new *civitates*, the foundation of two *coloniae*, encouraging the construction of public buildings in the Roman style, and promoting education and the spread of literacy. It is interesting to note that the man who was governor whilst the plan for the Chester fortress was being prepared was Sextus Julius Frontinus. In addition to being an extremely competent general and administrator, and holder of consulships in 73, 98 and 100, Frontinus also possessed extensive experience in the fields of land surveying, civil engineering and architecture. He was the author of a manual on land surveying, and wrote a treatise on warfare (*De re militari*) and a handbook for officers on military strategy (the *Strategemata*). When appointed manager of Rome's entire water-supply by the Emperor Nerva late in his career, he compiled a survey (*De aquaeductu*) covering the administrative, historical, topographical and technical aspects of the city's aqueduct system. Is it even possible perhaps to see the hand of Frontinus in the design of the Elliptical Building?

There are two final pieces of evidence to be adduced in support of the hypothesis advanced above. The first consists of the Agricolan lead water-pipes found in the fortress. One, as we have seen, served the fountain at the centre of the building (**colour plate 15**). The other, discovered in 1899, crossed the southern half of the *insula* (*XI*) occupied by the legate's residence. The cast inscriptions they bear (occurring twice on adjacent lengths of the second example) are identical and record their manufacture 'in the ninth consulship of the Emperor Vespasian and the seventh consulship of the Emperor Titus during the governorship of Gnaeus Julius Agricola' — that is, in 79 (before 24 June, the date of Vespasian's death). The two pipes could in fact have been part of the same water main, given that the section found in 1899 lay between the Elliptical Building and the reception/distribution tank of the fortress aqueduct located beside the east gate. They are in fact the only examples of water-pipes with an imperial inscription from the whole of Britain; nothing similar has been found in any other legionary fortress despite extensive investigations. Again, this could be attributed to the presence of *II Adiutrix* and its North Italian background where the epigraphic tradition was more widespread and comprehensive. Yet, like the other legions in this period, the Second did not stamp its bricks or tiles and of course it is not mentioned on these inscriptions. Perhaps, therefore, the inscribed water-pipes should be taken at face value as evidence of the governor's

1 *(left) A legionary of* Legio II Adiutrix Pia Fidelis

2 *(right) A legionary of* Legio XX Valeria Victrix *of* c.*AD 100*

3 *(left) A centurion of the early second century*

4 *(right) The* aquilifer *or bearer of the Eagle Standard*

5 *A* cornicen *or horn-player*

6 *A unit of auxiliary infantry commanded by a legionary centurion*

7 *The rear turf revetment of the fortress rampart, Linenhall Street 1964*

8 *The base of the fortress wall and exposed timber strapping of the turf rampart, St John Street Site 1989*

9 *Reconstructed interior of centurion's house based on evidence from Flavian building found on the Crook Street 1973/4 Site*

10 Culvert arch in fortress baths, Newgate/Pepper Street Site 1964

11 Concrete raft foundation for raised water tank in fortress baths, Newgate/Pepper Street Site 1964

12 Massive blocks of base of secondary water reservoir, fortress baths, Newgate/Pepper Street Site 1964

13 Intact hypocaust of tepidarium, *main baths-suite of fortress baths, Newgate/Pepper Street Site 1964*

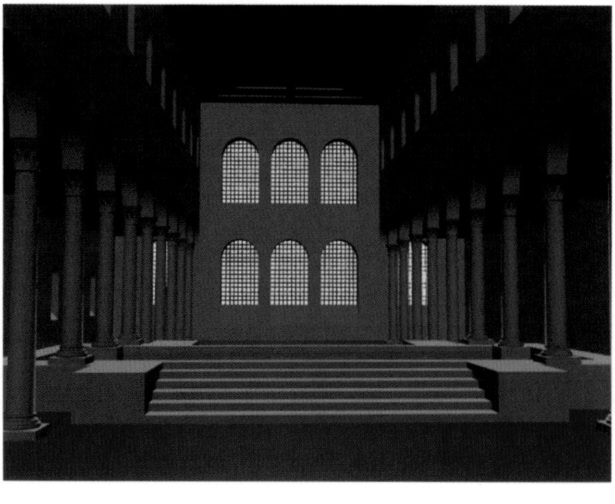

14 Computer-generated reconstruction of exercise-hall of fortress baths

15 *Lead water-pipe with cast inscription recording manufacture in AD 79, found leading to fountain-monument at centre of Elliptical Building 1969. Expanded, the inscription translates as: '(Made) when the Emperor Vespasian and Titus, acclaimed* imperator, *were consuls for the ninth and seventh times respectively and when Gnaeus Julius Agricola was Governor of Britain' i.e. AD 79 (before June 24)*

16 *Computer-generated aerial view of Elliptical Building viewed from the south-east*

17 *Computer-generated view along eastern frontage of Elliptical Building*

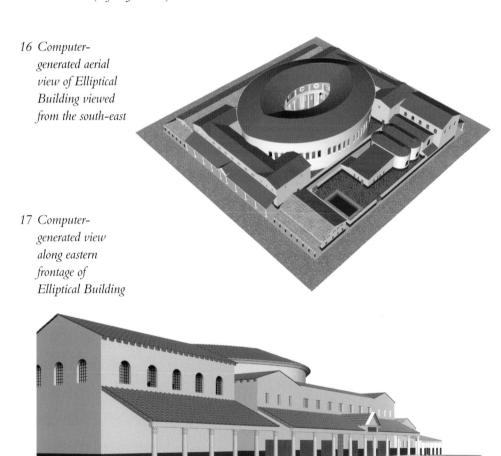

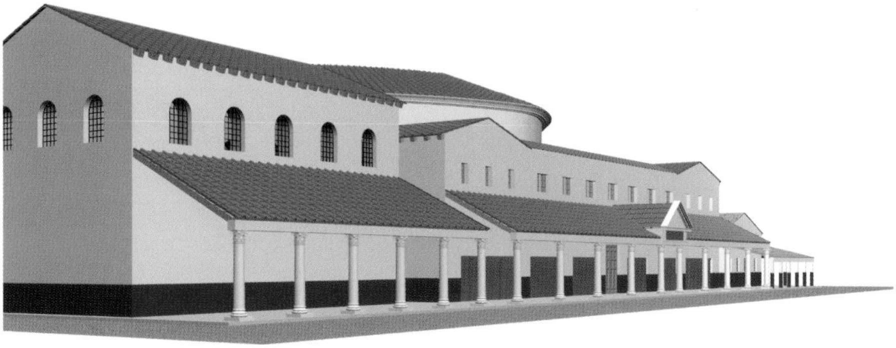

18 (left) Computer-generated view of Elliptical Building interior

*19 (right) Watergate Baths, early plunge-bath found during Sedan House excavation 1989. Note use of tiles with projecting bosses (*tegulae mammatae*) to construct hollow wall-jacketing around sides of bath. Hot gases passed through this from the hypocaust beneath and thus both floor and walls were heated*

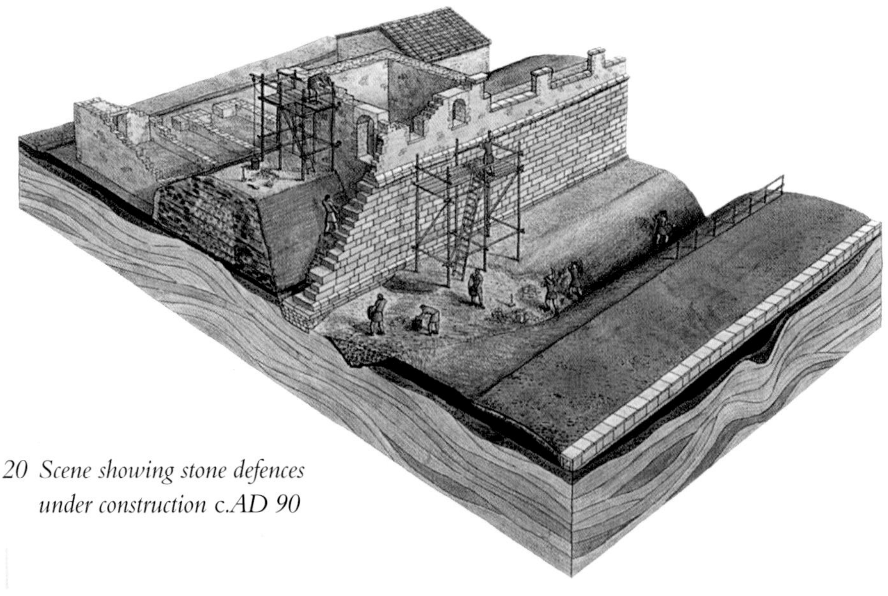

20 Scene showing stone defences under construction c.AD 90

21 Computer generated reconstruction of the fortress east gate — porta principalis sinistra. *The superstructure above the level of the wall-walk is shown with two storeys rather than the usual single level gallery as this seems more appropriate for what was one of the two most important gates of the fortress, the other being the south gate*

22 Computer generated view down a street between barrack-blocks with a rampart-building in the distance

*23 Computer generated view of the legionary shrine (*aedes*) in the headquarters building*

24 Sextius Marcianus making an offering in the Shrine of Nemesis at the amphitheatre

25 *Types of tile roof antefixes from Chester. Two bear the stamp of the Twentieth Legion along with an image of the boar, its emblem. Of the remaining pair, which are very finely moulded and which were most probably manufactured by the Second Adiutrix, one has the bearded and horned head of Jupiter Ammon (a conflation of the principal deity of the three major civilisations of the Mediterranean world - Roman Jupiter, Greek Zeus, and Egyptian Ammon or Amun — and thus expressing their unification under Rome) while the other bears a lion's head, the lion being the zodiacal sign particularly associated with Jupiter*

26 *Sarmatian cavalry of the early third century*

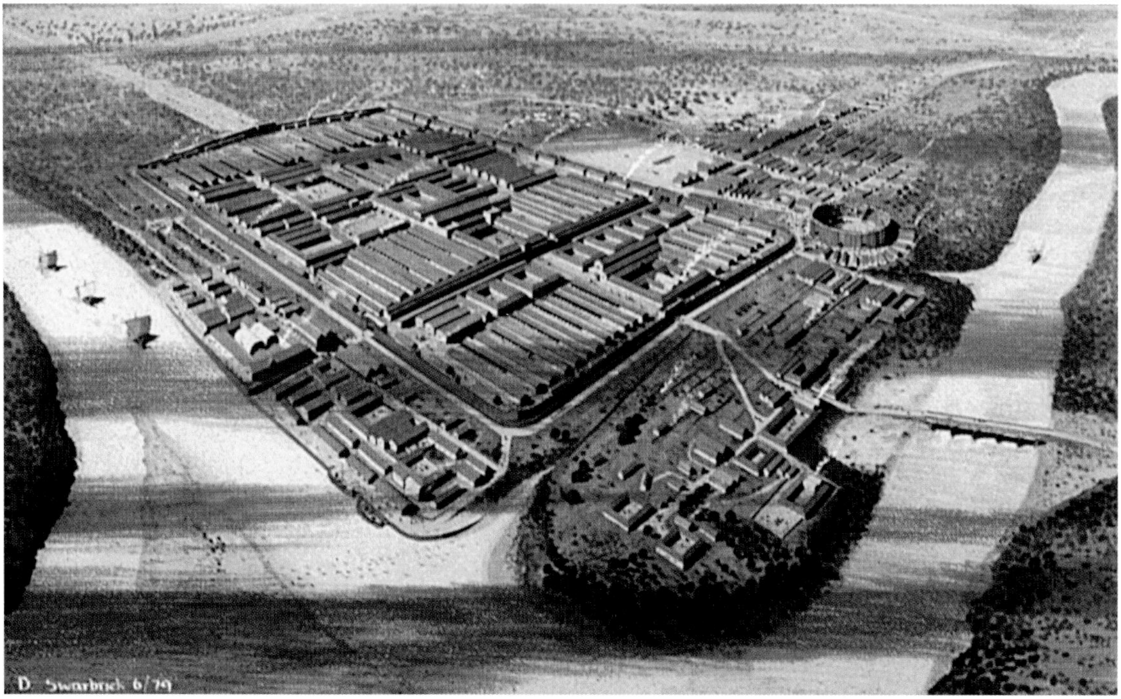

27 *Reconstruction panorama of Chester in its third century heyday. Recent research suggests it is unlikely that ships could approach as close to the fortress as shown here. Also, details of some of the buildings at the centre of the fortress need modifying*

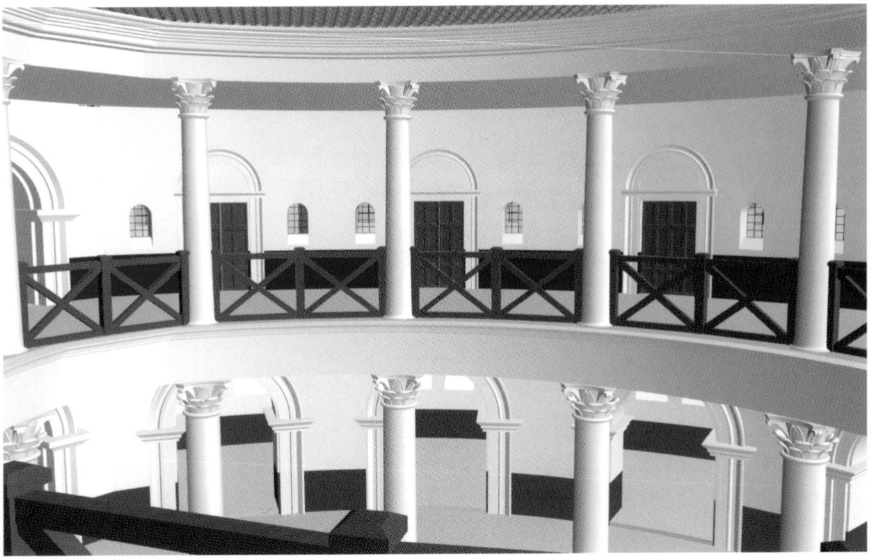

28 (above) Computer-generated view of the interior of the third-century Elliptical Building

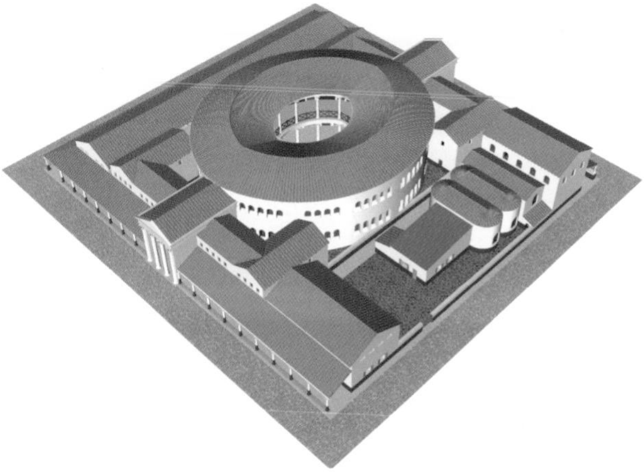

29 (right) Computer-generated aerial view of the third-century Elliptical Building viewed from the south-east

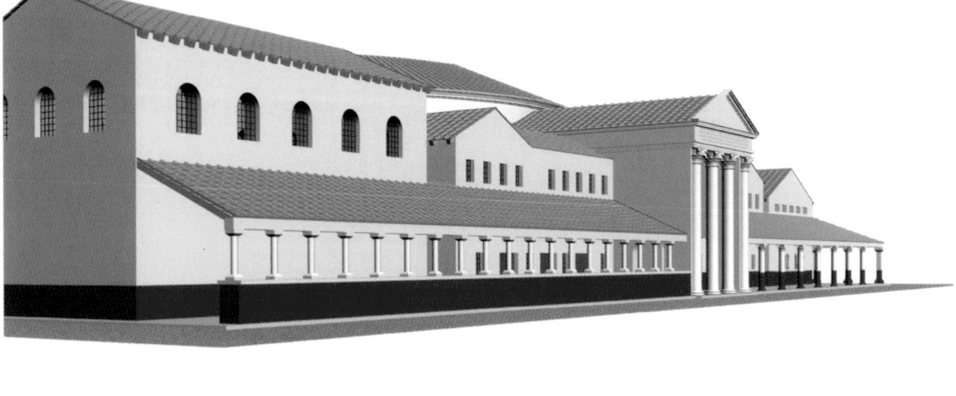

30 Computer-generated view along eastern frontage of the third-century Elliptical Building

31 Computer-generated view looking up the via praetoria *towards the entrance into the* principia *in the distance*

32 Samian vessels from the mansio *well*

33 Reconstructed glass vessel from the mansio *well*

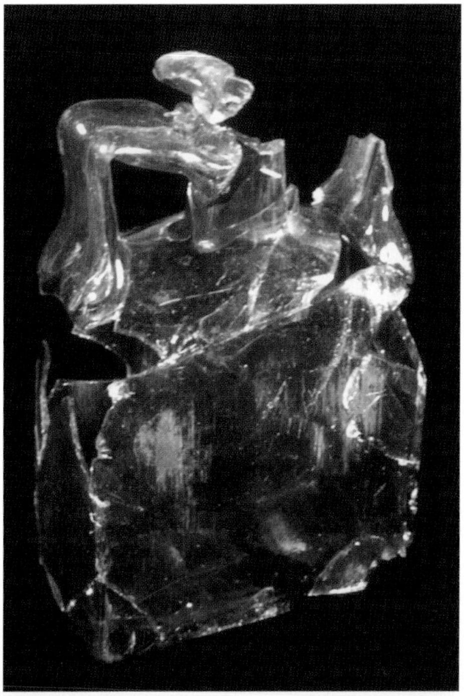

34 Bronze face-bosses, possibly fittings from items of furniture

35 *Small bronze brooch in the shape of a swan*

36 *Section across fortress defences showing ditch fill sealing foot of fortress wall, St John Street Site 1989*

37 *Gold coin of the Emperor Magnentius minted in AD 353*

55 The Old Market Hall slate inscription

presence, albeit of Frontinus's successor rather than Frontinus himself.

The second, and final, item is of even greater rarity and far more remarkable. It consists of three fragments of a slate-cut inscription found in 1968 during the Old Market Hall excavations (**55**). The letters, which are 2½ in (64mm) tall throughout, are finely carved and the inscription was obviously prepared by a master craftsman. The style of the lettering is consistent with a date in the early second century. The position and orientation of the fragments, face down on the street behind the north-west corner of the *principia*, suggests the inscription was originally affixed to the back wall of the portico running along the frontage of the large building to the rear. The remarkable thing about this inscription is that the text is set out in narrative prose rather than the usual formulaic and abbreviated language of military/imperial inscriptions; as such it is at present unique in Britain. It gives every indication of belonging to a very specialised class of inscription, which can broadly be described as administrative, set up as a public record of decrees and rulings taken at the highest level of government. Usually they concern the political and constitutional status of communities, along with detailed provisions for their internal regulation. The best known examples are the constitutions of *coloniae* and *municipia* and the regulations concerning gold-mining operations like those at Vipasca in modern Portugal. The fact that the stipulations of such documents were set out in great detail using legal or quasi-legal terminology meant that the inscriptions in this class could be very lengthy indeed. The text of a recently discovered example found near Seville, for example, which proclaims the municipal law of the *Municipium Flavium Irnitanum*, ran to 10 plaques of bronze each 3ft (90cm) wide and 2ft (60cm) high and thus covered a length of wall over 29ft (9m) long!

56 Legionary dispositions in Britain AD 79

Frustratingly, although the largest fragment of the Chester inscription carries parts of six lines of text, the purpose and meaning of the inscription is unclear; both its style and its prominent position, however, attest its importance. A few of the identifiable words provide clues as to its possible content. The term '*castris*' implies reference to the fortress, a word that potentially occurs twice is '*permissa*', perhaps referring to a grant of permission, while '*clause...*' would suggest something was either 'closed' or 'divided'. Another portion of the text runs '*contra regim[en]*' which could mean 'against the authority of' or 'a contrasting authority/governance', The overall sense of the inscription, as far as it can be gleaned from these few fragments, is that it records some fundamental change in the administrative or territorial arrangements for the fortress, or part of it, that was so important that it had to be effected by an imperial decree. Given the function and status suggested for the buildings in this area of the fortress, a possible explanation emerges which is bound up with the failure to complete these structures.

The grandiose scheme which included the Elliptical Building was brought to a halt early in 79 at precisely the moment when Agricola was embarking upon the conquest of Scotland (**56-8**). Originally it may have been the withdrawal of troops to participate in this endeavour that caused a temporary abandonment of work on the governor's complex. Yet as operations proceeded, Agricola may also have begun to wonder if the planned headquarters were in the wrong place and have issued an order not to recommence work at Chester. His recall to Rome in 84 was followed only a few years later by a gradual withdrawal from much of Scotland, perhaps prompted at least in part by the reduction in the number of legions in Britain to three with the transfer of II *Adiutrix* to the Danube

57 *Legionary dispositions in Britain AD 83*

58 *Legionary dispositions in Britain AD 88*

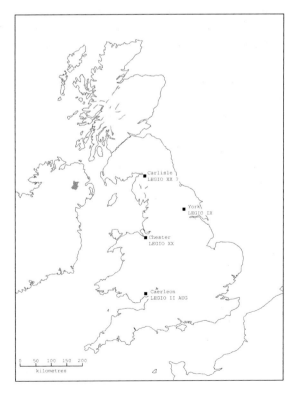

frontier *c.*88. This effectively marked the end of the great Flavian adventure in Britain. Thereafter its governors and its governance concentrated on administration rather than campaigning and as a consequence London became the more logical location for both the *procurator* and the *legatus Augusti provinciae Britanniae*. From what we know of the way in which power was exercised in the early Roman Empire, it is quite possible that the buildings comprising the governor's enclave and the land which they occupied differed in status and ownership from the rest of the fortress. As the personal appointees of the emperor, the buildings they occupied could well have been classed as belonging to the imperial *patrimonium*, whereas the rest of the fortress controlled by the legion was owned by the state and administered as part of the *aerarium*. Our inscription might therefore have been set up to record the formal transfer of jurisdiction over the land originally earmarked for the imperial buildings to the legionary command, at a time in the early second century when it had become clear that there was no longer any chance of the governor's headquarters being located at *Deva*.

7 Outside the fortress: the *canabae legionis*

Much of the area immediately surrounding the fortress was also occupied by buildings and structures (**59**). Some of these, like the parade ground and the amphitheatre, were 'official' facilities used largely if not exclusively by the military and sited beyond the defences because of their size and/or the nature of their function. Others, in particular the extramural bath-buildings, were frequented by soldier and civilian alike. In and around these, and particularly along the frontages of the roads leading to the fortress gates, were established the houses, shops, workshops, taverns and other buildings erected and occupied by civilians. The land around the fortress, just like the fortress itself, was under the direct control of the military; decisions about who was allowed to build what and where were taken by the *praefectus castrorum*. He would have selected the sites for the official extramural facilities and dictated those areas where civilian development could occur. Once the *canabae legionis* had begun to develop, however, the day-to-day administration of the community was left in the hands of an elected council which appointed officials with responsibility for specific aspects of its maintenance. Who actually built and paid for the earliest commercial buildings in such communities is uncertain. Most probably, some were erected by successful merchants as yet another branch of their business empires, some were built by occupier-traders, and yet others by property developers who leased them to other businessmen. All of these had to pay rent to the state which owned the land. Some of these properties, even from a fairly early date, would have been occupied by the unofficial families of serving soldiers and also by time-served legionaries who had retired to the *canabae* beside their place of service, possibly to set up in business. The bonds between *miles* and *canabensis* were strong and grew ever stronger with each decade that passed.

In later periods there was a 20pM (5.9m) wide patrol-track along the outer edge of the fortress ditch and there was very probably a similar arrangement as part of the primary defences. It also appears that it was the intention to maintain a zone free of buildings beyond the patrol-track so as to prevent civilian structures encroaching too close to the defences and thus compromising their effectiveness by providing cover for an enemy. On the west the width of this zone south of Watergate Street was *c.*165ft (50m) while south of the fortress it was at least twice this. Much of the east side was free of buildings in any case because of the presence of the parade-ground, while south of the road issuing from the east gate the clear zone may have been about 100ft (30m) wide. There was no need for such a zone outside the north defences as this area was not favoured by the inhabitants of the *canabae*. The earliest cemeteries were located along the approach roads beyond the

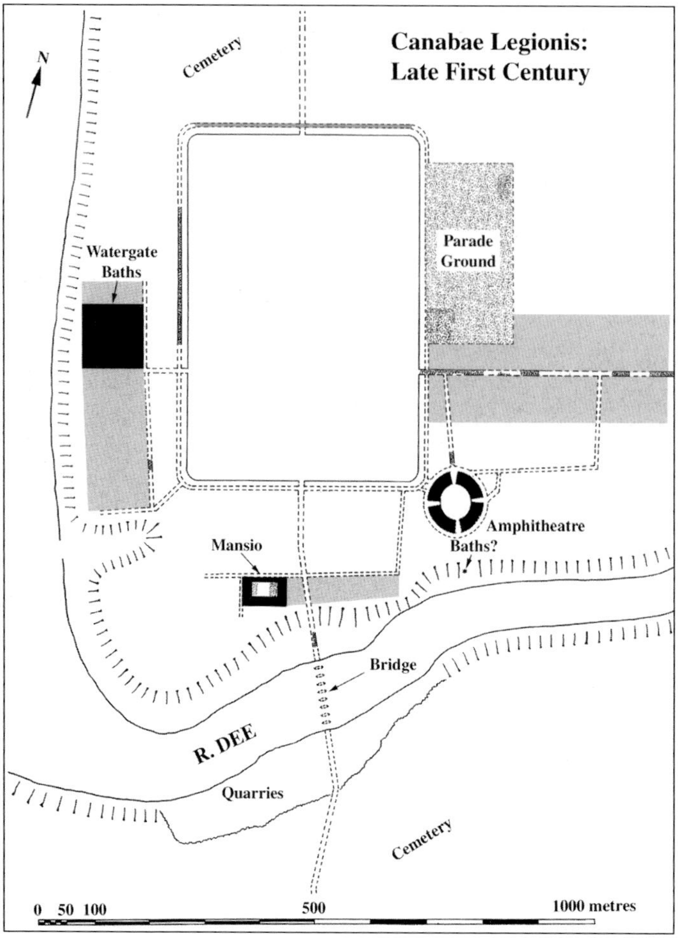

59 Plan of the extramural settlement — canabae legionis — *in the late first century. Solid black = excavated buildings; shading indicates general extent of built-up area*

built-up areas and also in the open areas around the fortress. Subsequently, the expanding *canabae* began to encroach upon them. New cemeteries were located further from the fortress, in particular on the opposite side of the river in Handbridge and lining the road heading south to the settlement at Heronbridge. Siting burials and building tombs beside main roads was customary as this ensured the dead would continue to be remembered and revered by passers-by, who in turn might reflect upon their own mortality.

The names and backgrounds of some of the earliest members of the extramural community are known from inscribed tombstones. Gaius Valerius Crispus was among their number as he was a veteran of *II Adiutrix* which had left Chester by *c.*90 at the latest (**60**). Another was Flavius Callimorphus whose memorial, set up by his brother Thesaeus, was found *in situ* overlying his grave on the south bank of the large gully south-west of the fortress (**61**). He died at the age of 42 and was buried along with his 3½-year-old son or nephew (the text is ambiguous on this point) Serapion. The names of all three are Greek which suggests the adults were freedmen or traders.

Given their ability to afford a reasonably impressive memorial and the location of the burial overlooking the harbour, it is tempting to believe Callimorphus and Thesaeus were

60 *Tombstone of Gaius Valerius Crispus, a veteran of* II Adiutrix, *found in the North Wall (west), 1891*

involved in mercantile commerce. Another man who could well have been a merchant is Pompeius Optatus. He paid for a tombstone to commemorate three of his slaves, the 10-year-old twin boys Atilianus and Antiatilianus and Protus, aged 12 (**62**). Their youth and the fact that they died within a short time of one another suggests either disease or accident.

East

The dominating feature of the eastern sector of the extramural area was the main road connecting Chester with Northwich, one of the two principal approach roads to the fortress. Little in the way of extensive excavation has been possible in this area and much of our information derives from observations of building works made in the first half of the twentieth century. The general impression is that this was the main commercial section of the *canabae* with settlement, at least in its earliest stages, confined to the frontages of the main road. Only fragments of the earliest buildings have been seen. The majority appear to have been of timber and, probably like their more substantial successors, conformed to the 'strip-building' type so common in the business sectors of towns and cities throughout the Empire. These were long, narrow buildings, generally no more than 35ft (10.5m) wide and 100ft (30.5m) long, with a shop at the front, a yard, workshop or store behind, and then the living-quarters right at the back. There is some evidence for industrial activities such as metal-working and pottery manufacture taking place in the areas behind the street-frontage buildings. There is also the likelihood of industrial activities undertaken by the legion continuing beyond the construction camp phase. There is, for example, evidence for the production of bricks and tiles in the City

61 (left) Tombstone of Flavius Callimorphus and his son Serapion, who died at the ages of 42 and 31/2 respectively, found at the Roodee Racecourse in 1874. The memorial was set up by Thesaeus, brother of Callimorphus. All three names are Greek and the brothers may have been freedmen and/or traders

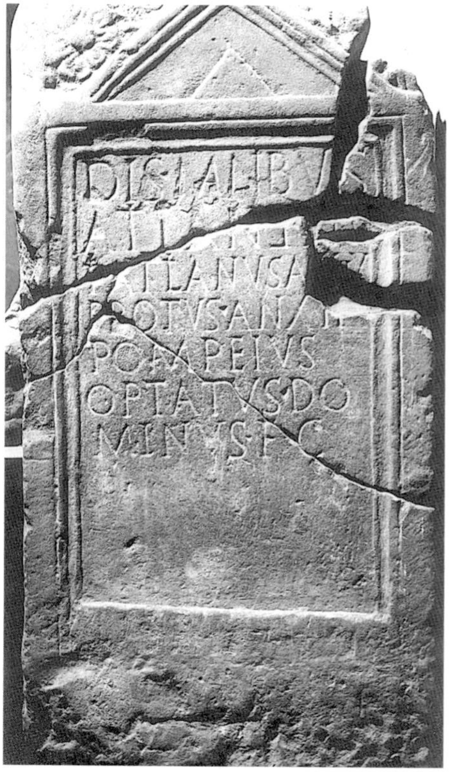

62 (right) Tombstone of the three slave-boys Atilianus and Antiatilianus, aged 12 (and probably twins), and Protus, aged 10, set up by their master Pompeius Optatus. Three deaths either simultaneously or close together implies either an accident or an outbreak of disease

Road area. By the end of the first century, the main road appears to have been lined with buildings for a distance of around 650-1000ft (200-300m) out from the defences. Beyond this point the road was lined with burials (almost exclusively cremations in this period) as far out as the source of the fortress water supply at Boughton, one mile out from the fortress. There is in fact a cluster of early cremation burials around the springs which supplied the aqueduct, perhaps a consequence of the veneration of water-divinities and the life-supporting properties of the medium over which they presided. These burials extend southwards for some distance as though lining a road running on the east bank of the Dee in the direction of the Farndon/Holt crossing and on to Whitchurch.

Another dominating feature of this part of the *canabae* was the legionary parade ground or *campus*. This was one of the more conspicuous features of any military site and one which would have had a major influence on the layout of the extramural settlement. It

63 Restored plan of the primary, timber amphitheatre of c.AD 75

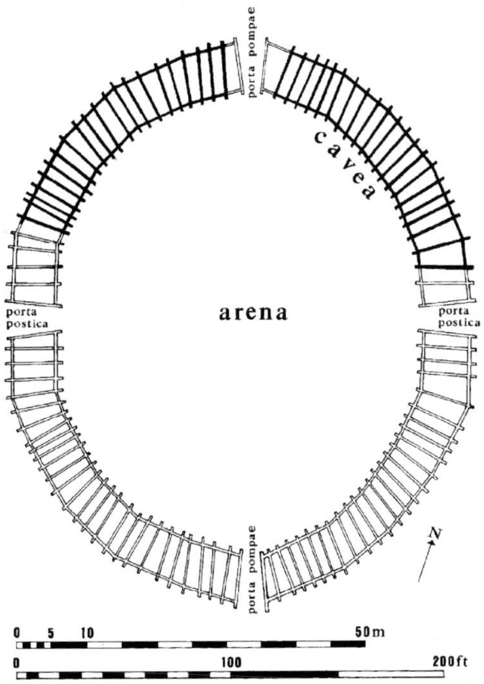

usually consisted of a large, artificially-levelled area provided with a hard surface and sited close to the defences. Most of the time it was used for weapons training and military drill under the instruction of the *campidoctor* but, because of its size, it was also the most suitable venue for assembling the entire garrison for inspections and parades on ceremonial occasions. Weapons training included attacking a target mounted on a post (*palus*) using dummy swords and practising javelin throwing. Drill not only familiarised recruits with executing battlefield manoeuvres in tight-knit formation and instilled discipline but also contributed to physical fitness as well as keeping the soldiers busy; allowing soldiers to have too much free time on their hands has never been a wise indulgence.

The *campus* at Chester, partially excavated in 1966, stood beside the east defences and north of the road leading out of the east gate (modern Foregate Street). Its sandstone metalling had been repaired and replaced many times and its lowest surface sealed traces of pre-Roman ploughmarks cutting the surface of the natural clay. Its overall size is unknown but as an indication, that at Caerleon measured 490 by at least 720ft (150 x 220m) and was enclosed by a massive perimeter wall. At the centre of one of the longer sides of the *campus* would have stood a prominent platform known as the *tribunal* from which the legate or the officer-in-charge might review and address the troops. This was sometimes flanked by lower platforms on which were placed altars to deities such as Jupiter Optimus Maximus, to whom a new altar would be dedicated on the Kalends of January (1 January) when the regiment renewed its oath of allegiance to the Emperor and the Roman People, Mars Militaris and Victoria Augusta. A fine altar found in Foregate Street in 1653 and dedicated to Jupiter Tanarus, Best and Greatest, by Lucius Bruttius, *princeps* of the Twentieth Legion, in 154, probably once stood next to the *tribunal*.

Another official facility stood close to the south-east angle of the fortress, positioned at the edge of the plateau and overlooking the River Dee. This was the amphitheatre or *ludus*. Military amphitheatres like that at Chester were multi-purpose structures. They were used for a variety of activities including weapons-training, the mounting of entertainments (*spectacula*) by troupes of professional gladiators, acrobats, wrestlers and so forth, the celebration of certain rites and religious festivals presided over by the legate in the presence of the entire legion, as well as the more bloodthirsty spectacles of wild beast fights, duels, grudge matches and public executions. The first hint of its location occurred in 1929 when a section of a curved and buttressed wall was uncovered during building work at the Ursuline Convent near St John's Church. This was observed by Mr W.J. ('Walrus') Williams, a member of the Chester Archaeological Society, and excavations were mounted soon afterwards to confirm its initial interpretation as the outer wall of the amphitheatre. This work took place on land farther to the north in an area across which it was planned to drive a new road. The trial excavations located not only further sections of the outer wall but also the arena wall, enabling a tentative plot of the amphitheatre's complete outline. A public appeal was launched by the Society which raised sufficient money to purchase the northern half of the amphitheatre with a view to total excavation. The Second World War intervened however and it was not until 1960 that excavation commenced. This was carried out by the Ministry of Works to whom the Society had gifted the site and was directed by Hugh Thompson. The Society also continued to contribute large sums of money towards the excavation costs. Only a few weeks into the first season of excavation in 1960 it was discovered that the stone amphitheatre had had a timber predecessor belonging to the earliest years of the fortress (**63**). The *arena* remained the same size in both phases, at *c*.190x160ft (57.9 x 48.8m), but the primary seating-bank (*cavea*) was only 22ft (6.7m) wide, much narrower than its replacement and with an estimated capacity of only *c*.3,000. The *cavea* of this period consisted of an open timber-framed structure such as depicted on Trajan's Column (**64**). This was raised on a grid of beams set into the ground, into which the uprights were mortised. There was an inner and outer line of beams connected by radial beams set 6ft (1.8m) apart at their outer ends and converging as they ran inwards. Judging by the quantity of material dumped around the base of the timber uprights, the arena was excavated to a depth of 2ft (60cm) below the normal ground surface. There were no signs of repair to the foundations of the timber *ludus* and this confirms the impression gained from both its modest size and its comparatively insubstantial construction that it was intended to have only a very limited life. Deposits associated with the construction of its stone replacement produced a small amount of Flavio-Trajanic pottery and, more importantly, a fragment of an antefix with the stamp LEGXX, on the basis of which a date in the period *c*.90-100 was proposed for the stone *ludus*. However, the small size of the primary structure suggests it was erected very soon after the legion, or rather that portion of it which constituted the construction workforce, arrived. It is difficult to see its use having extended over much more than a decade without major repair. The process of replacing it with a stone amphitheatre could have begun much earlier than suggested — perhaps even before 80 — and, as for several buildings inside the fortress, the construction programme was interrupted by external developments and only completed after an interval. Consequently, the design for the stone

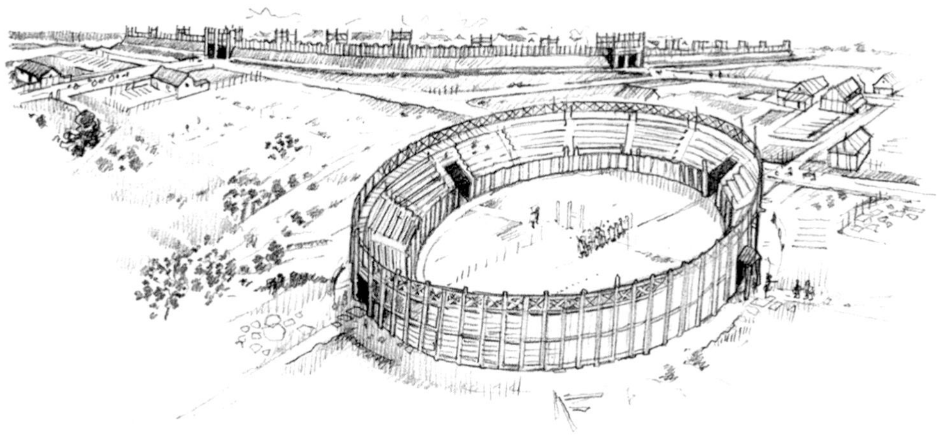

64 *Sketch reconstruction of the timber amphitheatre*

amphitheatre described in the next chapter might actually have originated in this period. Mechanical soundings taken at a spot about 200ft (61m) south of the amphitheatre in 1989 encountered a very substantial Roman concrete structure set on a terrace beside the Dee. This might indicate that the amphitheatre, like its counterpart at Caerleon, was provided with an adjacent bath-building.

South

Twenty-five years ago practically nothing was known about the area between the south defences and the Dee, except for the fact that it was traversed by the road, roughly following the line of Lower Bridge Street, which ran down to the bridge across the river on its way to Whitchurch. While there is much still to learn, excavations since then have begun to give us a broad outline of occupation in this area. Buildings always seem to have been largely confined to the area south of a line represented by present day Castle Street and St Olave's Lane, which may themselves perpetuate the alignment of Roman predecessors. There was some industrial activity including small-scale lead-working a little to the north of St Olave's Lane, while the discovery of a number of cremation burials shows that other parts of the land lying east of the road down to the bridge were used as a cemetery in the early years. As is described later, there is evidence for a number of quite substantial buildings, most probably residences, occupying sites along the edge of the plateau but these have yet to be explored in any detail. The cliff-face south of the fortress facilitated quarrying of the local sandstone and evidence of Roman quarrying operations has been found at various locations in this area. As the number of buildings constructed of stone increased during the course of the second century the demand for stone increased and quarries were also opened on the far side of the river, to either side of the bridge approach. Little is known of the bridge itself except for the fact that it stood more or less on the site of the present bridge, which itself dates back to the medieval period. What have been interpreted as the foundations of the bridge piers have been noted a few feet downstream of the existing structure and what was thought to be the eastern revetment of a raised causeway carrying the road to the bridge was found beneath Lower Bridge Street in 1959.

West of Lower Bridge Street, building works in 1976 on the south side of Castle Street exposed the remains of part of a large and hitherto unsuspected Roman building which led to a hastily mounted 'rescue' investigation. In estate agent's terminology, the building occupied a superb location affording extensive views, standing at the edge of the sandstone plateau and looking down on the bridge across the Dee. The earliest building, of timber, was erected within a few years of the fortress and was constructed using the usual post-in-trench type of wall foundation. Only its south-east corner was located, but this was sufficient to show it consisted of ranges of accommodation arranged on at least three sides of a courtyard with a pebble-surfaced external veranda 2.2m deep on the south and east sides. The building measured a minimum of 100ft (30m) north-south and at least 70ft (21m) east-west. In its later phases, its dimensions were *c.*131ft north-south by *c.*213ft (40 x 65m) east-west and it is probable that the primary building was of a similar overall size. Its internal arrangements and appointments are unknown because of the severity of the levelling operations undertaken during later phases of the building. What is clear, however, is that the primary building was destroyed by fire — whether accidentally (as happened at the end of the third century) or deliberately as part of the demolition process is uncertain. It was rebuilt immediately, again in timber, and the new building continued in use down to the end of the first century. During the earliest years of its existence this building was approached via a cobbled road which branched off that running down to the river at a point immediately outside the south gate of the fortress. This soon went out of use and access in later years is presumed to have been by a minor road roughly on the line of present Castle Street. The plan of this building, the military style of the construction methods, its prominent position beside one of the main approach roads to the fortress, and its early dedicated access road all imply an official function and it is thought that it belonged to the class of building known as *mansiones*. These were a sort of large coaching inn where those travelling on government business could, on production of a warrant, obtain accommodation and a change of horse, or carriage, at the expense of the imperial posting-service known as the *cursus publicus*. Such establishments were located at regular intervals along all the major highways of the Empire with smaller lodgings (*mutationes*) in between.

Mansiones were normally provided with their own bath-buildings and there are hints that those attached to the Chester *mansio* stood between it and the road running down to the bridge across the Dee. Further to the west and south-west, chance discoveries of Roman structures have occurred from time to time but their nature and date are unknown and the opportunities for further exploration are limited by the presence of the Castle buildings. The western periphery of the area was the site for a number of burials in this period. The grave of Callimorphus and Serapion was mentioned above and other interments of a similar date have been found farther north, at the point where the north side of the Nun's Field defile meets the Roodee. Private shrines and small temples are also likely to have been a feature of these outlying areas.

There is evidence of civilian occupation on the far bank of the Dee in what is now Handbridge later on in the Roman period. This could have begun soon after the fortress was founded. On present evidence, however, the main characteristic of this area in the Flavio-Trajanic period was the growth of cemeteries lining the road running south; these were eventually to become very extensive.

West

Excavations since the mid-1970s have shown that the 550ft-wide strip of ground lying between the fortress and the river channel was already crammed with buildings by the beginning of the second century. The space available for buildings was in fact further reduced by the 165ft (50m) wide clear zone extending out from the external patrol-track. An earlier hint of the potential of this area was provided by an excavation in 1959 at Watergate House, situated just inside the Watergate. This disclosed the existence of a Roman road following a line a little south of the present Lower Watergate Street, running from the harbour to the *porta principalis dextra*, with a late first-century timber building on its south side. The latter was a long narrow building and its stone successor was thought to have been a stable-block or a warehouse; given its position, the primary building may have served a similar purpose. Immediately to the south lay a deep gully which was filled in a few decades later to provide more building land. To the south again, the Greyfriars Court excavations of 1976-8 and 1981-2 constituted the first really extensive investigation in this part of the *canabae* and revealed a collection of buildings with a complicated structural history. Intensive development of this area does not appear to have begun until *c.*100 and so this will be discussed in the next chapter.

Moving on to the area north of Lower Watergate Street, evidence for the existence of a major Roman building in this area has been accumulating since at least the end of the eighteenth century. The area is now covered by terraces of Georgian properties and it was during clearance of the ground for their construction in 1778/9 that many impressive discoveries occurred. These included at least three chambers equipped with hypocausts and mosaic floors and another with a brick floor executed in *opus spicatum* style. Although the clearance work proceeded at such a pace that no detailed measurements let alone plans or sketches were made, it is clear from the accounts that elements of either a bath-building or the baths-suite of some residential building had been found. Other discoveries included bricks and tiles bearing the stamp of the Twentieth Legion as well as an attractive altar with a significant inscription (**65**). The latter, now in the British Museum, carries a dedication to Fortune the Home-Bringer (*Fortuna Redux*) and the gods of healing and good health Aesculapius and Salus, by the freedmen and slave-household of a man who holds the distinction of possessing the longest name of any recorded inhabitant of Roman Britain — Titus Pomponius Mamilianus Rufus Antistianus Funisulanus Vettonianus. This man is described as '*legatus Augusti*', that is imperial legate, and although it is normally assumed he held the post of legionary commander it is not impossible that he was actually

65 Altar found amongst the ruins of the Watergate Baths in 1778/9. This was dedicated to Fortuna Redux (Fortune the Home-bringer), to Aesculapius (god of Healing), and Salus (goddess of Good Health) by the freemen and slave-household of Titus Pomponius Mamilianus Rufus Antistianus Funisulanus Vettonianus, imperial legate — either commandant of the legion or just conceivably the provincial governor himself. Included on the right side are a cornucopia and a rudder set crosswise, symbols of Fortuna, while on the left is a rod with a twining serpent, the symbol of Aesculapius

the provincial governor. The style of the lettering suggests a date in the early second century, a time when the names of few of the governors of Britain are known.

Further discoveries took place later in the nineteenth century. The plinth-stones for two column bases were found *in situ* beneath Stanley Street in 1845, perhaps belonging to a *palaestra* situated east of the main bathing accommodation. A 6ft (1.8m) thick wall found running beneath Lower Watergate Street itself in 1866 could represent the southern perimeter wall of the entire complex. The mortar of this wall was so hard that the tools of the workmen could make no impression upon it and so instead it was blasted out using gunpowder: what the local residents thought of this is not recorded. A 17ft (5.20m) wide concrete platform found just inside the Watergate in 1958 seems likely to have been the base of the *castellum aquae* for the baths-suite. Elements of yet more hypocausts have been seen farther north in the Stanley Place area and taken together with the other discoveries indicate a baths-complex measuring *c.*330ft (100m) north-south by *c.*295ft (90m) east-west. One small portion of the 1778/9 discoveries still survives in the cellar of the end building on the north side of Lower Watergate Street. Re-discovered in 1894 and surveyed in 1927, this consists of a short stretch of north-south walling under the west wall of the modern building. It sits on a concrete floor and is pierced by an arched opening 2ft (60cm) wide and 2ft 3in (70cm) high and is itself overlain by another layer of concrete. Clearly part of a hypocausted chamber, the *praefurnium* for which must have lain to the west beneath what is now City Walls Road, this could have functioned as the dwarf supporting wall at the front of a plunge-bath. The first opportunity in modern times to examine part of this complex occurred in 1989 with a proposal to construct an extension to the rear of Sedan House which stands at the south-west corner of Stanley Place. The spot lies at the estimated middle of the west side of the complex about 100ft (30m) north of the surviving fragment just mentioned. Levels taken from the latter suggested that structural remains could lie quite close to the modern surface. In fact, because of the way in which City Walls Road drops down to meet Lower Watergate Street as it passes beneath the Watergate, the latest Roman floor level lay at a height which was actually above the pavement level outside the site. The structural sequence revealed was a very complex one (**colour plate 19**), with at least five major changes to the layout of the accommodation. The nature of the facilities encountered — hypocausts, a plunge-bath, brick flooring in a herringbone pattern (*testacea spicata*) and complex drainage-systems — confirmed the building's identification as a bathhouse (henceforth referred to as 'the Watergate Baths'). Once again, the structures continued westwards beneath City Walls Road and so the baths must have extended to within a few metres of the ancient shoreline of the Roodee. Indeed, studying a plan of this part of the city reveals that the ruins of this massive building influenced the course of the adjacent section of the City Walls, which have a distinct westward deflection at this point. The date of the baths' construction is unknown but the design characteristics of some of its primary features imply an origin in the late first century.

The area north of the baths has also yielded evidence of occupation but again this seems to belong to the closing years of the first century and is dealt with in the next chapter.

North

Despite widespread observation of building developments on the land beyond the north gate, no definite traces of occupation have come to light. The discovery of inhumation burials not far from the defences reinforces the impression that civilian activity was concentrated in the more attractive locations on the other three sides of the fortress.

The harbour

For today's visitor to Chester who strolls along the western city wall and looks out over the flat green sward of the Roodee racecourse, it must be difficult to imagine that in front of them lies the site of what was once the busiest port on the west coast of Britain. The leap of imagination required to visualise this is magnified further by two large constructions of the modern era which have increased the visual separation of the river from its estuary: the Grosvenor Bridge and the road embankment leading to it at the south end of the Roodee basin and, downstream, the railway viaduct lying opposite the north-west corner of the City Walls. The disappearance of the harbour and Chester's demise as the premier port of north-west England, eventually to be replaced by Liverpool, was caused by a process of silting both at Chester and throughout the length of the Dee estuary, which took place over many centuries. Ironically, the very same phenomenon brought an end to the maritime role of Ravenna, home to the fleet from which the legion first based at Chester — *legio II Adiutrix* — was recruited. The first area to be affected was at the south end of the Roodee where a small island had already formed by the late Saxon period. It was from the Anglo-Saxon name of this small island or 'eye' and the cross or 'rood' that was erected upon it that the area took its name. Severe problems navigating the upper reaches of the estuary were already being experienced by the late medieval period. The degree of silting can be judged from the fact that the Roodee had already been largely reclaimed by the end of the sixteenth century, when it began to be used for horse-racing. The general effect of the silting was the confinement of the Dee to a channel against the west side of the Roodee. This can be seen at the north-west corner of the City Walls where the Water Tower, built in 1322 at the end of a spur-wall projecting out into the channel, was eventually left high and dry. Various attempts at remedying the situation were made. These culminated in the canalisation of the Dee in the 1730s, when a new channel was cut between Chester and Queensferry that diverted the river from the north to the south side of its former estuary. New quays were built at the city — the New Crane Wharf — lying 650ft (200m) in advance of the Water Tower. A large area of salt-marsh lying to the north-west was reclaimed and was henceforth known as Sealand ('sea-land').

The natural and extensive anchorage that the Roodee once provided appears to have been the determining factor in the choice of this precise spot as the site for a legionary fortress. Principally during the subjugation of northern Britain in the Flavian period, but also on occasion later on, it would have afforded a useful assembly point for squadrons of warships and transports engaged in combined land and sea operations. There may indeed have been a flotilla of the British Fleet — the *Classis Britannica* — stationed here throughout the Roman period, patrolling the coastal waters of North Wales and north-west England and, especially from the late third century onwards, maintaining a constant vigil for seaborne raiding-parties from north of Hadrian's Wall and from across the Irish Sea. Alternatively, as the latter was known as the *Oceanus Hivernicus* and as the *Classis Britannica* appears to have operated chiefly if not exclusively in the Channel, perhaps there was a separate fleet for the western approaches — a *Classis Hivernica*.

While the harbour's capacity as a naval base was no doubt significant to the military, its real importance lay in the fact that it meant many of the supplies required by the legion could be brought in by sea. The transport of goods, especially when bulky and/or fragile, was usually cheapest, easiest and safest by water in the ancient world. In many cases it cost only a twentieth of transport by road, and although the Roman Army always tried to obtain as many as possible of its supplies locally much would still have had to be imported. This is why many of its main military bases were sited by navigable rivers. The region around Chester was very probably capable in time of supplying the legion with all the meat, dairy products and vegetables it needed. Yet it is very doubtful if the surrounding Cornovian countryside and farmers could ever have produced anything like the surplus of grain required. Consequently, throughout the life of the fortress, merchant vessels bringing cargoes of grain from both the south of the province and from abroad would have been a regular sight in the harbour. Other commodities required in bulk included pottery, especially the finer tableware such as samian from the factories in Gaul, glassware, chiefly from Germany, and of course wine, olive oil and fish sauce transported in the large storage jars known as *amphorae* from Spain, Southern Gaul, Italy and Greece. For the most part these were not shipped via the Straits of Gibraltar and up the Atlantic coast, but by the Rivers Rhone, Saone, Mosel, down to the mouth of the Rhine where they would be transferred from barges to sea-going vessels for the final leg of the journey to Britain. The majority of the latter were probably similar to the County Hall Ship found in the Thames at London, with dimensions averaging 100ft (30m) in length, 20ft (6m) in width and with a draft of less than 6ft (1.8m) at their fully-laden weight of around 150 tons. Unlike naval vessels, these were propelled by sail alone and were owned by private operators and merchants fulfilling contracts placed by the army. Ships of this type were also probably used for shorter, local journeys such as importing ingots of copper and lead from the refining centres along the North Wales coast, as well as lime, slate and perhaps coal. On the outward voyages from *Deva* the cargoes would have consisted of manufactured items such as weapons, other equipment, specialised building materials such as bricks and tiles and foodstuffs shipped on from the fortress. Sometimes personnel journeying to the auxiliary forts in the legion's command area travelled by ship. Sea travel was not of course without its dangers. One of the Chester tombstones commemorates an *optio*, name unknown, serving in the century of Lucilius Ingenuus, recently promoted to the rank of centurion and awaiting a suitable vacancy, who '*naufragio perit*' — perished in a shipwreck. Instead of cutting the full formula H.S.E. ('*hic situs est*' = 'his body lies here') on his tombstone, the mason had left a space for *H(ic)* in case the body lost in the shipwreck was recovered; this does not seem to have happened as the missing letter was never added (**66**).

Other vessels visiting the port of Chester would have included those belonging to merchants bringing in luxury and specialised goods for sale in the shops of the *canabae*. Fine metalwork and jewellery, clothes and textiles, lamps and religious figurines, exotic foodstuffs and rare wines were just a few of the commodities. Nor was maritime traffic restricted to the Mediterranean world. Trade with Ireland was well-established in the pre-Roman era and positively flourished in the Anglo-Scandinavian and early medieval periods. There is no reason why it should have declined with the advent of Rome. Indeed, Tacitus tells us that Agricola obtained useful information about Ireland's approaches and harbours from merchants who traded there on a regular basis. The mid-second-century geographer Claudius Ptolemaius had sufficient detailed information about Ireland to include it in his atlas. Items of Roman metalwork occurring throughout south-east Ireland attest such trade links, while the goods flowing in the opposite direction probably consisted largely of hides, furs, hunting-dogs and slaves.

Thus the area where today many people seek their own Pegasus was once under the sway of Neptune and Oceanus. Broad-beamed merchant vessels would have anchored alongside the sleek biremes or triremes of the navy. The flat-bottomed barges used for transporting goods up the Dee intermingled with them, together with the small, usually oared, native inshore boats used for catching fish and collecting the shellfish which formed such an important part of the diet of both the garrison and the *canabenses*. Given

66 *Tombstone of a shipwreck victim. The man in question, whose name is missing, held the rank of* optio ad spem ordinis *which means he was awaiting promotion to the centurionate. Instead of cutting the full formula H S E (*hic situs est *— 'he lies here') the space for the H was left blank indicating that his body was never recovered*

the spacious and protected nature of the harbour, its facilities may well have included dry docks for ship repairs and maintenance.

Despite the intensity of maritime activity at Chester little is known of the onshore infrastructure and installations which supported it. A wall built of large blocks of sandstone lying a little in advance of the city wall has traditionally been referred to as the 'quay wall'. Whether or not that was its true function — something which will be investigated in a subsequent chapter — this clearly belonged to a later stage in the history of the fortress. The most important discovery relating to the early history of the harbour occurred in 1885 during preparatory groundwork for the construction of a gasometer beside the present course of the Dee and immediately north of the railway viaduct.

The gravel bed of the ancient river channel was encountered below 17ft (5.2m) of silt and made ground at a level approximately equivalent to 0ft Ordnance Datum. Lying on this was a collection of worked oak timbers with an average diameter of 1ft (30.5cm) and still surviving in lengths exceeding 10ft (3.3m). Many had one end carefully shaped to a tapering point which had been encased in a protective iron sheath 1ft 3in (40cm) long attached with nails (**67**). Some of these sheaths had Roman concrete adhering to them while others only survived as casts in lumps of concrete. The iron-tipped timbers were obviously piles for some form of wharf or jetty. A 6ft (1.8m) deep excavation into the river bed found nearby had clearly functioned as the bedding-trench for a line of such piles, apparently secured in position with concrete. The deposits around the timbers produced a considerable quantity of Roman finds which included coins, water-worn fragments of pottery, several human skulls and numerous lumps of coal. There was also a lead ingot bearing a cast inscription with consular dates indicating its manufacture in 74 from ore mined in the territory of the Deceangli (**18**). Whether the skulls were Roman war trophies, the result of pre-Roman sacrifices to the water-gods, or the remains of individuals who were caught up in some catastrophic collapse of the timber jetty, it is clear that this structure belonged to the earliest years of the harbour's operation.

Those who wrote about the Gas Works discovery at the time linked it with the finding of similar piles outside the Watergate a few years earlier, also at a considerable depth and surrounded by Roman material. They suggested that the two discoveries represented opposite ends of a jetty extending out from the eastern shoreline of the Roodee for a distance of *c.*1,150ft (350m). In more recent times this idea fell into disfavour, due in part at least to the acceptance of the interpretation of the wall running along the east edge of the Roodee as a quay. Consequently, the timbers found on the Gas Works site were seen instead as belonging to a landing-stage projecting out from the west bank, the assumption being that the river channel lay farther east than it does today. But the river cliff here is high and steep and any goods offloaded at this point would have to be transported by cart through what are now the suburbs of Curzon Park and Handbridge, across the bridge over the Dee, and then up the steep slope to the south gate of the fortress. The results of recent research on sea level changes throughout history in general and river levels in the Roodee area in particular do in fact suggest that the Victorian antiquaries were correct. They also explain why the Romans considered it necessary to construct such an enormous pier-like structure (**68**).

The general shape of the Roodee area in the early Roman period can be reconstructed from the results of excavations, soundings and chance discoveries. The city wall stands roughly at the crest of the ancient riverbank. It was at this point that the comparatively gentle downslope of the land west of the fortress steepened rapidly falling from *c.* +42ft (13m) Ordnance Datum to *c.* +7ft (2.1m) OD. A layer of gravel at the latter horizon some 30ft (9m) in advance of the city wall marks the original river bed. It was the same layer that was found during the gasometer excavations of 1885 1,150ft (350m) to the west at *c.*0ft OD. The gravel was around 2ft (60cm) thick and in both cases overlay boulder clay

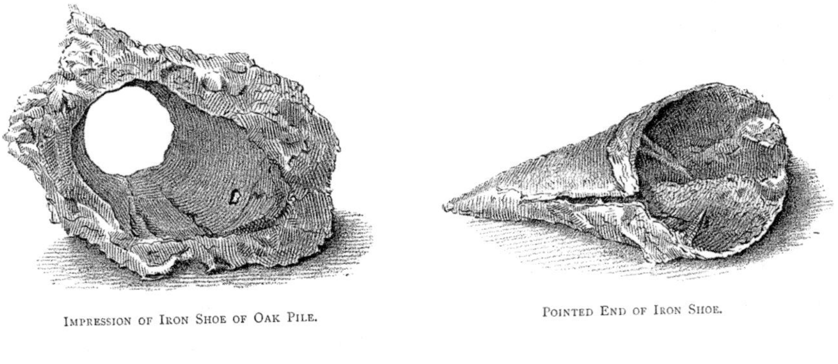
Impression of Iron Shoe of Oak Pile.
Pointed End of Iron Shoe.

67 Drawings of iron sheathing of timber piles found on the site of the Roodee Gasworks in 1886 belonging to the early Roman pier/jetty

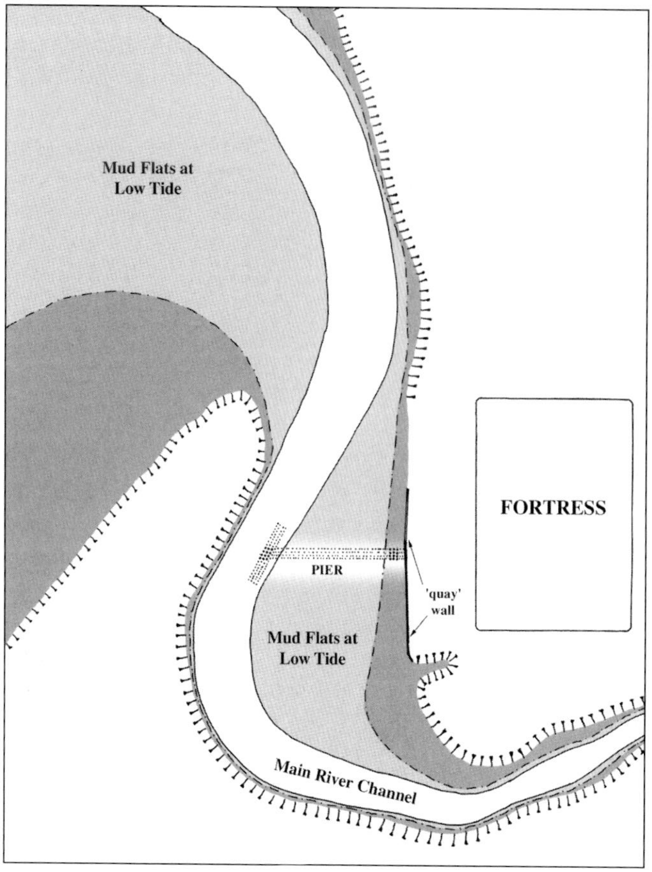

68 Plan of the early Roman harbour

demonstrating that the whole of the bowl-shaped Roodee was formed under periglacial conditions at the end of the last Ice Age. The location and depth of the grave of Callimorphus and Serapion mentioned at the beginning of this chapter demonstrates that the process of silting was already underway by the time the fortress was established, for it lay beneath the outer line of posts marking out the race track some 40ft (12.2m) in advance of the city wall. Clearly this spot and presumably a considerable area both to the south and to the north was dry land at the time of the interment. Indeed, another gravestone was found *c.* 650ft (198m) to the north in 1920 during the extension of the Dee Stand; this too probably lay *in situ*. The floor of Callimorphus' grave lay at *c.* +13ft (4m) OD and the earliest Roman surface found on a site immediately west of the north end of the Old Dee Bridge lay at *c.* +18ft (5.5m) OD. This implies that even the highest average tide did not reach these levels. This agrees with the results of research into historic sea levels on the west coast which suggests they were 5-6ft (1.5-1.8m) lower than today. Under normal conditions therefore the level of high tides at Chester at the beginning of the Roman period probably did not exceed *c.* +13ft (4m) OD. With a tidal range of at least 6ft (1.8m) in the Dee estuary, this means that heavily-laden ships would have found it impossible to get anywhere near the eastern shoreline of the Roodee except for short periods during the highest state of the tide. Given the vast quantities of goods and supplies that had to be

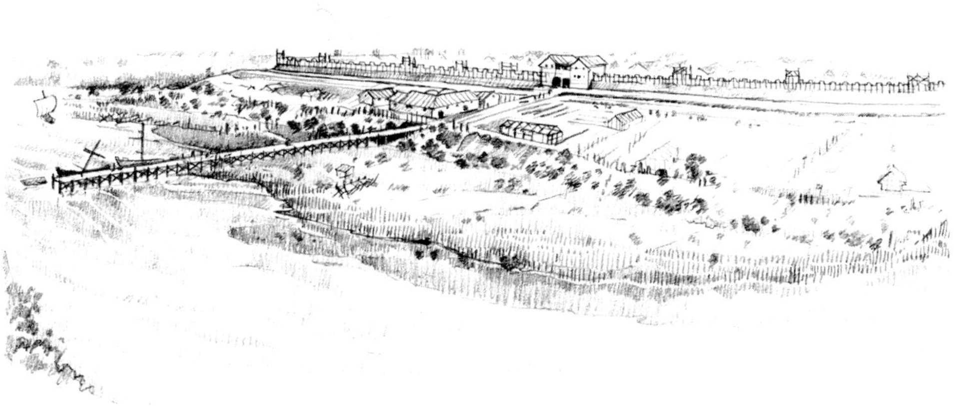

69 Sketch view of the early Roman harbour viewed from the south-west

offloaded by hand such a situation would clearly have been unacceptable to the military. The solution apparently adopted was the construction of a substantial jetty projecting out from the shore and across the Roodee basin as far as the deepest part of the river channel so that ships could tie up and their cargoes be offloaded under most if not all tidal conditions (**69**).

8 The hinterland and the command area

The *prata legionis* and *Deva*'s other civil settlements

On the analogy of the arrangements made in other provinces, the legion at Chester would have had a large tract of land assigned to it known as the *prata legionis* — literally 'the fields of the legion' — which came under its direct control. As a citizen body headed by a deputy or *legatus* of the Emperor, a legion could 'possess' territory on behalf of the Roman People. For administrative and legal purposes, it could be regarded as a locally sovereign *respublica* in just the same way as a chartered town or a formally constituted *civitas.* This is evidenced by examples where the boundaries of civil *territoria* run with those of military lands, implying equivalent status. Little is known of the territorial arrangements in the vicinity of legionary fortresses in Britain but the evidence from other provinces indicates that a legion's *prata* could be very extensive indeed. A useful source of information is the inscribed marker stones erected along the boundaries of a legion's lands. An example from *Burnum* in Dalmatia was set up some 11 miles (18km) from the fortress, while a whole series of such stones marking out the lands of *legio IIII Macedonica* in Northern Spain indicate an area covering no less than 216 square miles (560km^3). The choice of the word *prata* to describe these lands (denoting pasture as opposed to arable land) suggests that their primary purpose was the provision of grazing for the legion's animals: around 500 cavalry horses (including remounts), probably well over 1000 draught and baggage animals, large herds of cattle and flocks of sheep kept to ensure a plentiful supply of fresh meat. In fixing the extent of the *prata* the inclusion of natural resources required by the legion, especially water, stone, and timber, was probably taken into account, along with the need for land on which to practise battlefield manoeuvres and the construction of overnight camps — the ancient equivalent of a firing-range.

Unfortunately we do not possess any boundary-stones set up by the garrison at Chester and so any discussion of the extent of the *prata* here must be entirely speculative. The pattern of settlement in the hinterland of the fortress does however provide some clues as to the location, if not the size, of the legionary land-holdings (**70**). After crossing the Dee just below the fortress, the road south to *Mediolanum* (Whitchurch) ran alongside the west bank of the river until it crossed it again in the vicinity of Aldford. About $1\frac{1}{4}$ miles (2km) out from the fortress along this road, at a location now known as Heronbridge, there stood another civil settlement which in time grew nearly as large as the *canabae legionis*. Discovered in 1929, excavations followed in the early 1930s but it was not until the most recent large-scale work in the 1950s that a detailed picture of this settlement's

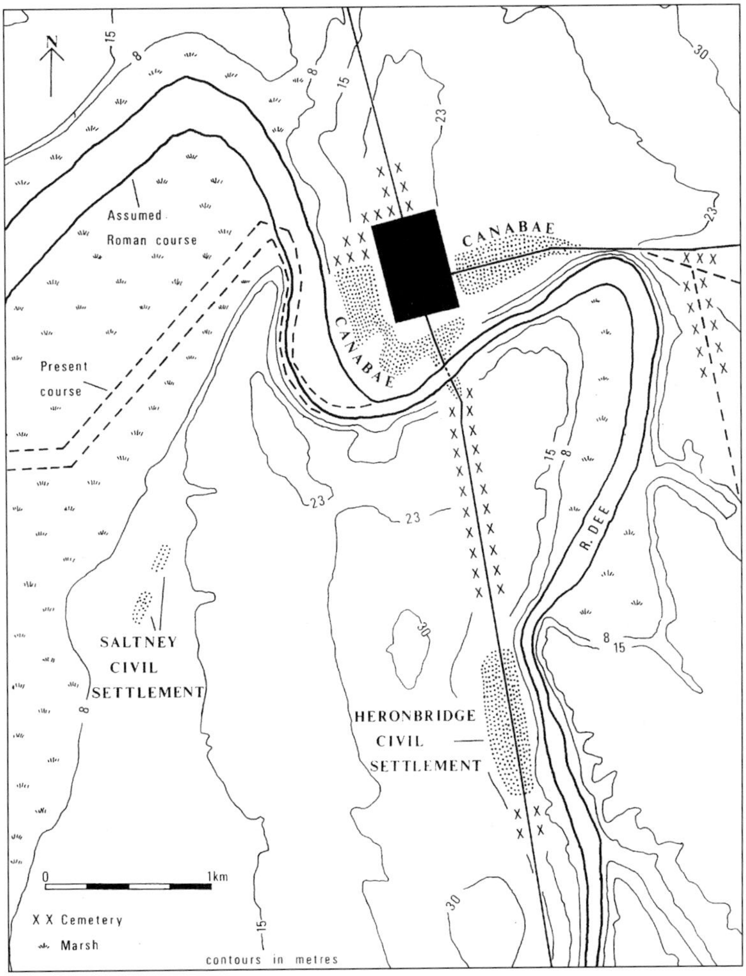

70 Map showing civilian settlements near the fortress

development began to emerge. On the evidence currently available the settlement was essentially linear in shape, consisting of typically civilian strip-buildings placed end on to the main road and lining it, ultimately, for a distance of nearly a kilometre. The primary buildings were largely of timber construction and quite a number were already in existence by *c*.90 if not earlier (**71**). Some were occupied by metalworkers including a bronzesmith whose products included fittings for small chests or boxes and thin plates with pierced crescentric decoration suitable for attachment to articles of leather. A small masonry building of this period and an associated circular kiln appear to have been used for either corn-drying or malting on a commercial scale.

The existence of a second civil settlement of urban character so close to the fortress puzzled the early investigators of Heronbridge. One suggestion was that it was a deliberate and planned settlement of veterans. Another saw it as a transhipment centre where the products from the legionary brick, tile and pottery works at Holt, 8 miles (12km) upstream, were transferred from barges to carts for the final leg of the journey to the fortress. This operation was thought to be necessitated by the probably unnavigable

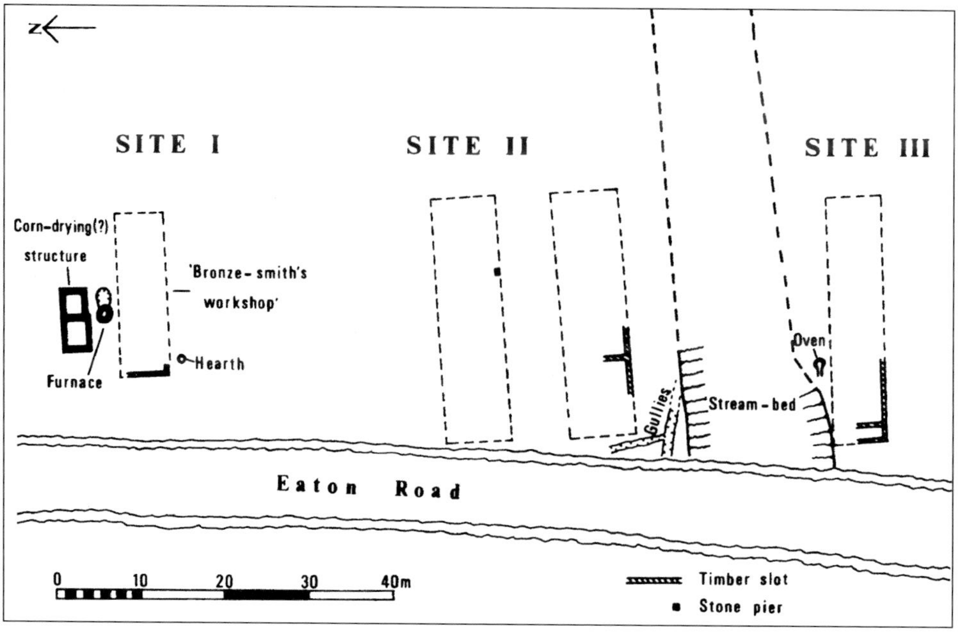

71 Plan of the earliest buildings at Heronbridge

character of the Dee between Heronbridge and Chester in this period. In fact, the phenomenon of two nucleated civil settlements in close proximity to a legionary fortress had been detected at some sites on the Continent as long ago as the 1920s. Work since then has shown that, rather than being the exception, this duality of settlement, or '*siedlungsdualität*' as it has been termed, was commonplace. It occurs at legionary bases all along the Rhine-Danube frontier from *Noviomagus* (Nijmegen) in the west to *Troesmis* (Iglita) in the east, and has also now been detected at the Caerleon fortress in South Wales where the equivalent settlement to Heronbridge lay at Great Bulmore. At all such sites the settlement pattern characteristics are the same. Immediately beside the fortress stood the *canabae legionis*, beyond which lay cemeteries shared by the civil population and the legion. At a distance of 1-2 miles (1.4-2.8km) from the fortress, and separated from both it and the *canabae* by a space that was neither built upon nor used as a burial ground, lay another sizeable civil settlement. It was easily distinguishable by its extent and character from the numerous minor settlements which developed in the fortress hinterland. Developing soon after the fortress was established, its cemetery was quite distinct from those of the military base and its suburbs. To distinguish the outlying settlement from that beside the fortress, Continental scholars have coined the terms '*zivilen Dorf*' (civilian town), '*zivil vicus*' (civil village), or simply '*vicus*' (village) to describe it, the last of these being the smallest unit of local government in the Roman system of administration. Where the civilian community near a fortress was elevated in status to a self-governing town with the rank of *municipium* during the second century, as happened at *Aquincum* (Budapest), *Carnuntum* (Petronell), and *Viminacium* (Kostolac) under Hadrian and at *Apulum* (Alba

Iulia) and *Durostorum* (Silistra) under Marcus Aurelius, it was always the outer settlement that was accorded superior civic status.

In trying to determine the reasons for the growth of such *vici* the range and type of goods used by the inhabitants, the architecture of their buildings and their grave goods have all been examined to identify their cultural origins, but no consistent pattern has emerged. In some *vici* people of native and local origin appear to have been in the majority, in others there was a considerable admixture of settlers from other provinces, while in yet others foreigners constituted by far the largest section of the population. There was no displacement of the native population from some local pre-Roman stronghold and there is no evidence of such communities having originated as the extramural settlement of a pre-fortress auxiliary fort. The explanation which seems to fit best with the known facts, especially the clear physical separation of *canabae* and *vicus*, is that the territorial and thus the legal and administrative status of the two communities differed fundamentally. In other words, whereas the *canabae* stood on the *prata legionis* under the jurisdiction of the legion, the *vicus* occupied land belonging to the neighbouring civil authority. In the case of Heronbridge this was the *civitas Cornoviorum*. This would explain why it was the outlying settlement that was selected for elevation to chartered town at some sites in the second century; promotion of the *canabae* would have resulted in the peculiar situation of the legion losing jurisdiction over the ground immediately surrounding the fortress. Thus the *canabenses*, most of whom made their living by providing goods and services for the legion, could only rent plots of land. Yet those living at Heronbridge, a more conventional and independent form of settlement, had the opportunity of owning the land where they lived and worked.

If Heronbridge did lie on territory belonging to the *civitas Cornoviorum*, then clearly the legionary *prata* at Chester cannot have extended south of the Dee much beyond the modest zone encompassing the quarries and cemeteries in the Handbridge area. The bulk of it must therefore have lain to the east and north. The Central Ridge would be an obvious boundary to the east. The existence of a villa at Eaton by Tarporley on its eastern slopes 10 miles (16km) east-south-east of the fortress, founded around the end of the first century, sets the absolute limit in this direction. Alternatively, the River Gowy, formerly known as the Tarvin, a name derived from the Welsh *Terfyn* and ultimately from the Latin *terminus* (a boundary), may have marked the eastern limit of the *prata*. The gently rolling landscape here and at the base of the Wirral to the north would have been well suited to the *prata*'s supposedly primary function of providing pasture. Perhaps confirming the notion of military control over this area, and also highlighting one of the other functions of the *prata*, aerial reconnaissance in recent years has revealed the existence of no less than 14 earthwork enclosures of Roman date to the east and north-east of the fortress at a distance of 1½ and 3 miles (2.4 and 4.8km) respectively. They bear all the hallmarks of practice camps.

Another civil settlement developed at Saltney, 1½ miles (2.4km) south-west of the fortress, situated along the edge of a slight cliff overlooking the marshlands bordering the Dee estuary to the north-west (**70**). From information recorded during the construction of a housing estate in the 1930s it would appear that occupation began before the end of the first century. The inhabitants' standard of living, however, was far below that of the

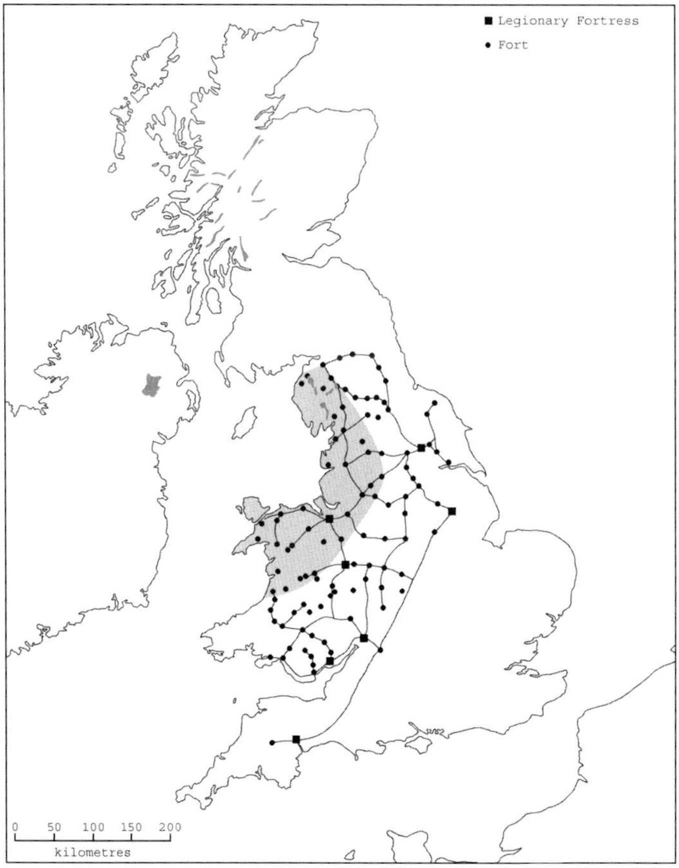

72 Map showing extent of the 'Chester Command' area c.AD 100

population at Heronbridge. The dwellings were crudely constructed with rubble footings, each one apparently set in a fenced and ditched plot of ground. The settlement seems to have been essentially agricultural.

The command area

Each of the legions stationed in the frontier districts of the Empire had a number of units of auxiliary troops attached to it which were stationed in forts. These were generally spaced one day's march apart (15-20 Roman miles) throughout the region or 'command area' for which that legion was responsible. It was to these (largely) non-citizen regiments which made up the second and less prestigious branch of the Roman Army that fell the routine police and patrol duties associated with maintaining peace and security in recently pacified areas. Contemporary with the establishment of the Chester and Caerleon fortresses, the pre-existing network of auxiliary forts was extended throughout the whole of Wales. In many cases, the more sophisticated buildings at these forts were built by legionary personnel using bricks and tiles produced by the legion to which they belonged. The distribution of these materials can be used to provide a more accurate picture of the

Table 6: Chester command AD 98 and 105

ala quingenariae (cavalry squadron 500-strong)

I Hispanorum Asturum
Gallorum et Thracum Classiana c.R.
Augusta Gallorum Petriana c.R.
I Tungrorum

cohors milliaria equitata (mixed infantry/cavalry regiment 1,000 strong; *c.*760 & *c.*240 respectively)
I fida Vardullorum eq. c.R.

cohortes quingenariae equitatae (mixed infantry/cavalry regiment 500-strong; *c.*380 & 120 respectively)
II Asturum eq.
I Celtiberorum eq.
II Delmatarum eq.
I Lingonum eq.
II Lingonum eq.
II Pannoniorum eq.
II Vasconum eq. c.R.
I Hispanorum eq.

cohortes quingenariae peditatae (infantry regiment 500-strong)
I Frisiavonum
I Nerviorum
II Nerviorum c.R.

* c.R. = civium Romanorum (Roman citizens)

geographical extent of a legion's command area. Unfortunately, the legions in Britain only began stamping such products from *c.*90, a few years after *II Adiutrix* had departed for the lower Danube. Thus this method cannot be applied in defining its command area. However, the distribution of its successor's stamped bricks and tiles, together with that of inscriptions recording the presence of either officers or construction parties from the Twentieth at auxiliary forts, indicates that the later command area of *Deva* encompassed North Wales as far south as the Severn along with the whole of north-west England (**72 & 73**). The extent of the Welsh portion of the command area in *II Adiutrix*'s time was probably somewhat smaller, as the Twentieth was based at Wroxeter and controlled mid-Wales. When *legio XX* moved forward to *Deva c.*88, its former command area was presumably divided between the Chester and Caerleon commands. Military diplomas, recording lists of units with men due for discharge at a given date, can sometimes be

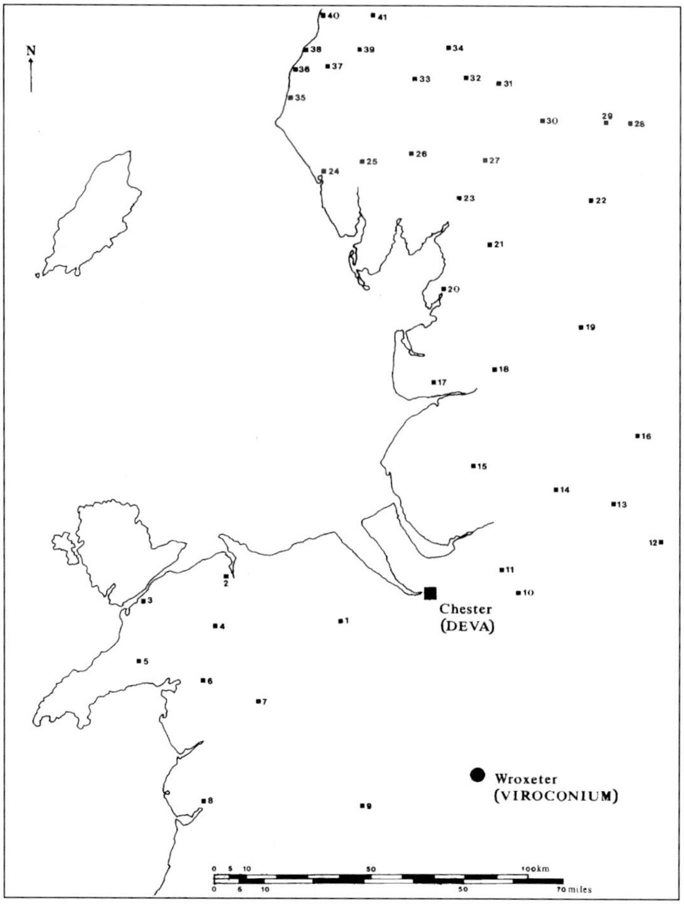

73 Map of auxiliary forts in the 'Chester Command' area. 1 Rhuthun 2 Caerhun 3 Caernarfon 4 Bryn y Gefeiliau 5 Pen Llystyn 6 Tomen y Mur 7 Caer Gai 8 Pennal 9 Forden Gaer 10 Middlewich 11 Northwich 12 Brough on Noe 13 Melandra Castle 14 Manchester 15 Wigan 16 Slack 17 Kirkham 18 Ribchester 19 Elslack 20 Lancaster 21 Burrow in Lonsdale 22 Brough 23 Watercrook 24 Ravenglass 25 Hardknott 26 Ambleside 27 Low Borrow Bridge 28 Greta Bridge 29 Bowes 30 Brough under Stainmore 31 Kirkby Thore 32 Brougham 33 Troutbeck 34 Old Penrith 35 Moresby 36 Burrow Walls 37 Papcastle 38 Maryport 39 Caermote 40 Beckfoot 41 Old Carlisle

attributed to a particular legionary command. It is thought that examples dating to 98 and 105 set out the auxiliary formations belonging to the Chester command. The units are shown in **Table 6**, although the list does not of course include all those controlled by *legio XX*, but only those with men due for retirement.

The region controlled from Chester contained areas rich in mineral resources. Their rapid exploitation during Vespasian's reign may well in part reflect that emperor's concern with improving the state finances in the wake of Nero's extravagances (**74**). Such areas

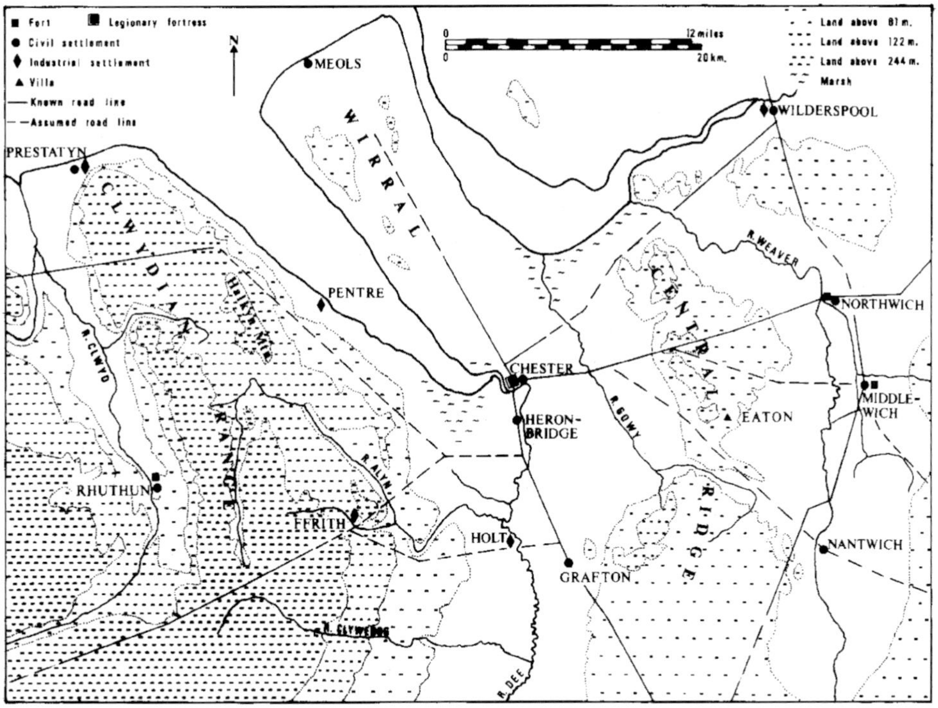

74 Map showing principal sites in the hinterland of Deva

were regularly appropriated as imperial estates with operations overseen by an official (a *procurator metallorum*) from the department of the provincial procurator (who was responsible for the financial aspects of the province's administration) and with troops on hand to enforce security. This was very probably the situation with the Flintshire lead-fields, where examples of stamped ingots datable to 74 and 76 attest the beginning of direct imperial exploitation. By *c.*90 refining and transhipment centres had been established at Pentre-Oakenholt near Flint on the Dee estuary and at Prestatyn farther down the coast. A third lay inland at Ffrith, some 10 miles (16km) south-west of Chester. Lead mining had an added significance in the Roman world as silver could be obtained — by the process known as cupellation — from lead ores with a medium-high argentiferous content. Silver coinage was fundamental to the Roman monetary system and economy. It is still unclear whether the low level of silver in the known Flintshire ingots reflects a naturally low silver content in the lead ore or the fact that the lead from which they were made had already been desilvered. Further into North Wales the copper deposits of the Great Orme near Llandudno and at Parys Mountain on Anglesey, both worked for many centuries previously, were also exploited fully. In the opposite direction the Cheshire Plain contained a resource vital to the Roman economy in general and the army in particular, namely salt. Its importance was far greater in the ancient world than today. Then, it was the chief means of preserving food to be used during the winter months, when herds and flocks were reduced in size because of the problems of feeding them and when sea-fishing was often impossible owing to adverse weather. The alternative method of sun-drying used in Mediterranean climes was impracticable in the north-western provinces with their poorer weather. Salt production was concentrated in the Weaver valley with its numerous brine-springs and this area too may have been formed into an imperial estate. Salt production was greatly increased above the level of pre-Roman native exploitation and industrial settlements were rapidly established at Middlewich (*Salinae* — whose name means 'salt-works'), Northwich (*Condate*) and Nantwich. The first two of these appear to have been the most important. An auxiliary fort was established at both, *c.*75, whose garrisons were to reinforce the authority of the officials in charge, to prevent theft and to make sure rents and taxes were paid by any commercial operators permitted in the area.

9 A change of garrison and the fortress rebuilt (*c.*90-*c.*120)

Around 88 the Emperor Domitian, Vespasian's second son who succeeded Titus in 81, ordered the transfer of *legio II Adiutrix*, along with a number of auxiliary units, from Britain to the Lower Danube to strengthen the forces ranged against the Dacians. This had a dramatic effect on military deployment in Britain. *Legio XX Valeria Victrix*, still busily engaged in the construction of a new fortress at Inchtuthil, was withdrawn from Scotland to garrison the now-empty fortress at Chester. All forts north of the Forth-Clyde isthmus were abandoned. The Twentieth was one of the oldest regiments in the Roman Army and had already been in existence for a century or more when *II Adiutrix* was formed in 69. It had seen service in Spain, the Balkans and Germany before being assigned to the invasion force launched across the Channel in 43. Prior to its being stationed at Wroxeter and subsequently Inchtuthil, it had been based first at Colchester and then at Usk in South Wales. Its titles *Valeria Victrix* — meaning 'Valiant and Victorious' — were probably awarded for its part in putting down the Boudiccan Revolt of 61. The wealth of tombstones from Chester show that the majority of the Twentieth's recruits continued to come from colonies in Spain, southern France, northern Italy and the Balkans well into the third century.

Of the men known to have been serving with the Twentieth in its early years at Chester, one of the more interesting is the centurion Titus Claudius Vitalis. Originally from Spain, he began his career with *legio V Macedonica*, then stationed in the Balkans, subsequently transferring to *legio I Italica* in the same region. Next, he served with *legio I Minervia* in Dacia before transferring to Britain where he saw service successively with the Twentieth *Valeria Victrix* and the Ninth *Hispana*, followed by a final posting as centurion with *legio VII Claudia* stationed on the Danube. A man who held the office of *praefectus castrorum* in the opening decades of the second century, and would thus very probably have been closely involved in the fortress reconstruction, was buried in the Eaton Road cemetery on the far side of the river. The fine slate-cut memorial inscription which once adorned his doubtless impressive tomb survives only in part and so his name is unknown. However, the extant fragment reveals that immediately prior to his arrival at Chester he had been *primus pilus* with *legio XXII Deioteriana* in Egypt. Two men who were very probably with the Twentieth when it moved to Chester are Quintus Cassius Secundus and Geminius Mansuetus. They are mentioned on a writing-tablet found at Carlisle dated 7 November in the year 83 which records that the former owed the latter a sum of money. A Cassius Secundus does in fact appear on a tombstone found at Chester (**75**). A veteran

75 Tombstone of the veteran Cassius Secundus who died aged 80. Found in North Wall (west) 1891

who married in retirement, he lived to the ripe old age of 80. If not the same man perhaps he was a relative of the man recorded at Carlisle. Also possibly from this early period is the armourer Julius Vitalis, whose tombstone was found at Bath. He had presumably been sent there, like Gaius Murrius Modestus of *legio II Adiutrix* before him, to try the healing powers of the hot springs. His funeral was paid for by the Guild of Armourers ('*collegium fabricensium*') at Chester.

Following the Twentieth's arrival, a programme of building work was instituted which was to last a decade or possibly longer. It entailed the replacement of many of the now ageing buildings erected some 15 years earlier. Some, perhaps the majority of those affected, were rebuilt in timber initially but by the end of the first century the gradual process of replacing all the fortress buildings with masonry or part-masonry successors had begun. The impressive stone defences, possibly already partly built, seem likely to have been completed by the opening years of the second century (**76**). The grandiose scheme for a group of special buildings at the centre of the fortress was however abandoned. Most of the area continued to lie derelict, although the large building to the rear of the *principia* was eventually completed to a modified plan and possibly with a different function from that originally intended. For at least the next 150 years Chester was the regimental headquarters of the Twentieth Legion. The legion's cognomen eventually became attached to the placename, to give '*Deva Victrix*' as it occurs in the late antique document known as the Ravenna Cosmography.

The defences

The character of the fortress curtain wall has been found to be the same on all four sides of the fortress. On the south and west only the lowest few courses survive because the fortress defences were demolished in the early medieval period when the line of the city's defences was extended down to the river. On the east and north, however, considerable stretches of the wall can still be seen projecting out from beneath the medieval wall. The longest and most impressive section is that immediately east of the Northgate where the Roman masonry survives up to and including the moulded cornice at the level of the parapet walkway. The wall was of course accompanied by stone corner and interval towers but whereas the wall and, on the evidence of antiquarian drawings (*see* **4**) and accounts of their remains, the gates too, were built of massive blocks (**colour plate 20**), these were constructed employing the more conventional double facings of small blocks in *opus vittatum* style (**77**). The date of the completion of the stone defences is unknown but is usually assumed to lie in the opening years of the second century. A fragmentary imperial inscription of large size recovered from a point close to the east wall and dating to the reign of Trajan has been thought to derive from the *porta principalis sinistra* nearby, but this is far from certain (**78**). The evidence from the Abbey Green excavations of 1975-8 beside the eastern sector of the north wall does however demonstrate that the process of converting the rampart buildings to stone was underway by *c.*100. It seems very likely that the provision or completion of the stone defences was contemporary.

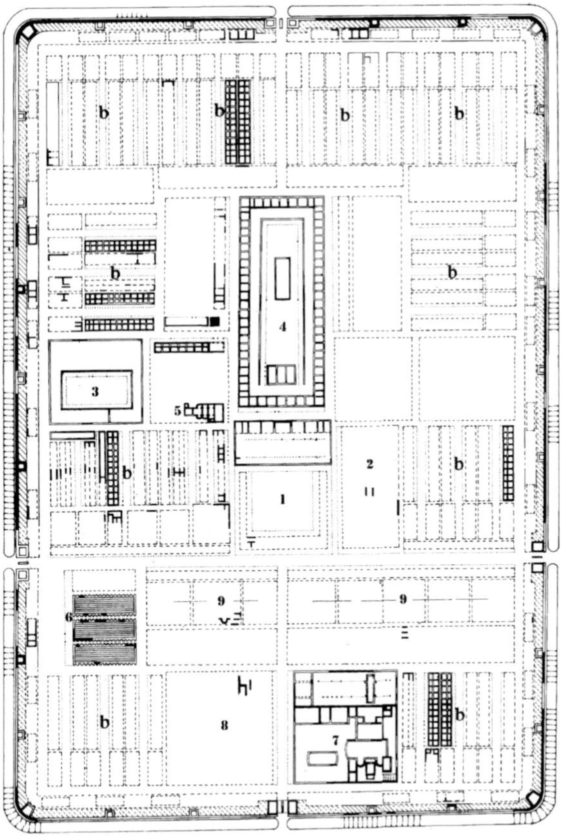

76 Plan of the fortress in the early second century. KEY: 1 headquarters building; 2 legate's residence; 3 workshops; 4 stores; 5 minor baths; 6 granaries; 7 major baths; 8 hospital(?); 9 senior officers' residences; b barracks

As mentioned in chapter 6 the fortress wall was an elaborate and unusually monumental construction executed in a style known as *opus quadratum*. In this, large blocks of stone measuring up to 6ft (1.8m) long and $3\frac{1}{2}$ft (1.05m) broad were laid without mortar in regular courses varying between 10 and 15in (25 and 36cm) in height. The wall averaged $4\frac{1}{2}$ ft (1.35m) in width, reducing to $3\frac{1}{2}$ ft (1.05m) at the level of the parapet walkway. The space between the wall and the face of the rampart was filled with rubble which had an admixture of mortar in the sector between the south and east gates and clay elsewhere on the circuit. Similarly, the foundation, set in a rock-cut trench, consisted of rubble which was bonded with mortar on the south and east sides but with clay on the

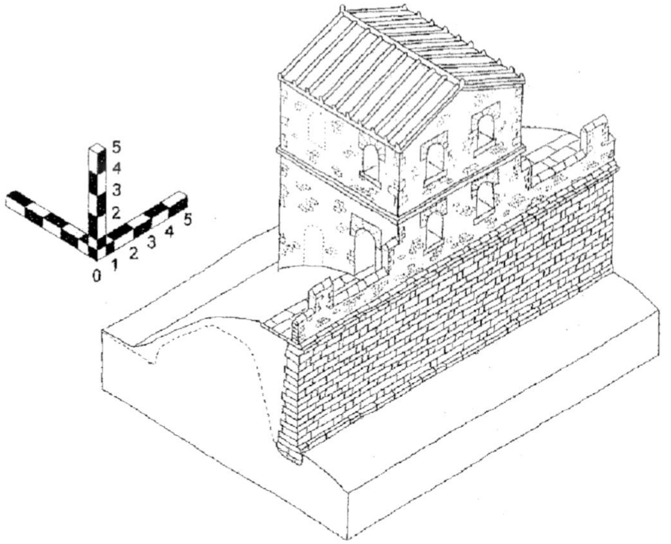

77 *Reconstruction of the stone fortress defences*

78 *Fragment of monumental slate inscription, with partial restoration, dating to the reign of Trajan (AD 98 - 117) which may have adorned the east gate and recorded the completion of the stone defences*

west. These differences could be explained by the varying techniques employed by the work-parties or they might indicate two phases of construction. The foundation was oversailed at the front by the lowest course which projected 20in (50cm) out from the wall face. The next course was a chamfered plinth which projected by about half this amount, above which was 14ft (4.2m) of masonry arranged in 13 courses. Next came an elaborate projecting cornice, whose multiple mouldings can be seen, and then a slab rebated to take the stones of the parapet. The remaining thickness of the wall was insufficient by itself to carry a walkway of practical width. Extra material was therefore added to the top of the earlier rampart to bring it up to the same height and thus allow the construction of a walkway about 6ft (1.8m) wide, perhaps with a fence along its inner side. The ditch running in front of the wall, already re-cut at least once, was replaced by a larger one of V-shaped profile measuring *c.*24ft (7.5m) wide and 8ft (2.45m) deep and with a vertically-sided cleaning or 'ankle-breaker' slot in the bottom.

The interval towers, of which there were 22, were spaced approximately 194ft or 200pM apart and measured 22ft (6.5m) square on average. Their walls were 4ft (1.2m) thick, probably narrowing to something like 3ft (90cm) in the second storey above the level of the parapet walkway, and were set in foundation trenches which cut through the earlier rampart. Thus their lower level was solid. The angle towers, with their splayed side-walls, were slightly larger, measuring 31ft (9.5m) wide overall by 28ft (8.5m) deep. The south-west and north-west angle towers were examined in the 1960s while that at the south-east angle, first investigated in 1929, has been on public display for many years (**79**). The chamber at walkway level was roofed and above it would have been either an open lookout platform with crenellated parapet or another roofed chamber. As well as providing cover for sentry patrols and space for weapons storage, such towers would also have housed small artillery pieces such as *ballistae*. Little is known in detail of the gate-structures at Chester. Only fragments of the south and north gates have been seen. Information about the east gate is derived largely from antiquarian sketches and descriptions made when the remains of the Roman structure, along with the medieval gatehouse into which it had been incorporated, were demolished to make way for the present gate in 1768. Although contradictory in places these accounts are in sufficient agreement to suggest that the gate was a double-portalled affair and executed in the same monumental style as the curtain wall. The arched portals were about 12ft (3.65m) wide and around 20ft (6m) high separated by a *spina* of *c*.5ft (1.5m). The accompanying towers, on the evidence of masonry surviving in cellarage on the south side of the gate, were approximately 24ft (7.5m) wide overall. The total width of the gate structure was thus in the order of 77ft (23.5m). The passageways would have been surmounted by a crenellated fighting-platform linking the two towers, the latter rising one or possibly two storeys higher still. The antiquarian sketches depict a pronounced cornice just above the crown of the arches like that which adorned the curtain wall but at a higher level and there was a statue, perhaps of the god Mars, positioned high

79 The south-east angle-tower

up between the two passageways on the front elevation. Although the gate as recorded was probably a reconstruction of the third century, if it is like the rest of the defences its form is unlikely to have differed much from the original design of a century or more earlier, with the possible modification of an additional storey (**colour plate 21**).

In the strip immediately behind the defences the process of replacing the rampart buildings with stone successors was begun, although not completed, in this period. The *via sagularis* was renewed, including the main sewer running beneath its inner edge.

The barracks

All of the barrack accommodation sampled to date has exhibited evidence of at least one rebuilding in timber, probably on the arrival of *legio XX c.*90, before their eventual replacement with stone or part-stone buildings in the first two decades of the second century. The only exception is the cohort group in the *praetentura* next to the *thermae*, where stone barracks appear to have replaced the primary timber ones without any intermediate reconstructions. The first cohort barracks underwent one rebuilding in timber and those in *insula XXII* to the north possibly two. Those in the right (western) half of the *retentura* were rebuilt twice in timber and the same may also have been true of those in the left (eastern) half. What is also clear is that the replacement of the *retentura* barracks with stone successors had only just begun when the legion, or most of it, was posted north to participate in the construction of Hadrian's Wall. As far as can be judged, the new timber barracks erected by *legio XX* replicated the plans and dimensions of their predecessors built by *legio II Adiutrix*. When the time came to replace these with masonry structures, modifications were introduced, due in part at least to the extra space taken up by stone walls compared with their wooden precursors. The Deanery Field barracks occupying the outer *insula* (*XXVII*) in the left part of the *retentura*, excavated by Newstead and Droop in the 1920s and '30s, have long been taken to represent a typical second-century stone barrack at Chester. However, not only does the evidence from recent excavations elsewhere in the *retentura* imply that these barracks are in fact third-century, but it can be seen from the examination of barracks in other parts of the fortress that they are in fact atypical in that they contain only 11 *contubernia* whereas the majority have 12.

Because of their more substantial remains rather more is known about the stone barracks than their timber predecessors (**80**). While the overall length and width of each *hemistrigium* remained about the same at 280 and 40pM (82.5 and 11.8m) respectively, there were detailed changes to the arrangement of the accommodation. The length of the centurial quarters was increased by 10pM to 90pM or 26.5m at the expense of the space allotted to the men's accommodation. The latter was in fact reduced further by an increase in the width of the alley or recess which separated the two from 3 to 5pM. Thus the length of the men's block was now 185pM (54.6m). As already mentioned, the number of *contubernia* was reduced from 14 to 12 although the proportion of space allotted to inner room, outer room and veranda remained unchanged from the arrangements of the timber barracks. The *arma* and veranda were allotted 10pM (2.95m) each with the *papilio* having

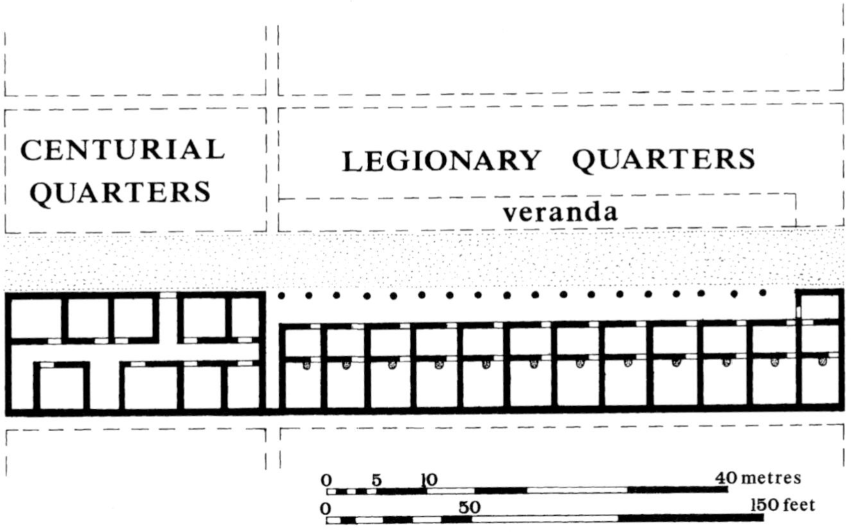

80 Restored plan of second-century stone barracks

twice as much (*see* **24 & 80** for comparative plans of timber and stone phase barracks). As to the actual dimensions of the rooms, both were 13.5pM (4m) wide while the inner was 16.5 and the outer 9.5pM deep (4.85 and 2.8m). Commonly, the end of the veranda was enclosed by an extension of the gable wall, and the chamber thus formed housed a latrine. The floors in the men's block were generally of sand or clay, the walls rendered with plaster, and each inner room was provided with a U-shaped open hearth placed centrally against the spine wall which was used mostly for heating and cooking (**81**). Two doors, about a metre wide and placed in line against the wall dividing one pair of rooms from the next, gave access to the outer and inner rooms respectively. In some cases the socketed stones in which the doors pivoted have been found. Few other details of the living arrangements are known, although given that eight men had to be accommodated in each *papilio* it seems safe to assume that bunk-beds were used (**82**). The walls were faced with sandstone blocks bonded usually with either clay or mortar and were about 2ft (60cm) wide at the level of the footings. Owing to the extent of later reconstructions it is still uncertain whether the superstructure of these walls was of stone or timber. The former might be thought more likely, as such buildings were now roofed with heavy terracotta tiles whose combined weight on a single barrack block roof was somewhere in the region of 350 tons. A masonry superstructure also seems more likely because stone columns instead of timber posts were now employed as supports along the front of the veranda (**colour plate 22**).

As one would expect, the accommodation for the centurion was more lavishly appointed. A regular feature of the interior was a central longitudinal passage with rooms opening off to either side and at the ends of the building. The floors were of a higher grade than in the men's quarters, being either concrete or mortar (**83**). One room at the end of

81 Hearth in barrack of the first cohort, Crook Street 1974

82 Sketch reconstruction of inner room in barrack

the building was set aside as the centurion's private latrine. In the first cohort centurial block examined at the 1990 Crook Street site, this was located at the north end of the building. It emptied into a branch sewer which ran beneath the recess separating the centurion's and mens' blocks, eventually flowing into the main sewer running beneath the *via principalis* (**84**). Only fragments of the interior decoration have survived but the standard can have been no less than existed in their Flavian counterparts, as represented by the example found on the Crook Street 1974 site described in chapter 5. Later on some rooms in the centurial houses were equipped with hypocaust heating, a trend which may have begun in this period.

83 Concrete floor with skirting, centurial quarters Crook Street 1974

84 Lead-lined latrine outflow, centurial quarters Abbey Green 1975-8

The *principia*

Richmond & Webster's excavation of 1949 located elements of the west side of the stone *principia*. These included the south-west corner of the *basilica principiorum* and a colonnade to the south of it belonging to the external portico of the range of offices enclosing the west side of its courtyard. The former exhibited two phases of construction, confirmed by

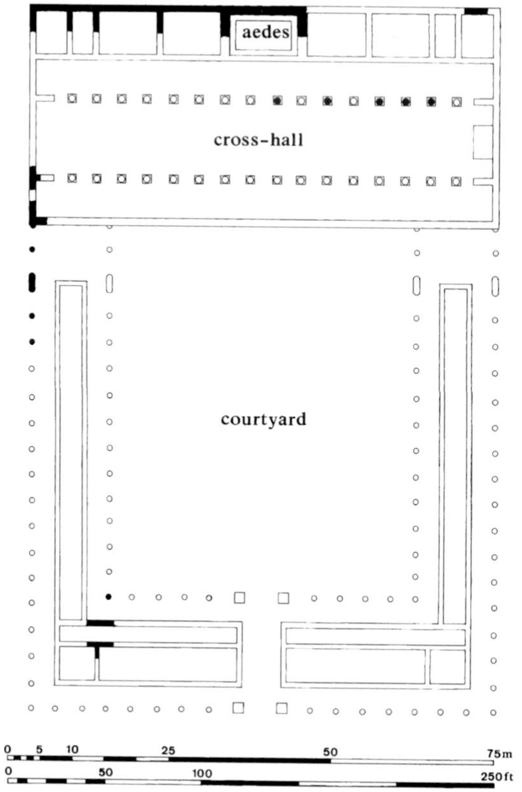

85 Plan of early second-century headquarters building

the Goss Street 1973 excavation, and it is clear that most of the surviving structures then seen belong to the reconstructed *principia* of the third century. This was also the situation found during the examination of the west half of the range of rooms along the rear of the *basilica* during the excavation of Phase V of the Old Market Hall site in 1969. It is equally clear from these investigations however that the third-century building was a straightforward reconstruction of its second-century predecessor with only minor changes in plan. To the excavations just mentioned can be added another at 12 Watergate Street in 1985, which located the south-west internal corner of the *principia* courtyard, and the remains of the *basilica* columns on display in premises on the west side of Northgate Street. The cumulative information from these is sufficient to give us an outline plan of the second-century *principia*. When the time came to replace the original *principia* the opportunity was taken to increase its size in both dimensions (**85**). Thus its width was increased from 220 to 245pM (65 x 72.4m) by encroaching 12.5pM (3.7m) on to both of the adjacent side streets; its length was expanded to 360pM (105.8m) by taking in 8pM (2.3m) of the street to the north. The courtyard in front of the *basilica* was approximately 150pM (44.25m) square and was lined on all four sides by a colonnaded portico. That fronting the *basilica* was about 15pM (4.4m) deep while those on the other three sides were all 20pM (5.8m) deep. The range of rooms behind this on the east and west sides of the building appears to have been 20pM (5.8m) broad whereas that along the south side was around 40pM (11.8m) across and contained a double range. There was also an external colonnaded portico 12pM (3.75m) wide down the east and west sides of the *principia* and probably along the southern frontage. The main entrance to the complex would have been set centrally within the south range. Minor entrances into the courtyard existed where the east and west ranges met the *basilica*. The exterior colonnades did not continue beyond this point as the basilica occupied the full width of the *insula*.

The great aisled hall or *basilica principiorum* was 245pM (72.4m) long and 115pM (33.8m) wide. As before, it stretched the full width of the *principia* but now had two rows of columns instead of timber posts down its centre, supporting a wall incorporating clerestory windows rising to a ceiling some 40-50ft (12-15m) above floor level. The columns belonging to the north aisle of the *basilica* discovered and partially preserved on the west side of Northgate Street are evidently third-century in style. Yet the absence of any other foundations in the vicinity implies that their second-century predecessors occupied exactly the same positions, spaced at intervals of 10pM (2.95m). The precise location of the southern row of columns is not known. The beginnings of an internal return wall were seen during examination of the western gable wall of the *basilica* in 1973. This could be the north wall of a range of rooms about 20pM (5.90m) deep running along the south side of the hall. If so, the two rows of columns would have been spaced 30pM (8.85m) apart with the neighbouring aisles being 15pM (4.4m) wide. Alternatively, it might represent the southern edge of a platform positioned in line with a row of columns, in which case there would have been no range of rooms along the south side and the nave and aisles would have been 40pM (11.8m) and 20pM (5.8m) wide respectively. Depending on which of these two possibilities is preferred, the range of rooms along the rear of the *basilica* would have been either 35 or 30pM (10.32 or 8.85m) deep. There were nine chambers; the central one, the *aedes* or legionary shrine containing the eagle and other standards, was 40pM (11.9m) across (**colour plate 23**). Beneath its floor was a rock-cut strongroom or *aerarium*, probably added during the Severan reconstruction. The next two chambers to the west were both 30pM (8.85m) wide and the pair beyond those 12 and 15pM (3.5 and 4.4m) wide respectively (**86**).

The rebuilding in stone of the *principia* appears to have occurred at a date well into the second century. The accumulation of street surfaces sealed by the room at its north-west corner, for example, was quite substantial, while the pottery from make-up levels below the floors in the south range revealed on the 12 Watergate Street site indicate a date after *c.*AD 120. This must raise a question mark as to whether the building had actually been completed by the time that most of the legion went north to participate in the building of Hadrian's Wall.

The building behind the *principia* (39)

When work on the large building behind the *principia* stopped, construction had only got as far as the laying of the first few courses of walling on the foundations, and that only in a few places. The interval which passed before work resumed was certainly significant and pottery recovered from levels associated with the building's eventual completion indicates this did not occur until well into the reign of Trajan. Thus the gap between the initial work and final completion may have been as long as 30 years (*c.*80-*c.*110). The finished building featured a number of modifications to the original plan, confined largely to the outer ranges. These were increased in width from 20 to 30pM (5.8 to 8.8m) and were divided into rooms conforming to a standard width of 17pM (5m) in the west range and varying from 20 to 24pM (5.9 to 7.1m) in the south range. The walls were constructed of neatly coursed and faced masonry and where they were placed over the line of the earlier cobble-concrete foundations, they oversailed them either side by 4in (10cm). Elsewhere they sat

86 Sunken strong-room beneath legionary shrine in headquarters building, Old Market Hall Site Phase V, 1969

on new, more substantial foundations of rubble and clay. The chamber occupying the south-west corner was equipped with a hypocaust but this was the only one so treated. All of the other rooms in the outer ranges had simple flagged floors and all were provided with doorways 10pM (2.95m) wide opening internally onto the courtyard (**87**). These may have been closed with either doors or shutters. The only means of access to this enormous building found so far was a 24pM (7.1m) wide entrance passage set centrally in the south range. As the penultimate chambers at both ends of the east and west ranges were narrower than the rest, it is possible they contained staircases giving access to an upper storey. The space between the outer ranges and the structures at the centre of the complex was surfaced with heavy stone flags and appears to have been an open yard. This fits with the character of the outer ranges as a whole, suggesting that, whatever their originally intended function, these were now used for the storage of equipment of some form brought into and taken out of the building on wagons. In this context, the hypocausted chamber in the south-west corner would have been the office of the man charged with responsibility for the building's contents. Perhaps it is no mere coincidence that the number of rooms in the outer ranges is sufficient to permit an allocation of one per century. If, as suggested in Chapter 6, this building was no longer required for the purpose originally envisaged, then it would seem that its plan was modified so that it could provide additional storage space. This in turn could be connected with the reduction in the number of *contubernia* per barrack from 14 to 12. The fragments of the important slate-cut inscription also mentioned in chapter 6 were found face down on the street in front of the west end of the south range in a context associated with the dereliction of the building in the later second century. Its unweathered state suggests the inscription could have been attached to the front wall of the building under the shelter of its colonnaded portico.

87 *Wide doorway in outer range of large store building behind headquarters building, Old Market Hall Site Phase I, 1967, showing progressive narrowings*

The structures at the centre of the complex were completed to the original design, comprising a three-chambered building opposite the main entrance and a free-standing colonnaded portico delineating and enclosing a long narrow rectangular court with a single building sitting in its northern half. The function of these elements of the complex is unknown.

The *praetorium* and houses of the senior officers

The legate's residence, if not built of masonry from the very beginning, would have been accorded priority in the programme of reconstructing timber buildings in stone along with those of the tribunes. Only fragments of the *praetorium* have been seen under far from ideal circumstances and so the date of the structures observed is unclear. Near the centre of the complex, a herringbone tiled floor and an adjacent mosaic executed with black and white *tesserae* discovered on the north side of Music Hall Passage might belong to this period. So too might the hypocausted chamber found immediately to the south although the stone *pilae* within it clearly belonged to a later, probably fourth-century, reconstruction. A different form of hypocaust, one with radiating flues instead of *pilae*, was found closer to Eastgate Street beside the spot where the inscribed lead water-pipes were uncovered in 1899, while a small apsidal structure exposed to the north-east the previous year most likely belonged to the legate's private baths-suite.

Exploration of the residences of the tribunes and the *praefectus castrorum* located along the south side of the *via principalis* has been equally piecemeal to date. Part of the first building west of the *via praetoria,* consisting of a small apsidal chamber equipped with a hypocaust, probably belonging to a baths-suite, was seen in 1894 and what appears to have been a section of its central courtyard was examined in 1985. East of the *via praetoria*, fragments of walls of both Trajanic and third-century date have been seen along with portions of hypocausts and mosaic floors, but insufficient for any coherent building plan to be reconstructed.

The workshops — *fabricae*

Insula XVIII lying immediately west of the Elliptical Building, was partially and hastily examined during the 1963-5 Crook Street/Princess Street excavation conducted shortly in advance of the start of the Central Redevelopment Scheme. Only fragments of the timber buildings belonging to the primary phase of the fortress were recorded and it was not possible to deduce their function. However, the building which succeeded them, apparently in the early second century, can confidently be identified from the abundant quantities of slag and other industrial waste encountered as the principal legionary workshop complex. This measured 240pM east-west by 210pM north-south (71 by 62m) and took the form of a large courtyard at the centre surrounded on all four sides by ranges of varying depth. That on the south was 40pM (11.8m) across, that on the north 80pM (23.6m), with the two side ranges probably the same size as the first of these. There was a colonnaded portico along the north side of the courtyard. It was in this building that all sorts of metal objects, ranging from swords to cart axles and from spears to belt-buckles, were made and repaired.

Other major buildings

The site of the unfinished Elliptical Building was left derelict for a while. Some of the stonework was removed for reuse elsewhere and parts of the site were used for the dumping of refuse and spoil from neighbouring sites. After a short interval, two timber workshop buildings were erected over the northern part of its site with metalworking debris and industrial waste deriving from their operation being dumped over the remainder. By contrast, the bath-building at the south end of the *insula* and the *tabernae* at the other end were completed and used. By 110 the two timber workshops had been demolished and the *tabernae* had been replaced by a stone building of similar plan, the east end of which contained several large hearths apparently used for iron-working. The site of the Elliptical Building remained as open ground used for rubbish disposal for the next 120 years. On *insula XXI* to the north, the timber buildings occupying the east and south sides were replaced by stone structures of similar form early in the second century and a 20ft (6m) square platform of masonry, probably the base for a water reservoir, was inserted in the south-east corner. The remainder of the *insula,* however, lay unused until *c.*230.

Although only fragments have been seen from time to time, the *praetorium* and the houses of the senior officers bordering the *via principalis* were clearly rebuilt in stone during the opening decades of the second century. Examples of tribunes' houses in other fortresses conform to a standard design of four ranges of accommodation arranged around a central square or rectangular courtyard. No major changes affected either the *thermae* or the granaries. Whatever the function of the building occupying the north end of *insula III* opposite the baths, it underwent a number of rebuildings in this period as revealed by an excavation to the rear of 30 Bridge Street in 1988. On the first two occasions the building was reconstructed in timber, the stubs of the lath and plaster internal walls of the second of these being well-preserved. The third rebuilding, executed in the Hadrianic period, saw it converted to stone with solid foundations of rubble set in clay.

The *canabae legionis*

The early second century was a period of steady development in the *canabae legionis* which saw the gradual replacement of the early timber buildings, both civilian and military, with more sturdy versions of masonry as well as the expansion of the settlement onto new areas (**88**). A few individuals can be identified as being among the increasing population of the *canabae* in this period. There is for example the veteran of *legio XX*, Lucius Ecimius Bellicianus Vitalis, whose tombstone was found amongst those reused in the North Wall. The fact that the stock phrase *Dis Manibus* is only partially abbreviated suggests an early second-century date. Another veteran, although from which legion we are not sure, is the

88 Sketch reconstruction of view along what is now Foregate Street looking back towards the east gate with shops of canabae legionis *in foreground*

Cassius Secundus mentioned at the beginning of this chapter who lived to the age of 80 and married in his retirement. East of the fortress the shopkeepers with premises fronting onto the main road had them rebuilt in stone, some perhaps now two-storey. This part of the *canabae* was becoming so popular that side-streets were laid out with stone shops built alongside them. This was the situation revealed by an excavation at Priory Place in 1989. Here, at a spot about 330ft (100m) south of the predecessor of Foregate Street, a section of north-south street was examined along with the front halves of two buildings bordering its east side. These were typical civilian strip-buildings about 30ft (9m) wide and upwards of 100ft (30m) long with open frontages which could be closed with shutters at night. Possibly occupied at one stage by metal-workers, the distance of these buildings from the main street illustrates the rate at which this part of the *canabae* was expanding in the early second century. The shops fronting onto what is now Foregate Street were very similar. One example excavated in 1961, situated immediately west of the junction between the main street and the side-street serving the Priory Place buildings, was 34ft (10.37m) wide and more than 78ft (24m) long. A yard in the central part of the building contained a metal-working furnace while at least one of the residential rooms at the rear was equipped with a concrete floor. The existence of stone eavesdrip gutters and a southwards-heading branch pipeline from the fortress aqueduct demonstrate the level of infrastructure now provided for the *canabae*. The settlement began to thin out about 1,300ft (400m) from the fortress. Trackways and ditches found beyond this point are probably connected with horticultural or agricultural activity.

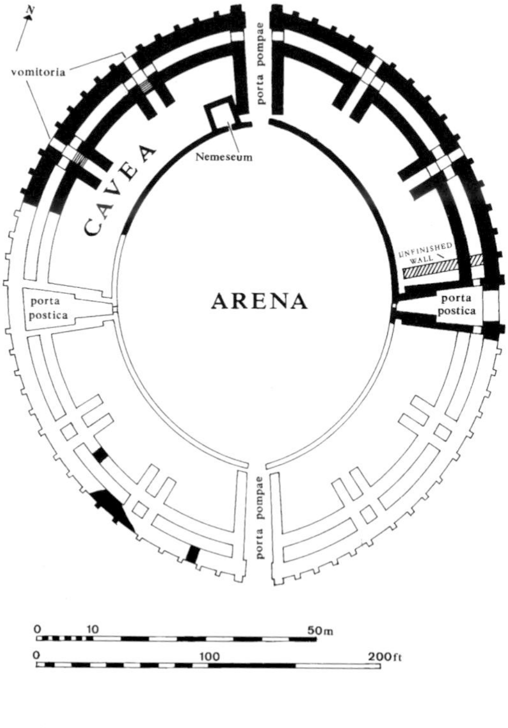

89 Plan of the early second-century stone amphitheatre

A development which had a major impact on the visual appearance of the eastern sector of the *canabae* at the beginning of this period was the replacement of the modestly sized timber *ludus* by a far larger and much more impressive stone amphitheatre. The size of the arena remained the same as before at 190 x 160ft (57.9 x 48.8m) but the depth of the *cavea* was enlarged from 22ft (6.7m) to 63ft (19.25m), nearly tripling the seating capacity and increasing the overall dimensions to *c*.325 x *c*.287ft (99 x 87.5m) making it one of the largest amphitheatres in Britain (**89**). The arena floor was lowered 6ft (1.8m) by excavating into the natural clay and rock and the resultant material was spread over the surrounding area as a base for the new seating bank (**90**). The arena wall averaged

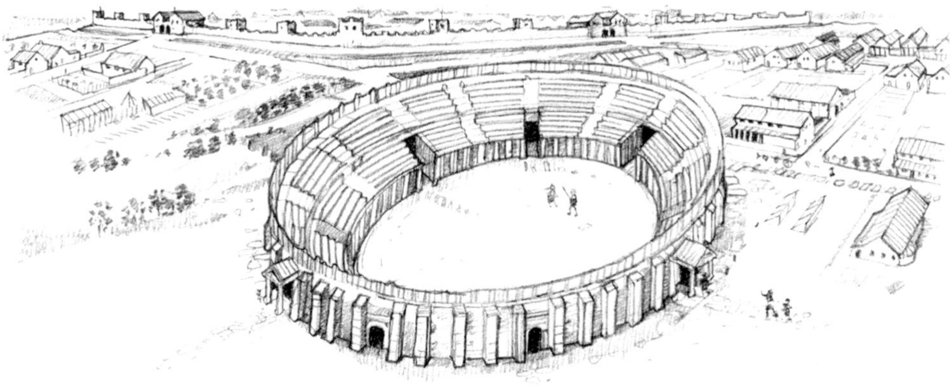

90 Sketch reconstruction of stone amphitheatre

3ft (90cm) in thickness while the outer wall, equipped with buttresses every 12ft (3.65m), was 8ft 10in (2.7m) thick. Both were built with facings of small blocks in *petit appareil* style and the outer wall had a plinth course of massive blocks. The processional entrances or *portae pompae* which gave direct access to the arena were situated at the ends of the north-south long axis. On the evidence of the excavated north entrance, this narrowed from 17ft 5in (5.3m) to 10ft 6in (3.2m) at the inner end where the lead sockets for the iron pivots of its two gates were still preserved. Just behind these gates a narrow flight of steps led up to a gangway running immediately behind the arena wall parapet. A covered drain ran beneath the entrance passage and continued across the arena on its long axis beneath a paved pathway. Near the centre of the arena the drain veered to the west to avoid a raised timber platform, while the path continued on towards it. The precise purpose of the platform, which was about 10ft wide and 20ft long (3.3 x 6m) long, is unknown but was presumably associated with the performance of certain formal ceremonies.

To the west of the entrance into the arena and originally covered by the auditorium was a small chamber measuring 12 x 14ft (3.6 x 4.2m) internally, to which access was gained via a small doorway set in the arena wall (**91**). This was the shrine of Nemesis, Goddess of Fate and Divine Retribution, as indicated by the discovery still *in situ* of an altar dedicated to this deity. The room had a raised timber floor laid on joists and its walls had been rendered with plaster and painted with a scheme of decoration in which orange played a major role. The south-west wall of this room had a 8in (24cm) wide offset at a height of 1ft 6in (46cm) above the floor which seems to have functioned as the rear support of a low bench. Centrally placed at the rear of the room was a sandstone plinth on which rested an altar dedicated to the Goddess Nemesis by the centurion Sextius Marcianus *ex visu* 'as the result of a vision' (**colour plate 24**). Shrines to this goddess were commonplace in amphitheatres but normally they were situated close to the outer wall. The fact that access to the example at Chester was gained from the arena might indicate it

91 The Shrine of Nemesis

was those actually engaged in contests, rather than the audience, who made offerings to the goddess to secure retribution or the downfall of those whose success had made them conceited. Equally, as amphitheatres were used for the public execution of criminals the goddess who represented divine retribution would be an appropriate deity to preside over such a place.

The entrances on the short axis were known as the *portae posticae* and that at the east end was encompassed by the 1960s excavation. These entrances had a dual function. Firstly, they afforded communication with the arena by means of a flight of steps leading down to a small door set in the arena wall, and secondly they provided access via a narrow upward flight of steps set each side of the passageway both to the auditorium in general and to a box or tribunal for senior officers set above the entrance (**92**). Judging by the architectural fragments recovered from the debris in the entrance passage, this probably took the form of a covered but open-fronted platform with a tiled roof supported in part by small columns. It was from one of these that the legate, accompanied by his guests, would preside over the proceedings. Each quadrant of the *cavea* was also provided with two minor entrances (*vomitoria*) spaced at regular intervals which gave access from the exterior to the seating bank.

Some aspects of the amphitheatre's superstructure are still open to debate. What is clear is that in order to provide tiered and raked seating of the required form the outer wall must have risen to somewhere in the region of 36-40ft (11-12m) above ground level. It is also clear that the buttresses were too insubstantial to have performed any meaningful structural function and were instead probably associated with some form of decorative architectural scheme such as mock arcading. It is when we come to the actual form of the auditorium support that the uncertainty begins. The 1960s' excavations disclosed the

92 Amphitheatre east entrance showing flight of steps leading up to box for senior officers

existence of a concentric wall 7ft (2.1m) wide located close to the outer wall and separated from it by a gap of 7ft (2.1m). It was suggested that the gap functioned as a corridor linking the 12 entrances and was covered by masonry vaulting which supported the highest tiers of seating, the lower rows being supported by a timber framework as in the primary amphitheatre. It is not impossible, though, that the lower rows of seats were also of stone, here resting on an earth bank, all of which had been removed in later centuries for use in the construction and then successive reconstructions of nearby St John's Church.

There are also hints that the supposed corridor arrangement at the perimeter of the *cavea* may have resulted from the modification of an earlier and different design. Examination of the east entrance disclosed the existence of an earlier, unfinished wall a few metres north of its northern side wall. It seems that it was the original intention either to make the entrance wider or to position it slightly farther north than where it was actually built. The second possibility is the more likely as this would make the interval between the east entrance and the neighbouring minor entrance the same as that between the north entrance and its neighbouring lesser entrances. Consequently, assuming that the amphitheatre as built was symmetrical, it would seem that the dimension on the long axis was increased by a matter of *c.*12ft 3in (3.75m) as the result of a modification introduced at an early stage of the construction process. Furthermore, the 'concentric wall', the abandoned north wall of the east entrance and the walls of the minor entrances all have relatively shallow foundations and a less than impressive constructional quality in comparison with the outer wall and the masonry of the main entrances as completed. Quite possibly therefore the 'concentric wall' began life as the intended outer wall of a rather more modest amphitheatre, with dimensions of *c.*292 x 256ft (89 x 78m). It was

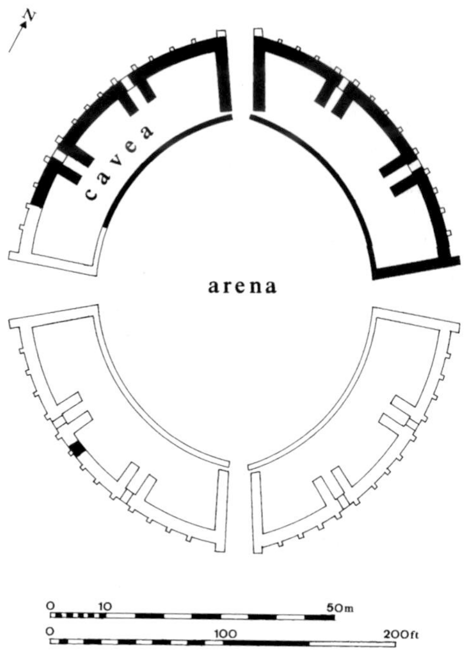

93 Plan of stone amphitheatre as it may originally have been intended

adapted to function as the inner wall of a corridor when the decision was taken before it had been completed to make the structure both larger and more impressive (**93**).

In addition to the altar to Nemesis, other inscriptions from the amphitheatre record participation in the construction work of the centuries commanded by Burricus and Refidius. Another, incised into a coping-stone from the arena wall, reads '*Serano locus*', meaning 'Seranus's place'. A fragment of a slate frieze depicting gladiatorial scenes was found not far from the amphitheatre in 1738. Purchased soon after by a London collector of antiquities, its whereabouts in later years were unknown until its rediscovery among the collections of the Saffron Walden Museum in 1978. The full size of the frieze when complete is unknown, as is its original context, although it has been suggested it could have adorned the tomb of a gladiator. The surviving piece depicts a *retiarius* carrying his distinguishing equipment of net and trident (**94**). The identity of his opponent is unknown though it was usual to match *retiarii* against the more heavily armed *secutores* and the remains of a sword and shield on the relief would suggest this was the case. Although now plain, the frieze was probably brightly painted originally. Stylistically, it belongs to the mid-second century. Another representation of a gladiator was found during the excavation of the large building behind the *principia* in 1967/8 and takes the form of a small bronze statuette, the lower half of which has been lost (**95**).

South of the fortress and east of the road leading down to the bridge, fragments of masonry buildings have been noted on occasion. Although undated it is probable that more substantial structures began to appear on the prime sites overlooking the river in this period. West of the road the timber *mansio* had already been rebuilt twice by the opening years of the second century, keeping more or less to the original plan on both occasions,

94 Fragment of relief depicting gladiatorial scene, found near amphitheatre in the eighteenth century. The figure at right holds a trident (tridens) *and net* (rete) *and can thus be identified as a* retiarius *or net-thrower*

95 Fragmentary bronze statuette of gladiator found on the Old Market Hall Site Phase I 1967

although during the first rebuilding the opportunity had been taken to extend it in an easterly direction. In the decade 110-120 a further rebuilding of the *mansio* was instituted, this time in stone and to a different plan. However work had only got as far as laying the foundations when the order was given to halt construction. After a short interval a start was made on a new stone building whose plan closely followed that of the third timber phase layout. Culverts found on the lower ground to the south probably served the *mansio*. The laying down of surfaces beside them suggests the spread of civilian occupation to the area around the north end of the bridgehead. Further to the west and south-west discoveries of fragments of tessellated floors as well as substantial concrete foundations during the construction of new buildings at the Castle in the late eighteenth century indicate the presence of important buildings in this area, but their date and purpose is obviously unknown.

The area west of the fortress was the scene of intense activity in the late first/early second century. A considerable proportion of the area lying north of the Watergate Baths was used as an inhumation cemetery in the later second century. During its investigation in 1912-17 the remains of a late first-century hearth or kiln together with large amounts of waste derived from iron smelting and bronze and lead working were found. Another excavation nearby in 1977 found evidence of early occupation in the form of fences and drainage gullies, followed by abandonment and the dumping of large quantities of refuse during the second century. Further north, opposite the north-west angle of the fortress, excavations in 1957 located a sizeable but isolated building with stone footings which had probably carried a timber superstructure. Measuring 40 x 50ft (12.2 x 15.25m), cross-walls divided its interior to provide rooms arranged around a small open court and the building has every appearance of being a house. Associated finds point to occupation spanning the period *c.*90-*c.*125. The picture north of the baths thus appears to be one of early colonisation followed by abandonment. South of the baths, however, the story is rather different.

The Watergate Baths underwent many phases of structural alteration in their history and although undated one at least of these is likely to belong to the period under discussion. Beyond the baths a massive retaining wall was built across the mouth of the minor east-west valley which crossed this area and henceforth it began to be filled in with refuse and building debris. The timber building next to the baths was rebuilt in stone in the early second century. It appears to have functioned as a stable block for draught-animals used to carry goods from the harbour up to the west gate of the fortress.

On the far side of the valley, the Greyfriars Court excavations of 1976-8 and 1981 showed that one of the earliest buildings in this area was an impressively constructed stone building aligned north-south occupying a position at the edge of the *c.*30ft (10m) high bluff overlooking the harbour area (for location, *see* **117**). Only its rear wall and a small portion of the interior were examined, the remainder lying beneath Nun's Road, but this was sufficient to show it had a mortar floor with the refinement of a quarter-round moulding around the edge. Positioned to the east and north-east of this structure, on ground about 2ft (60cm) higher and aligned at right-angles to it, stood two contemporary timber buildings both more than 70ft (21m) long, facing one another across a 36ft (11m) wide space. These were very similar in plan, consisting of a range 16ft 4in (5m) broad divided up into a series of rooms averaging 13ft (4m) wide interspersed with narrow passageways which gave access to another range at the rear. Along the frontage was a 7ft (2.1m) deep veranda. Raised timber floors were provided in some rooms and the interiors of both buildings were rendered with plaster painted white. All three buildings appear to have been erected more or less contemporaneously around 100. Although the two timber buildings were very probably residential, the arrangement of their accommodation is far too regimented and repetitive for individual households, unless they are the wings of a single and much larger residence. This does not seem very likely on present evidence. Possibly, therefore, these buildings served some official purpose. Around 120 there was a major reorganisation of the area. The masonry building facing out over the harbour was rebuilt on more substantial lines, while the two timber buildings to the east of it were demolished. Over the remains of the southern one, two stone buildings aligned north-south were constructed, while the site of the northern one remained as open ground for the rest of the century. The two new buildings were arranged facing one another across a 23ft (7m) wide open space, the western 40ft (12m) wide and its easterly neighbour 46ft (14m) wide; both consisted of a single range of rooms fronted by a corridor. One of the rooms in the western building was equipped with a hypocaust, reinforcing the impression that both were residential in nature. Again, such a drastic rearrangement is suggestive of official involvement. Are we perhaps looking at barrack accommodation for a detachment of the fleet?

The maximum length of the buildings just described can be fixed at *c.*180ft (55m) as to the south of them was another masonry building, this one aligned east-west, revealed by building works at Greyfriars House and Blackfriars House in the mid-1980s. About 56ft (17m) broad overall, its rooms had mortar floors set off by quarter-round mouldings at the edges and one, some 26ft (8m) square, was later equipped with a channelled hypocaust. What may have been the eastern gable wall of this building, or of its neighbour, was found 230ft (70m) to the east during an excavation at the corner of Nicholas Street in 1974. Both sites produced high quality wall-plaster and a notable find from the 1974 excavation was a section of finely carved slate architrave. Clearly the buildings in the area were of superior quality. On both sites, traces of late first-/early second-century timber buildings were also encountered. As their demolition deposits also included large amounts of good quality wall-plaster they too seem to have been comfortable residences. A hypocausted room with an apsidal west end encountered below the west end of Blackfriars Lane in the 1880s seems likely to belong either to a minor bath-building or a private baths-suite set on a lower terrace overlooking the harbour. If the latter, it could well have formed a west wing to the building lying below Greyfriars and Blackfriars Houses (**117**).

Little is known about the development of the harbour during this period, although one assumes its facilities were improved and expanded. A few years after the discovery of the remains of the collapsed timber jetty on the Gasworks site, excavations for another gasometer revealed a section of a substantial wall about 165ft (50m) closer to the river. Built of large sandstone blocks without mortar and rising from what was taken to be the ancient bed of the river, this followed a slightly curving course which when projected would have taken it close to the site of the jetty remains and ultimately to the east side of the Roodee somewhere in the vicinity of the Watergate. There seems a strong possibility that this was a Roman construction, presumably a more permanent replacement for the timber jetty of the Flavian period.

By the opening years of the second century, the cemeteries around the fortress were beginning to become quite extensive, especially that on the south bank of the Dee. Cremation was still the most common form of burial although inhumation was beginning to become more popular, as the grave of Callimorphus and Serapion demonstrates. Cremations were normally placed in a pot no different from those in everyday use; one however was found in a cylindrical lead *ossuarium*, with a tile or thin piece of stone over the top. They were sometimes protected in a stone or tile lined cist. Goods placed with them for the deceased's journey to the underworld included coins (the Ferryman's fee), ceramic and glass vessels, small phials of perfume, and pottery lamps. As with inhumations, an inscribed and sculptured stone was placed above the grave. These are rarely found *in situ*, usually having been removed for reuse as building stone. Both types of burial commonly included a small lead pipe, set vertically so that those visiting and feasting at the tomb on festival days devoted to the remembrance and worship of ancestors, such as the *Parentalia* or *Rosalia*, could pour offerings to the deceased and thus symbolically enable them to participate in the banquet. Indeed, the funerary banquet was one of the most popular subjects for tombstone reliefs, depicting the deceased reclining on a couch with a small table in the foreground set with the food and drink to be consumed (**120**).

The hinterland

The excavations of the mid-twentieth century produced evidence for widespread renovation of the Heronbridge settlement in the Hadrianic period. As well as the replacement of the original timber constructions by far sturdier stone buildings, the layout of the settlement was regularised by the grouping of buildings in blocks of three; neighbouring buildings were separated by only a narrow eavesdrip and adjacent blocks by side-streets averaged 20ft (6m) wide (**96**). The majority of buildings, at least those along the road frontage, were of the same type as before: long, narrow strip-buildings 25-32ft (7.6-10m) wide and about 115ft (35m) long divided into an open-fronted shop, a yard behind it, and a suite of living accommodation at the rear. Many were equipped with concrete floors and glazed windows. It is possible that each block of three houses together with an adjacent street was designed to occupy an *insula* 120pM square, the equivalent of one *actus*. The widespread appearance of stone street and eavesdrip gutters at this time is a further indication of a well-ordered and closely regulated community. It is possible that it was attracting an increasing number of legionary veterans, although this is pure speculation. Architectural fragments, including a competently moulded column capital, found reused in later structures point to the presence of at least one building of a more elaborate character somewhere in the settlement, which the results of recent geophysical survey suggest now lined the road heading south for a distance of nearly 1 mile (1.6km).

The only inscription recovered from the site so far is a small altar dedicated to the Matres Ollototae — the Foreign Mother Goddesses — by Julius Secundus and Aelia Augustina. Dedications to this particular variant of the Mother Goddesses are rare in Britain. The only other place where they are known is Binchester, Co. Durham, where they were worshipped by the garrison the *Ala Hispanorum Vettonum civium Romanorum*. In the first century this wing of auxiliary cavalry was part of the forces garrisoning Wales. Just possibly Julius Secundus, if not the centurion of *legio II Adiutrix* mentioned on the tombstone at Bath described in chapter 4, may have been a veteran of that unit who chose on retirement to settle down in the neighbourhood of the Chester fortress. If so then Secundus would not have been alone, for we know from the chance discovery of bronze discharge diplomas at Middlewich and near Malpas that there were a number of auxiliary veterans settling down in Cheshire in the opening decades of the second century. One such was Reburrus, son of Severus, a junior officer in the *Ala I Pannoniorum Tampiana* who received his *diploma*, that found near Malpas 15 miles (24km) south-south-east of Chester, on 19 January 103. Other regiments discharging men on the same day are mentioned on the diploma. Among these is the *Ala Hispanorum* mentioned above, so it is not impossible that Secundus retired on the same day as Reburrus. A Julius Secundus, recorded as the heir of a soldier on another tombstone, is possibly the same man. Another veteran, discharged from the *Ala Classiana civium Romanorum* two years later in 105, retired to Middlewich. His identity is unknown but his wife went by the name of Amabilis = 'loveable' or 'lovely'.

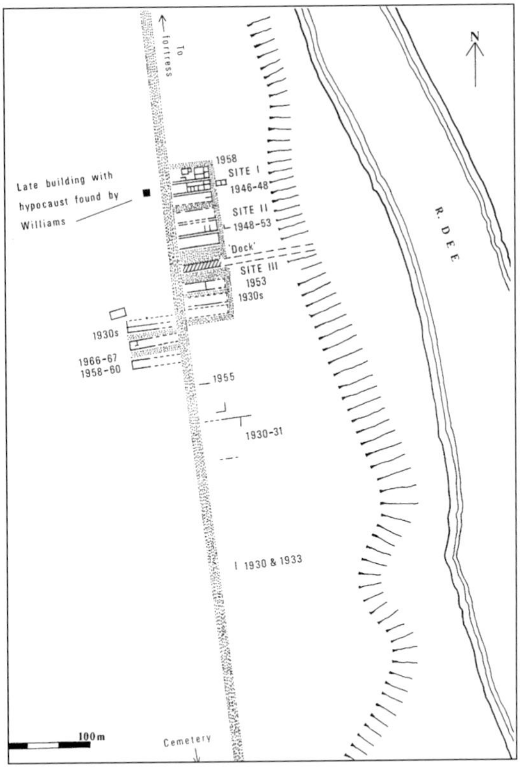

96 Plan of the Heronbridge settlement in the Hadrianic period

A little over 5½ miles (9km) upriver from Heronbridge, on the west bank of the Dee near the present village of Holt, the Twentieth Legion established a works-depot soon after its arrival at Chester. Its main function was the production of brick and tile but the manufacture of a range of pottery was also undertaken (**97**). Numerous tiles, bricks and antefixes bearing the stamp *LEG XXVV* and variations thereof identify the owners of the manufactory and several building stones attest work by centuries of the same legion (**colour plate 25**). It was also operated by legionaries although the discovery of a tile graffito referring to *Cohors I Sunicorum* indicates that auxiliary units also furnished working-parties. It was long thought that the site was the *Bovium* of *Iter II* of the Antonine Itinerary, described as lying 10 Roman miles from *Deva* on the road to *Viroconium*. This now seems more likely to have been the roadside settlement at Grafton a few miles south-east of Holt on the English side of the Dee. Discovered in 1907, excavations were carried out continuously over the next eight years with the consequence that Holt provides us with a detailed picture of a legionary brickworks equalled by only a few other sites throughout the Empire. The siting of this facility so far from the fortress is presumably to be explained by the absence of clay deposits of suitable quality and quantity any closer. These Holt had in abundance, as well as plentiful supplies of building stone from the rock outcrops above the Dee at this point and of timber for use as fuel for the kilns from the surrounding woodlands. A location beside the river was no doubt chosen because it offered an easy and cheap method of

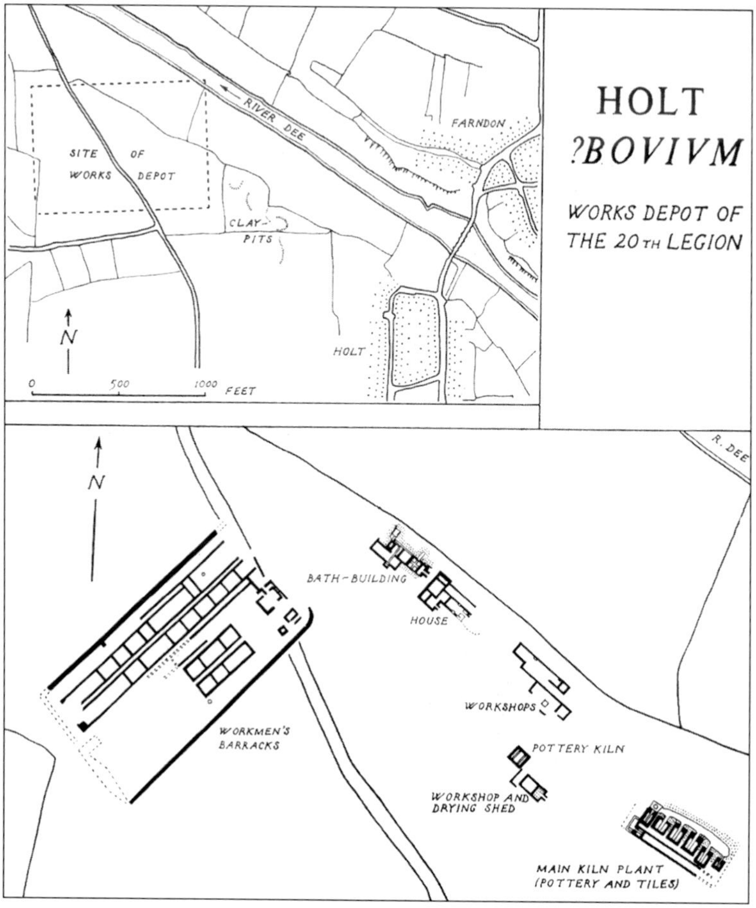

97 *Plan of the Twentieth Legion's brick, tile and pottery works at Holt*

transporting the heavy and bulky products to *Deva*. It is also possible that this spot was selected because some of the land hereabouts was already owned by the army. The Holt/Farndon crossing is one of the few obvious bridging-points on this stretch of the Dee and may well have had a strategic significance during the early stages of the Roman advance into the north-west Midlands in the 50s and 60s of the first century. If so, the crossing may have been guarded by an auxiliary fort and there are numerous examples from around the Empire of the military retaining ownership of territory long after the garrison had been removed. Certainly the coin evidence from Holt could be taken to indicate activity here in the late pre-Flavian and early Flavian periods.

The installations covered an area of about 24 acres (10ha) on ground sloping gently down to the river. The industrial structures included workshops, drying-sheds and of course the kilns themselves. The level of output can be judged from the scale of the main kiln-plant, which contained a total of eight kilns and incorporated a covered woodstore. It measured 136 x 58ft (41.5 x 17.5m) overall while the internal dimensions of the individual kilns ranged from 9 x 8ft (2.74 x 2.43m) to 17ft 6inx14ft 6in (5.33 x 4.42m), all served by a common stokery. The kilns were built of bricks within a casing of sandstone masonry and each had a main longitudinal flue opening into the stokery. Dwarf cross-walls formed side flues to aid even distribution of the heat. The floor laid on top of these usually consisted of rectangular tiles or a layer of broken tile and clay perforated by vent-holes at regular intervals. The range of building materials produced included various forms of hypocaust, revetment and voussoir bricks, roofing tiles (flat *tegulae*, semi-circular *imbrices* and the roughly triangular antefixes bearing the wild boar emblem of the Twentieth) and water-pipes. As well as the fortress at Chester, bricks and tiles were also supplied to auxiliary forts in the Twentieth's command area (such as Caerhun, Caernarvon, Caersws and Manchester) and certain industrial sites (described below) where they were required for the more elaborate buildings. These were probably also constructed by detachments of skilled legionary craftsmen. Most Holt pottery was made in a coarse orange fabric and included jars, bowls, jugs, dishes, cups, mixing-bowls (*mortaria*) and flagons coated with a white slip. Some vessels, however, were given a superior finish. These included jugs, bowls, dishes, cups and beakers which were either burnished (the so-called 'Legionary Ware'), mica-coated, red colour-coated, or, very occasionally, glazed. There were also examples of 'Eggshell Ware', thin walled vessels of white clay. The exotic forms of these vessels, which also occur at other contemporary legionary sites in Britain and the western provinces, can be traced back to the Aegean area. It has been suggested that groups of skilled industrial slaves were transported to the West to produce fineware in the wake of the collapse of the South Gaulish samian industry at the beginning of the second century.

Accommodation for the workforce was contained within a compound 200ft (61m) wide and about 400ft (122m) long surrounded by a wall 7ft (2.1m) thick. Within were three barrack-like buildings and two smaller structures, which may have been cookhouses and mess-rooms. Standing on the river-bank opposite the north-east corner of the compound was a small bath-building of simple *reihentyp* design containing *frigidarium*, *tepidarium* and *caldarium* and with an attached changing-hall. Another building beside it containing three hypocausted chambers. Once interpreted as a residence for the officer in charge of the depot, it is now thought more likely to be a second and later bath-building. Pottery production at Holt stopped *c.*130 as it did at many military-operated kilns elsewhere. The reason may have been an improvement in the output and quality of civilian potteries, but an additional factor in the decision to cease production at Holt may have been the secondment of a large contingent of the Twentieth to assist in the construction of Hadrian's Wall. Detachments of the Twentieth were also active at more distant locations within the command area.

Around 100 a major industrial facility was established on the coast of the Dee estuary at Pentre-Oakenholt near Flint, where lead ore mined at Halkyn a few kilometres to the south was brought to be smelted and cast into ingots for shipment 12 miles (19km) upriver to Chester. There had in all probability been industrial activity here since the early 70s but the earliest structures found so far date to a slightly later period. The remains of ancient furnaces were found at Pentre Ffwrndan (the name means 'village of the furnaces') as long ago as the mid-nineteenth century, and excavations in the 1920s and '30s confirmed their Roman origin. More recent excavations, from 1976-81, at the Pentre Farm site lying *c.*700ft (210m) north-east of the main industrial area, located a large and well-appointed residence which, on the evidence of stamped tiles, was constructed by the Twentieth Legion. Although the latter clearly built some of the facilities and may have furnished a detachment to provide security and guard the workforce, the person overseeing operations from this residence is more likely to have been a member of the procurator's staff than an army officer. A similar complex existed 12 miles (19km) further down the coast at Prestatyn. Excavations in the mid-1980s showed this was established *c.*75 and had had its facilities upgraded around 120 when the Twentieth constructed a small bathhouse. Roman lead mines are known at nearby Meliden and the settlement at Prestatyn, which probably possessed a small natural harbour in this period, was most likely the transhipment centre if not the actual focus of ore-smelting. On present evidence, therefore, the ingots of Deceanglican lead stamped 74 and 76 are more likely to have originated here than in Pentre-Oakenholt. Again, a small military force may have been present but the supposed identification of a fort next to the industrial site has been shown to be erroneous. The official activity here encouraged a group of native blacksmiths, bronze-smiths and enamellers to set up in business supplying the inhabitants and the traders who used the harbour; their output included brooches decorated with multi-coloured enamels alongside more mundane items such as harness fittings. Yet a third site connected with lead extraction lay at Ffrith, located 10 miles (16km) south-west of Chester on the road heading for the fort at Caer Gai. Limited excavation has located two masonry buildings, one of which was a bathhouse constructed, again on the evidence of stamped tiles, by *legio XX*. Occupation appears to have begun in the late first century and traces of lead extraction operations have been noted on the surrounding hills. A possible fort site lying on higher ground to the south-west of the known settlement has been identified from the air, but has yet to be proved by excavation.

The fortress was well served by the installations along the coast just listed for information about shipping in the Dee estuary. The legionary command would also have found it useful to have intelligence regarding estuarine traffic on the Mersey and a recent discovery suggests how this was achieved. In 1992 a double-ditched enclosure *c.*0.35ha (0.84 acres) in size was spotted by aerial reconnaissance occupying an elevated site on the south bank of the Mersey near Ince, nearly 7 miles (11km) north-east of Chester, which subsequent excavation dated to the late first/early second century. Its size and location suggest it was a look-out post and probably contained a watch/signalling tower, by which information could be rapidly communicated to the fortress, perhaps via one or more intermediate stations.

10 *Legio XX* goes north: *Deva* in the doldrums (*c.*120-*c.*210)

It has long been recognised, from the numerous inscriptions attesting its participation in the construction first of Hadrian's Wall and then the Antonine Wall, that a considerable proportion of the Twentieth Legion was absent from Chester for long periods during the second century and that this probably led to a decrease in the intensity of occupation inside the fortress. What has become clear from the excavations of the last 40 years however is that this period witnessed not just a decline in military activity in certain parts of the fortress, but the complete abandonment of large areas of the interior and a widespread failure to maintain the fabric and infrastructure of the base as a whole (**98**). Indeed, the need for such a fundamental reconstruction of the fortress in the opening decades of the third century was very probably directly attributable to its thoroughgoing neglect in the second. It is evident that not just part but the majority of the legion was absent for many decades with the fortress, still nominally the regimental headquarters, becoming little more than a rearward depot functioning as an arms and equipment manufactory, stores compound and transhipment centre. That a legionary presence of some form continued is proven by the dedication of an altar to Jupiter Optimus Maximus beside the parade-ground by the *princeps* Lucius Bruttius in 154 and by the production of tiles bearing a consular stamp of 167. In addition to the quartermaster's and headquarters' staff, detachments would probably have returned to *Deva* from time to time. Some of the legionaries, perhaps with relations among the extramural population, may have spent their leave here; however, the absence of such a high proportion of the legion, and the money they had to spend, must have had a detrimental effect upon the economic and social development of the *canabae*.

Building inscriptions from both Hadrian's Wall and the Antonine Wall attest the involvement of detachments of the Twentieth in their construction. Those from the former reveal the names of many of the centurions who oversaw the construction work as well as the identity of the cohorts involved. Thus, Atilius Maior of *Cohors II*, Ferronius Vegetus of *Cohors III*, Marcus Liburnius Fronto and Terentius Magnus fellow centurions in *Cohors IV*, and Julius Florentinus of *Cohors X*. In some instances it is possible to identify a centurion who achieved promotion during the course of the construction of Hadrian's Wall, as happened to Olcius Libo who started in *Cohors II* and progressed to the first cohort. In other cases the same man appears on inscriptions both at Chester and on Hadrian's Wall. For example Julius Candidus' name occurs on a silvered bronze disc found in the Deanery Field barracks and also on three centurial stones discovered near Housesteads. Similarly, the centurion Claudius Augustanus is mentioned on a breadstamp at Chester and three building inscriptions in the vicinity of Carvoran. A few years later, the centurion Flavius Betto was seconded to command the Sixth Cohort of Nervians garrisoning the fort of Rough Castle on the Antonine Wall. A contemporary of his, Gaius Arrius Domitianus, was doing similar duty at Newstead where he commanded a joint garrison consisting of a detachment of *legio XX* and the cavalry regiment the *ala Augusta Vocontiorum*. During the mid-second century the Twentieth was also called upon to provide vexillations for campaigns overseas such as that despatched to aid in the suppression of a revolt in Mauretania in the 140s. The man in charge of the vexillation, the senior centurion Sextus Flavius Quietus, was rewarded for his success by being placed in overall command of the British Fleet as *Praefectus Classis Britannicae*, the last posting of his career after which he retired to Rome, as attested by his tombstone there.

There was rebellion and warfare in the North in the 180s during which the frontier was breached and a general was killed along with his troops. Punitive campaigns followed in which the Twentieth is likely to have played a major role. The assassination of the Emperor Commodus in 192 set in motion a chain of events which was to have unfortunate consequences for the men of the Twentieth and the other British legions. The Praetorian Guard's auctioning of the throne to the highest bidder was an act to which the provincial armies quite understandably took exception and soon three main contenders for the purple emerged: Lucius Septimius Severus, governor of Pannonia; Pescennius Niger, governor of Syria; and Decimus Clodius Albinus, governor of Britain. Albinus, with the support of only three legions in Britain and one in Spain, came to an agreement with Severus, who had the backing of 16 legions, whereby he became his junior partner with the title of Caesar (to Severus' Augustus) with the implied right of succession. After Severus had defeated Niger in 194 it became clear he had no intention of honouring this agreement, leaving Albinus with no other option but to prepare for war. In the autumn of 196 Albinus crossed to Gaul with a large army which, given the restricted choice of units available to him, must have included a considerable proportion of *legio XX*. The final confrontation took place near Lyon in February the following year. It was a long battle in which both sides suffered heavy losses but eventually Severus' army won the day and Albinus, seeing all was lost, committed suicide.

After the battle the British legions were sent back to their bases. They were undoubtedly depleted in strength. This may explain why the new governor of Britain, Virius Lupus, sent by Severus, bought off rather than campaigned against the grouping of tribes in central-southern Scotland known as the Maeatae who had attacked the frontier. What is certain is that there must have been many families at Chester who looked in vain for fathers, uncles, sons or brothers among the returning cohorts of the Twentieth. There is no evidence for an immediate restoration of the fortress; this is something that did not happen until a decade or so later, as is described in the next chapter. Given the parlous state of the province's security, it would be understandable if most of what remained of *legio XX* was stationed along or close behind the northern frontier, rather than allowed to return to its regimental headquarters at Chester.

The fortress

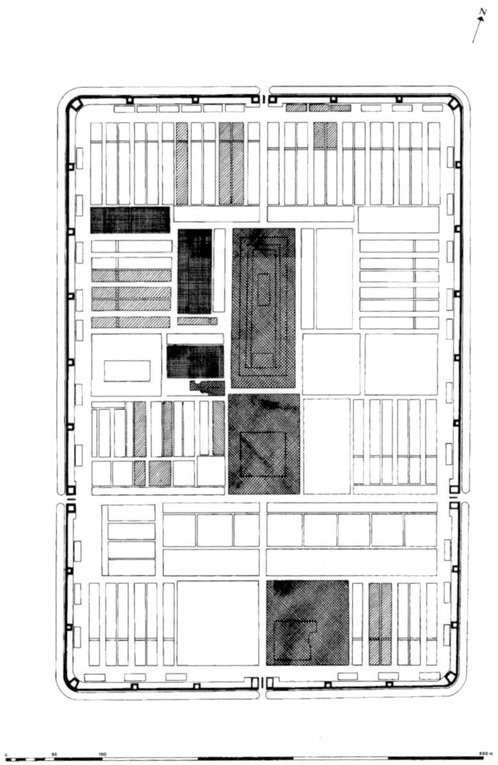

98 Plan of the fortress in the mid-second century, areas/buildings shaded are those which have produced widespread evidence of dereliction in this period

The history of the barrack accommodation during the second century provides the most striking evidence for the absence of legionaries for much of this period. The barracks in *insula XXII* in the right *latus praetorii* were abandoned shortly after they had been rebuilt in stone *c.*AD 120 and were left to decay. In the right *retentura* (*XXVIII*) a centurial block in the process of being rebuilt in stone was left unfinished and in the other half of the *retentura* (*XXVII*) barracks not yet converted to masonry were allowed to fall into a derelict condition. In both cases the sites of these buildings were subsequently used for the dumping of refuse and in the case of the barracks in *XXVII* examined during the 1975-8 Abbey Green excavation, several cremation burials were inserted through their remains. The accommodation of the first cohort (*XII*) tells a similar story. The barrack lying at the centre of the block examined by the Crook Street excavation of 1974 was demolished before the middle of the second century and its site became covered with a thick deposit of brown sandy soil. The building immediately to the east, partially explored in 1990, suffered the same fate. In its case, a kiln or oven was constructed over the stubs of the adjacent end walls of the men's block and the centurion's house. The range of *tabernae* at the east end of this *insula* was now converted into a latrine block, perhaps used by the staff still manning the administrative offices in the *principia* opposite, while portions of the intervening street were stripped of paving before becoming overlain with soil and refuse. The barracks at the other end of this *scamnum* in *insula X* have also yielded hints of disuse in this period. Thus it would seem that at least seven of the legion's ten cohorts were absent for the greater part of the second century. There are indications of some form of reoccupation in certain of the barracks mentioned above but full-scale reconstruction clearly did not occur before the Severan era.

This long period of neglect had equally detrimental effects upon many of the major buildings. In the massive stores building (*XVI*) behind the *principia*, the surfacing of the courtyard between the inner and outer ranges gradually disappeared beneath a layer of mud, silt and humus which accumulated to a depth of 1ft (30cm) and spilled into a drain running below the courtyard when its roof finally collapsed. A similar quantity of this material also accumulated over the floor of the westernmost of the three rooms in the block at the south end of the inner courtyard. The extent of the dereliction is indicated by the fact that an infant burial had been inserted through this deposit. The paving in the rooms of the outer ranges deteriorated and eventually part of the south range was destroyed by fire. Some parts of the building appear to have been reconstructed soon after 160 but it does not seem to have been brought back fully into commission until the Severan era. Most of the Elliptical Building *insula* (*XXVII*) and that to the north (*XXI*) remained as open ground throughout this period, used largely for the dumping of refuse and debris from industrial operations, which appear to have continued in the adjacent *fabrica*. Towards the end of the second century a very large rectangular pit, at least 16ft (5m) wide, 50ft (15m) long and 6ft (1.8m) deep, was dug in the north-eastern quadrant of *insula XXI*. This pit had vertical sides, a flat base and had emplacements for vertical timbers 8in (24cm) square inserted at regular intervals along its sides. The filling contained no clues as to its function and there was no discoloration of the sides as might result from industrial use. The most plausible interpretation based on the evidence would be a saw-pit, perhaps associated with the production of prefabricated structural units for shipping out to other military bases. The extent to which the *principia* was affected by the general lack of maintenance is unclear, but the fact that it was rebuilt from ground level in the Severan reconstruction of the fortress must surely be significant. There is little information from buildings in the *praetentura* relating to this period, although extensive rebuilding of the *thermae* in the Severan period, including replacement of its vaulted concrete roofs, might indicate previous and serious neglect. Across the street from the *thermae*, the building at the north end of *insula* III exhibited no signs of structural work within the period *c*.120-*c*.210.

The move north by much of the legion saw an end to pottery production at Holt. Already by *c*.120 civilian pottery manufacturers were beginning to flourish and the army soon found it more convenient to have pottery supplied under contract than to continue making it themselves. The everyday vessels such as jars, bowls and dishes now came in the form of the so-called black-burnished wares produced in both Dorset and at Rossington Bridge, near Doncaster. These came to dominate military and civilian markets throughout most of Britain, doing so until the middle of the fourth century, when they were replaced by the shell-tempered wares of east Yorkshire and the south-east Midlands. Closer to home, civilian potteries based at Wilderspool and Northwich enjoyed considerable success while another, whose principal product appears to have been mixing-bowls or *mortaria*, was established in the *canabae* east of the fortress. The latter declined towards the close of the second century, as *mortaria* in a hard white 'pipe-clay' fabric from the Hartshill-Mancetter kilns near Nuneaton took over and retained their dominant market position for the rest of the Roman period. Jars and bowls from the Severn Valley factories also appeared in significant numbers in the mid-second century. Regarding products of a more refined quality, samian continued to be imported from the factories in central Gaul alongside black, colour-coated beakers and cups from the same region and also from the Rhine. The east Gaulish kilns took over the samian supply at the end of the second century, gradually being replaced by red colour-coated fine wares from Oxfordshire half a century later. The latter, along with the products of the Nene Valley industry, provided the bulk of fine wares reaching Chester thereafter.

The *canabae legionis*

While the absence of much of the legion for most of the second century must have had a detrimental impact on the economic development of the extramural settlement, it nonetheless continued to prosper and expand, if not to the extent it would have had the whole of *legio XX* been in residence. In this it was probably helped by *Deva*'s twin additional roles as regional market centre and focus for mercantile trade. The eastern part of the *canabae* shows no sign of decline. A significant conflagration towards the end of the second century destroyed a number of properties bordering the south side of Foregate Street, but rather than rebellion, as was once thought, this seems far more likely to have been an accident: an all-too common occurrence where timber-framed properties and industrial activities existed side by side. By contrast, official extramural buildings appear to have suffered a similar degree of neglect to that which affected the internal buildings. Refuse and naturally accumulated deposits were allowed to cover the floor of the amphitheatre arena and, as already mentioned, the *mansio* rebuilding was left incomplete until the latter part of the second century. By the middle of the second century, civilian settlement had spread to the south bank of the Dee along the approach to the bridge where at least one masonry building was erected on the west side of the road as it passed through the quarries on its way to Heronbridge. The intensity of occupation in the western sector of the *canabae* appears to have continued much as before, although there was no actual expansion onto areas previously open. In fact much of the land to the north of the Watergate Baths was now put to use as a cemetery. Excavations in 1912-17 examined a sample area containing 40 burials, all inhumations, the majority belonging to the second half of the second century. Nearly all the burials had been made in wooden coffins but the construction of the graves varied: some were simple trenches dug in the clay; others were lined or covered with roof-tiles or masonry, and one had been covered with a sheet of lead. Males predominated although female and child burials were also encountered. Grave-goods included glass and pottery vessels, metal trinkets, coins and occasionally sandals. Some of these displayed signs of deliberate damage, probably a feature of the burial ritual.

The hinterland

Following the widespread rebuilding and replanning carried out early in the reign of Hadrian, the *vicus* at Heronbridge continued to prosper throughout the remainder of the second century. Occupation at Saltney carried on much as before but there is no evidence for any other civilian settlements springing up in the fortress hinterland. Operations at the lead-processing centres in north-east Wales also appear to have continued unabated, with security now presumably provided by auxiliary rather than legionary troops. Just as the larger part of the Twentieth went north in the 120s so too did a considerable proportion of the auxiliary units in its command area. The garrisons of a number of forts in North Wales had already been reduced or withdrawn earlier in the second century for service in the North, and this process was now taken further along with the removal of units from forts elsewhere in the southern half of its command area such as those at Northwich and Middlewich.

It was mentioned previously that tiles datable to 167 have been found in the fortress. The *tegulae* in question, two in number, were found in the *retentura* during the Northgate Brewery excavations of 1972 and bear the stamp *TEGULA(M) A VIDU(CUS FECIT) / VERO III CO(N)S(ULE) LEG(IONI) X(XVV)* — 'Aulus Viducus made this roofing-tile for *Legio XX Valeria Victrix* in the third consulship of Verus'. Four more examples were discovered in 1993; not at Chester, however, but at Tarbock on Merseyside, about 3½miles (6km) north-west of Widnes. They were recovered together with a large collection of tiles from the site of a Romano-British enclosure containing a single rectilinear timber building. Associated pottery suggests a brief occupation, while the occurrence of overfired and distorted tiles and blocks of fired clay indicates that the tiles were actually being manufactured on the site. In the absence of any other known function for the site it appears it was established simply and solely to produce bricks, tiles and pottery over a very limited period by the workshop of Viducus and presumably to fulfil a specific order placed by the legion. The equivalent products found at Chester may also have been manufactured in the vicinity by the apparently peripatetic Viducus and again in response to a specific contract.

11 *Deva* restored and revitalised: the heyday of Roman Chester (*c*.210-*c*.260)

99 Sestertius *of the Emperor Severus Alexander (AD 222-35)*

The years around 200 saw the implementation of a programme of rebuilding in the frontier zone of Britannia and by 207 Hadrian's Wall, the outpost forts beyond it, and those in its hinterland had all been overhauled and brought back into full military effectiveness. The time was now ripe to punish the rebels, and the governor Lucius Alfenus Senecio wrote to the Emperor requesting reinforcements or, even better, an imperial expedition led by Severus himself. Senecio had of course received imperial instructions to submit such a request beforehand, as Severus was keen to find an excuse to get his sons Geta and Caracalla away from the temptations of court. Severus arrived the following year accompanied by the Empress Julia Domna, his two sons, a large retinue of (probably disgruntled) courtiers, and reinforcements which included vexillations from legions based in other provinces and new levies raised in both Gaul and Britain. The imperial headquarters were established at York where the campaigns were planned and directed for the next three years until Severus' death on 4 February 211. The war was brought to a swift conclusion the following year and the military situation settled down into a period of calm that was to last most of the remainder of the century. To reduce the size of the military forces under the control of any one provincial governor, and thereby minimise the risk of revolt, Severus had instituted a process of dividing provinces containing large armies into smaller units. In line with this policy Britain was split into two provinces by Caracalla; Britannia Superior with its capital at London and including the legions at both Chester and Caerleon, and Britannia Inferior controlled from the base of *legio VI Victrix* at York.

We do not know the extent of the Twentieth's involvement in Severus' campaigns but it was probably considerable. On the other hand, the concentration of marching-camps attributed to these campaigns up the eastern coastal plain of Scotland makes it unlikely that Chester played the role of transhipment centre as it had done in connection with earlier expeditions. Following the cessation of warfare, the bulk of the legion returned to its old base at Chester and began the process of completely rebuilding the fortress. All the

Table 7: estimated fortress construction statistics
Severan rebuild – stone requirement

Building	**Volume (cu ft)**	**Weight (tons)**	**Wagonloads (1,763lbs)**
Barracks	1,754,417	122,170	155,155
Rampart buildings	151,519	10,551	13,400
Building behind *principia*	174,735	12,167	15,453
Granaries (x6)	127,244	8,860	11,253
Principia	312,084	21,732	27,600
Elliptical Building	263,251	18,332	23,280
Minor baths	18,021	1,255	1,594
Store behind Elliptical Bldg	99,223	6,909	8,775
Equivalent bldg in east *latera praetorii*	99,223	6,909	8,775
Praetorium	176,678	12,303	15,625
Other bldgs. in *latera praetorii*	123,675	8,612	10,938
Main *fabrica*	79,364	5,527	7,019
Assumed store	88,339	6,152	7,813
Hospital	123,675	8,612	10,938
Senior officers houses	265,018	18,455	23,438
Other bldgs in *praetentura*	265,018	18,455	23,438
Tabernae	150,035	10,447	13,266
Gates & towers (partial) excluding curtain wall	168,481	11,733	14,900
Totals	**4,440,000**	**309,181**	**392,660**

buildings still standing were replaced and those which had earlier been demolished or become derelict rose from the ground anew. Furthermore, even those plots which had remained as open ground for the century and a half since the abandonment of the early Flavian grand scheme for the centre of the fortress now had buildings erected on them. By the time the programme of works was complete, the fortress had a full complement of buildings for the first time in its history (**100 & colour plate 27**).

This work was finished within a few decades despite the fact that elements of the Twentieth continued to be absent in the North, where they were based at Corbridge and Carlisle. At both sites these were brigaded with a detachment from *legio II Augusta* though at Corbridge, if not at Carlisle also, each was provided with its own separate compound. We know from inscriptions that for part of the reign of Caracalla the officer commanding the detachment at Carlisle was the tribune Marcus Aurelius Syrio whose family came from Nicopolis in Thrace. He set up an altar to Jupiter, Juno, Minerva, Mars, Victory and 'all the other gods and goddesses' as well as a statue-group dedicated to Concord. The former carries a motif of clasped hands and the latter a depiction of two legionaries

Table 8: estimated fortress construction statistics

Severan Rebuild – Tile and Brick Requirements

Building	**Tile** **Tegulae**	**Imbrices**	**Antefixes**	**Ttl Weight** (tons)
Barracks	377,664	446,205	27,486	5,667
Rampart Buildings	42,560	50,160	4,180	630
Principia	34,102	41,385	2,834	516
Store behind *principia*	53,578	65,466	3,484	810
Granaries (x6)	31,760	37,908	1,957	476
Elliptical Building	6,536	43,035	1,570	210
Store behind Elliptical Bldg	7,680	9,508	771	116
Building equivalent to above in east *latera praetorii**	7,680	9,508	771	116
Assumed store in east *latera praetorii**	17,940	22,020	1,160	272
Building behind *praetorium*	16,146	19,800	1,044	244
Main *fabrica*	24,288	30,008	1,898	369
Senior officers houses	50,416	63,824	5,528	773
*Praetorium**	25,200	31,500	2,000	384
Other buildings in east *praetentura**	24,528	28,780	2,144	368
Hospital	36,628	47,098	1,446	560
Other buildings in west *praetentura*	6,132	7,195	436	92
Other buildings *retentura**	12,264	14,390	872	184
Tabernae	60,780	74,926	4,050	924
Gates & towers	13,360	15,820	1,236	201
Major baths	33,176	40,001	1,800	499
Minor baths	2,364	3,064	100	36
Totals (including +5% for breakages)	**929,021**	**1,156,681**	**70,105**	**13,447**

Brick

	Pedales	***Sesquipedales***	***Bipedales***	***Box***	
Major baths	70,000	2,800	2,200	54,736	1,094
Minor baths	3,200	236	183	1,600	44
Other bath-suites & hypocausts	12,000	1,000	800	1,600	120
TOTALS (including +5% for breakages)	**89,460**	**4,237**	**3,342**	**60,832**	**1,258**

Total weight brick & tile = 15,423 tons = 19,588 wagonloads (1,763lb capacity) or 309 bargeloads (50 ton capacity)

* = form of building estimated.

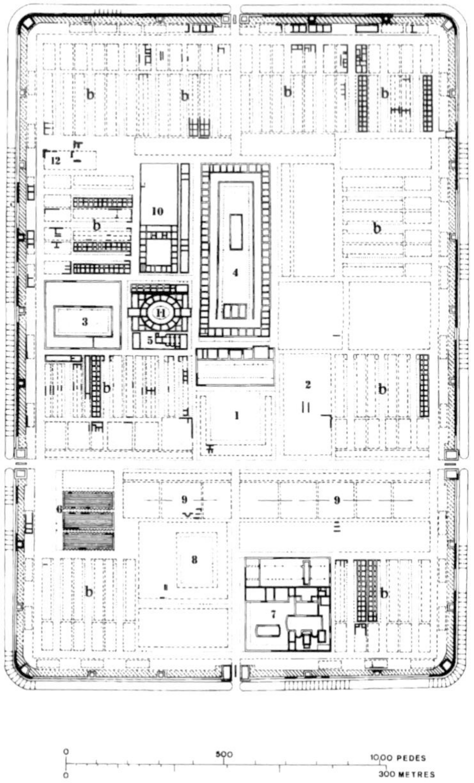

100 Plan of the rebuilt fortress of c.AD 235. KEY: 1 headquarters building; 2 legate's residence; 3 workshops; 4 stores; 5 minor baths; 6 granaries; 7 major baths; 8 hospital(?); 9 senior officers' residences; 10 stores; 11 Elliptical Building; 12 granary(?); b barracks

embracing, suggesting that Syrio was in charge of both detachments and not just that from the Twentieth. Elements of both legions are also recorded undertaking building work at Netherby and Maryport in this period. Possibly command of the 'brigade' at Carlisle passed between the two legions on a rotational basis. Also seconded for duty in the North was the centurion Lucius Maximius Gaetulicus, who set up an altar to Jupiter Dolichenus at Greatchesters and another, to Apollo, at Newstead whilst he was commanding their garrisons. A near contemporary of his and a fellow centurion was Valerius Martialis who was in charge of the Second Cohort of Asturians at the time it was rebuilding a granary at Greatchesters in 225.

That the process of rebuilding at Chester was underway soon after Severus' death is shown by the widespread occurrence of stamped bricks and tiles on which the legion is given the abbreviated cognomen *ANTO*, short for *Antoniniana*, or 'Caracalla's Own' (**101**). This was awarded to regiments in Britain in 213 following their declaration of loyalty to Caracalla who had become sole emperor the year before after engineering the death of his elder brother, an act which caused widespread resentment amongst the army in Britain. The title continued to be used under Caracalla's successor Elagabalus (218-22). The reconstruction of almost the entire fortress from ground level was an enormous task, as the accompanying tables illustrating the logistics involved demonstrate, and it is hardly surprising that it took several decades to complete. Coin evidence indicates the length of

101 *Third-century tile-stamps of the Twentieth Legion. Upper —* Anto *stamp an abbreviation of the title* Antoniniana *reflecting loyalty to Caracalla (Marcus Aurelius Antoninus) current during his reign (AD 212-16) and that of Elagabalus (AD 218-222). Lower —* De *stamp expanded as either* Deciana, *an honorific title bestowed during the reign of Trajan Decius (AD 249-51) or alternatively as* Devana *or* Devensis, *with the legion adding the place-name* Deva *to its titles*

the process. For example, a *denarius* of Elagabalus was found in the make-up of the courtyard paving at the centre of the second version of the Elliptical Building while counterfeit copies of coins of the reign of Severus Alexander (222-35) were recovered from the foundations of a new building in the *insula* immediately to its north. Similarly, an *as* of Severus Alexander datable to 231 was discovered in the footings of the western outer wall of the rebuilt cross-hall of the *principia*.

Alongside substantial and successive increases in both pay and retirement gratuity, Severus and his immediate successors also introduced major improvements to the ordinary soldier's conditions of service. Although in some cases these merely accorded official recognition to a situation which had long existed in practice, their net effect was to bind legion and *canabenses* closer than ever before. Soldiers were now allowed to contract legal marriages while still serving and to maintain a family home (*domum comparare*) in the extramural settlement. They were also permitted to operate businesses, although as leave was not granted for the purpose of *negotia privata* this was usually done via agents. However, it should not be thought that there was any relaxation of the military regimen; the routine of drill, training, patrolling, guard duty, record keeping, supplies' acquisition and the hundred and one other duties and fatigues remained as before for the ordinary soldiers. They were still expected to spend the greater part of their off-duty time in barracks.

The year 213 saw the enactment of the *Constitutio Antoniniana* or Edict of Caracalla which awarded Roman citizenship to every free-born person in the Empire, all of whom now had to give a specific town as their *origo*. Previously it had been sufficient for a non-citizen to give only his or her *civitas peregrina*. This was not pure generosity on the part of Caracalla but rather a means of simplifying the administration of the Empire by placing the overwhelming majority of its inhabitants into a single category and thus removing any real distinctions between the various types of self-governing community which had evolved over earlier centuries. The garrison towns in the frontier provinces were perhaps affected more than most by these constitutional and administrative reforms. The evidence from the Danubian provinces in particular illustrates how the territorial arrangements of the civil settlements around legionary bases were modified in this period. Where the outlying civil settlement had already been granted the status of a *municipium* the *canabae* was in some cases subsumed as a constituent *vicus* of the *municipium* but in others it became a self-governing community in its own right. By contrast, where the outlying settlement had remained as a *vicus* it was common for the *canabae* to be elevated in status and the *vicus* attributed to it much in the same way as the ward of a parish. Whichever solution was chosen the effect was the same: recognition of the *canabae* settlements as 'proper' communities and the regularisation of their constitutional status. Henceforth, they were self-governing towns like any other. The legal position of their inhabitants reflected reality for they were now classed as citizens of the community where they lived, not those of a town or city in another province where their ancestors had originated decades earlier. A major corollary of these changes was a reorganisation of legionary land-holdings and there is evidence for their severe reduction and possibly even complete abolition in the early third century. The territorial reforms and the resultant end to the phenomenon of two civil settlements in the vicinity of legionary fortresses is demonstrated by the new bases established in the late second century such as *Castra Regina* (Regensburg) and *Lauriacum* (Lorch) where only one civil settlement — that immediately outside the defences — developed.

One man who was very probably closely involved with the rebuilding of the Chester fortress, or at least some aspect thereof, is Marcus Aurelius Alexander. He held the post of *praefectus castrorum* at some stage in the first half of the third century. His tombstone, found reused in the North Wall, records that he died at the age of 72, seemingly still on active service, and that he came originally from northern Mesopotamia. The majority of the large collection of funerary monuments at Chester belong to the third century and attest its thriving character in that period. One of the more intact examples, standing nearly 6ft (1.8m) high, is that commemorating the centurion Marcus Aurelius Nepos who died aged 50 (**102**). Figures representing him and his wife are contained in a flat-topped niche above the inscription. Nepos, bareheaded with clipped beard, grasps the centurion's baton in his right hand and a scroll — probably his will — in the left. He wears a cloak draped over both shoulders, fastened on the right by a knee-brooch and, while neither tunic nor corslet are distinguished, emphasis is given to a wide belt fastened low by a circular clasp above a full kilt falling to the knees. His 'most devoted wife' ('*coniunx pientissima*') paid for the monument and although space was left for her name to be added when she died it was left blank; possibly she remarried and was eventually buried with her second husband. She stands higher in the niche, as if in the background. Her legs, even more attenuated than her husband's, peep out from below a full skirt partly covered by an over-skirt which she holds up with her left hand. In her right hand she holds what is probably a weaving comb while her hairstyle, arranged in tight waves, was popular in the early third century. Other members of the Twentieth at this time whose tombstones have survived include the *optio* Caecilius Avitus (**103**), the legate's orderly Titinius Felix and the record-clerk Gaius Valerius Justus who died at the respective ages of 34, 45 and 30. The last two left widows, Julia Similina and Cocceia Irene.

The importance and status of cavalry increased during the course of the third century with the need for a more rapid response to the numerous incursions across the frontiers of the Empire. Troopers are quite well represented in the sculptural collection at Chester, although owing to the vagaries of survival the stones in question are missing most of their inscriptions. One recording a 26-year-old trooper mentions that his unit was organized into *turmae*. This was the sub-division of auxiliary cavalry and was only applied to legionary cavalry when the strength of the *equites legionis* were increased from 120 to *c.*720 under Gallienus. Thus, either he was an auxiliary cavalryman or a legionary trooper of the late third century. In view of the poor style of his memorial the latter is perhaps the more likely. Another stone depicts a cavalryman galloping to the right holding a sword in his right hand and a long oval shield in his left (**104**). He wears a long shirt of chain mail (*lorica squamata*) as well as mailed breeches extending to the knees, a style of armour which became popular in the third

102 Tombstone of the centurion Marcus Aurelius Nepos, serving with the Twentieth Legion, who died aged 50. Nepos holds the centurion's baton in his right hand. The hairstyles of both Nepos and his wife indicate a third-century date. His wife's name was never carved on the stone so perhaps she remarried and/or moved away from Chester

103 Tombstone of Caecilius Avitus, from Emerita Augusta *(modern Merida in Spain), an* optio *in the Twentieth who died aged 34*

*104 (below) Tombstone depicting horseman wearing a long mailed tunic (*lorica squamata*) and mailed breeches of third-century style. A naked barbarian lies prone below the horse. Found North Wall (west) 1890*

century. A third stone carries a relief of a *draconarius*, the bearer of the dragon standard (**105**). These were introduced into the Roman Army in the later second century by Sarmatian cavalry units and consisted of a hollow, open-mouthed dragon's head to which was attached a long tube of material shaped something like a windsock, the whole contraption mounted on a pole. With the horseman travelling at speed such devices emitted a hissing sound meant to strike fear into the enemy. A force of 5,500 Sarmatian cavalry was transferred to Britain in 175 and a troop of them may have been brigaded with the Twentieth at Chester as our horseman is attired in Sarmatian style (**colour plate 26**). Very noticeable is the tall conical helmet with a vertical metal frame while both rider and horse are protected by scale armour (*lorica squamata*). A final stone worthy of mention is the fragmentary tombstone of the horseman Aurelius Lucianus (**106**). The bearded and moustached Aurelius is shown in the usual funerary banquet repose but here wearing a corslet of scale armour and trousers. On the wall behind him hang his helmet, with crest and cheek-pieces, and his sheathed sword, notable for its large pommel. In the lower register of the scene stands Aurelius' servant holding a rather ghastly trophy — the severed head of an enemy.

105 *Tombstone of a Sarmatian* draconarius *(the bearer of the dragon-standard). The material tail of the standard is shown streaming out behind the rider's head. Found in the North Wall (west) 1890*

106 *Tombstone of the cavalryman Aurelius Lucianus. Aurelius is shown reclining on a low-backed couch wearing a corselet of scale armour. He is bearded and moustached with long hair brushed stiffly back. In the background hang his helmet, with crest and cheek-pieces, along with his sheathed sword with large pommel. On the lower and much damaged portion of the tombstone a human head is depicted, possibly a war-trophy. Found in the North Wall (east) 1887*

The defences

The curtain wall appears to have required little in the way of restorative work at this time although there are signs that a number of the interval towers were rebuilt in the early third century, with subsidence of the rampart made good by the addition of new material. The ditch was cleaned out and its profile re-cut so that now there was little or no berm left at the foot of the wall, a modification that ultimately was to have unfortunate consequences. The inaccessibility of the gate structures means that we have no information about possible reconstruction or modification works effected at this time. The cookhouses against the rear of the rampart were rebuilt, in some cases incorporating one or more ovens which replaced the earlier free-standing examples situated between the buildings.

Streets and sewers

Most streets in the fortress had suffered from the long period of hiatus, either through neglect or deliberate damage, and the opportunity was now taken to renew the entire street system. As a logical preparatory step to this the network of drains and sewers was also overhauled with all the principal culverts being enlarged to a standard depth and width of *c*.6ft and 2ft (1.8m and 0.6m) respectively, with a mortar or clay bonded lining of masonry and a capping of large stone slabs. The Roman drains greatly impressed the fourteenth-century monk Ranuph Higden who wrote: 'There be ways under the ground vaulted marvellously with stonework, chambers having arched roofs overhead, huge stones engraved with the names of ancient men'. Antiquarians of the nineteenth century were equally admiring, although the drains were often misinterpreted as mysterious underground passages, a tradition which persists to this day in certain quarters. A 100ft (30m) long stretch of the exterior drain running from the *porta praetoria* in the direction of the Nun's Field gully was exposed in May 1821 when the debris resulting from the collapse of a building at the corner of Cuppin Street and Bridge Street was cleared. It is described thus: — ' It is uniformly, throughout its whole extent, five feet wide, and sixteen feet deep in the rock. The bottom was filled with soil, and at the depth of eight feet it appeared to have been boarded across with three inch oak plank, dividing it into an upper and lower road, each eight feet high. The direction of it is nearly due east and west . . . and at intervals there were small square recesses.'

The barracks

All barracks investigated so far have provided plentiful evidence of a reconstruction from ground level in the opening decades of the third century. Where previously of timber they were now built of stone, or at least with stone dwarf walls supporting a timber superstructure, and where the conversion had already occurred they were rebuilt to the same plan as their predecessors. For whatever reason, the barracks in the left *retentura* (*XXVII*) were slightly shorter than the rest and as a consequence contained only 11 instead of the more usual 12 *contubernia*. The period of disuse between the two structural phases was graphically demonstrated in the barrack of the first cohort excavated on the Crook Street 1974 site, where a thick layer of brown sandy soil intervened between the Hadrianic and Severan footings. The centurial quarters too were rebuilt to more or less the same plan as before but now refinements and comforts such as hypocaustal heating began to be added. As the third century wore on and the production of ceramic tiles ceased, thin, hexagonal-shaped slabs of micaceous sandstone or north Welsh slate were used for the roofing of barracks and other mundane buildings.

The excavation of sizeable portions of barracks conducted in the 1970s and 1980s yielded many examples of pieces of military equipment along with a wide variety of items illustrating aspects of everyday life. In the former category, the buckles, hooks and hinges of *lorica segmentata* are commonplace. Spear-heads and *ballista* bolts were a fairly frequent find and even a few dagger blades were recovered. Because of their rusted condition, iron dagger scabbards are deeply unimpressive objects on first inspection but x-raying them can reveal hidden details of inlay work as **25** demonstrates. Gaming-counters indicate one of the popular off-duty pastimes of the legionaries, while samian ink-wells, enamelled seal-boxes and bronze *styli* reflect their literacy and prodigious correspondence. Pottery oil-lamps and their lead holders remind us of the flickering light in the barracks after dusk. A bronze disc from one of the barracks on the Abbey Green site bears a *graffito* of punched dots indicating that the object to which it was attached belonged to Lucius Junius Abenus while another label, of lead, was used by Lucius Vanius of *cohors IX* to attach to goods he was sending by pack-animal to someone called Setinus. A clay die from the Hunter Street barracks in *insula XXII* with retrograde recessed lettering was used by Lucilius Sabinanus to mark the loaves he had made for the century of Malius Crassus. Occasional finds have included miniature altars of the type associated with the shrine of the household spirits or *lararium*. An example from one of the centurial houses in the Abbey Green barracks was accompanied by two, miniature columns suggesting the shrine took the form of a model of a classical temple.

The *principia*

Excavations at the north end of the *principia* in 1969 on the Old Market Hall site demonstrated that the building had been completely dismantled and rebuilt from ground level in the 230s (**107**). Both here and along the west side of the building as examined in the Goss Street excavations of 1948/9 and 1973 the plan of the second century building had been followed without major deviation. Now, if not earlier, a strong-room (*aerarium*) to house the legionary treasury was provided below the *aedes*. This was cut into solid rock to a depth of 6ft (1.8m) below ordinary floor level with its sides set in from the face of the enclosing walls by some 2ft (60cm). Although only a small portion could be examined its north-east corner was located during subsequent contractor's excavations, allowing the overall width of the excavation to be determined as 35ft (10.7m). As its north-south dimension can be estimated as lying between 25 and 30ft (7.6 and 9.1m) the *aerarium* could clearly accommodate a considerable number of pay-chests as well as bullion and other 'treasure'. A 1ft 6in (48cm) wide strip of mortar around the edge of the rock floor indicated the site of an original screen wall erected to conceal the rock face behind. This had been dismantled in a later phase and the rock face itself plastered over (**86**). In order to provide ample headroom in the *aerarium* and to emphasise the importance of the *aedes*, the floor of the latter would have been raised above that of the rest of the cross-hall. The front of the *aedes* would have been open so that the standards, the focus of religious

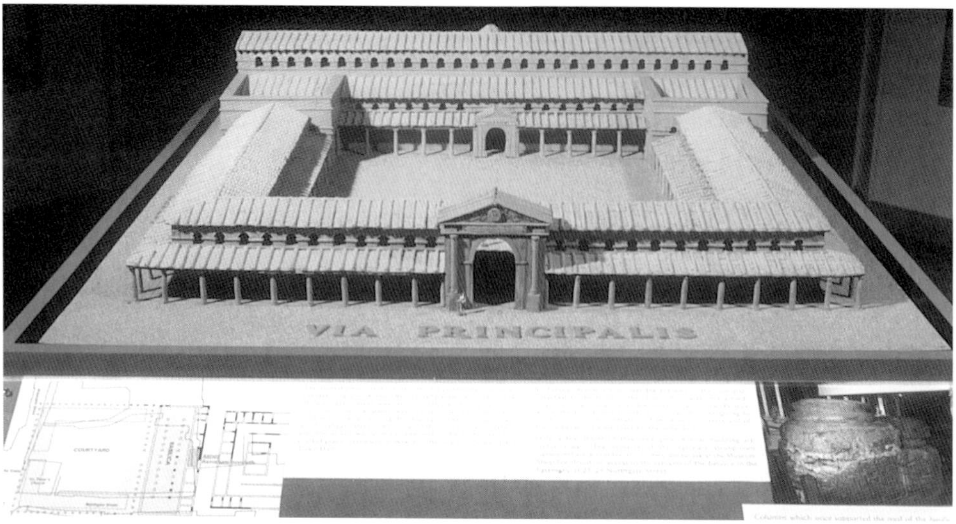

107 Model of the third-century headquarters building

attention along with images of the emperor and the imperial family, were always visible. They were, though, protected by metal grills set on decorated stone screens like those still to be seen in the auxiliary *principia* at Housesteads and Chesterholm (**colour plate 23**). Both the rear and side walls of the *aedes* were considerably thicker than their neighbours at 4 vs $2\frac{1}{2}$ft (1.2 vs 0.75m) and it is clear that the legionary shrine was given distinctive architectural treatment by being taller than the other rooms in the back range, its roof probably rising to the full height of the cross-hall aisle at around 25ft (7.6m). The masonry at the north-west corner of the room provided a clue as to the form of its superstructure. Here, in the surface of the uppermost surviving layer of mortar of the north wall was the impression of a large stone block measuring 3ft x 2ft (90 x 60cm). The block's function can only have been to support one of a series of either four, or more probably six, columns belonging to a blank pedimental entrance enlivening the otherwise fairly dull exterior of the rear of the *principia*. Observation of utility excavations further to the east in the 1980s revealed that the room next-but-one to the *aedes* was at some stage enlarged so that it projected a few metres out from the back wall. Possibly this served as a subsidiary shrine or perhaps a *schola*, a meeting-room for the legion's officers like those found in the *principia* at the fortress of Lambaesis.

Column bases belonging to the north aisle of the *basilica* were found during the excavation of a cellar at No. 23 Northgate Street in 1897. Altogether five bases were found, with spaces for two others, of which three can still be seen *in situ* together with the shafts of two fallen columns and a capital (**28**). The bases are set directly on the surface of the rock, which is quite high in this part of the fortress, and are of Attic type with two convex and close-set mouldings or *tori* of almost equal size. In this they contrast with the bases having a single large *torus* moulding of Flavian date found in the *thermae*. It would seem that the double *torus* type, which have been recovered from many fortress buildings, belong exclusively to the third century. The column drum from the *principia* displays considerable entasis (a convexity designed to counteract the optical illusion of concavity which results if it is carved with straight sides) while the capital is of Corinthian style but executed in a highly distinctive way. The acanthus leaves are plain and squat without the slightest embellishment and the double volutes above are stout and stumpy. This is the classical model reduced to its most simplified and basic form. Capitals of varying sizes recovered from other parts of the *principia* exhibit the same characteristics and illustrate the degree to which the classical orders had already become debased by this period (**142**). Indeed, so crude is the finish of these capitals that earlier writers thought them unfinished, but as identical examples have turned up in buildings throughout the fortress it is clear that it was never intended to refine their carving further.

The building behind the *principia*

The Old Market Hall excavations of 1967-9 and those at Hunter Street in 1978-82 demonstrated that this building had undergone a thorough reconstruction at some time in the first half of the third century. All elements of the complex were rebuilt, new floors and surfaces laid and the only modification introduced was a narrowing of the doorways of the rooms in the outer ranges. Presumably the building continued to be used as a store.

The Elliptical Building and associated structures

One of the major features of the rejuvenated fortress was the completion, albeit with a number of important modifications, of the Elliptical Building. The foundations and footings of the original, unfinished building had long since vanished from view, buried beneath nearly a metre of refuse and industrial debris from the neighbouring *fabricae*. It is clear from divergences between the plans of the two phases of the building, with the foundations of the new version sometimes coinciding with those of the Flavian structure and sometimes not, that the Severan builders had not simply dug down to the original foundations and placed their structure upon them but rather had surveyed out the building afresh. This means that the surveyors must have had access to the original plans for the Elliptical Building. These they presumably retrieved from the fortress archives where they had laid gathering dust for 150 years; an interesting insight into and confirmation of the meticulousness of the Roman Army's record-keeping.

The basic form of the building was much as before but with significant alterations (**108 & 109**). It was less sophisticated architecturally but nonetheless imposing owing to the robustness of its construction which featured walls up to 5ft (1.5m) thick. The fountain monument at the centre of the courtyard was retained from the original design and a new drainage culvert was built to serve it which exited beneath the west entrance. The courtyard itself was given an impressive paving of large sandstone slabs (**110**) and the surrounding colonnaded portico, whose columns now stood on a continuous stylobate foundation instead of separate plinths, was made somewhat deeper at the expense of the

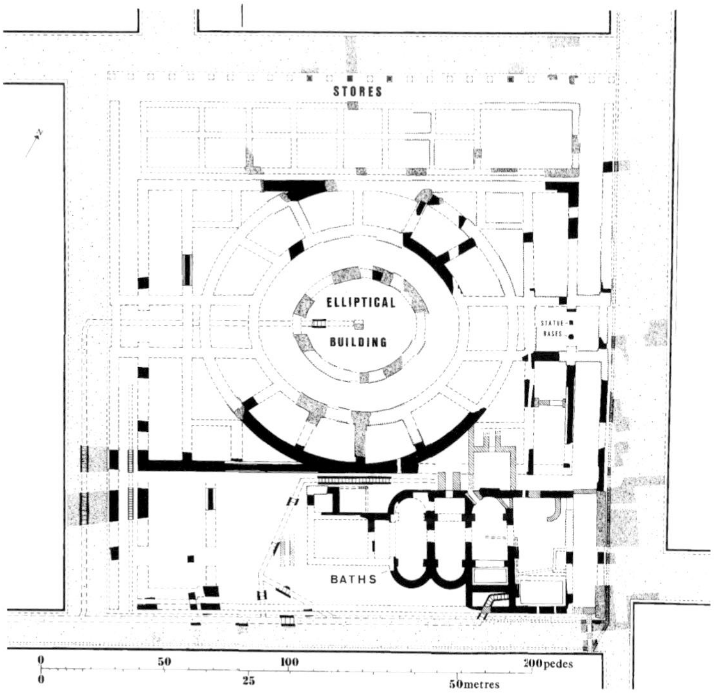

108 The third-century Elliptical Building as excavated

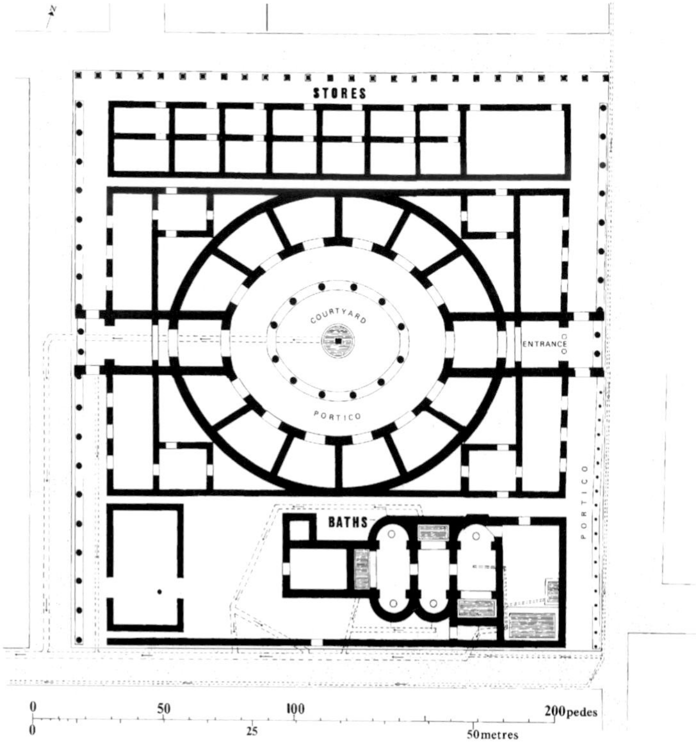

109 Restored plan of the third-century Elliptical Building

110 Paving of Elliptical Building courtyard, Old Market Hall Site, Phase IV, 1969

range of rooms beyond. As well as being slightly smaller the latter were simpler in design, lacking both the monumental entrances and the interior balustrade which characterised the original design. There were 12 rooms of equal size in the oval range as before but this was now separated structurally from the street-frontage ranges along the ends. Potentially most significant was the near tripling of the width of the two entrance passages, along with their architectural embellishment with a four-columned pedimental entrance. Clearly the building was intended to be used by a greater number of people than the original while the increased width of the entrance passages might also have been due to the need to incorporate staircases giving access to an upper storey (**colour plate 28**). Excavation revealed two statue bases occupying prominent positions in the eastern entrance passage but the identity of the images they supported is unknown (**111**). The street frontage wings were equipped with colonnades as before, but now placed on stylobates rather than separate plinths, and these continued in front of the neighbouring buildings to give the whole *insula* a more structurally integrated appearance (**colour plates 29 & 30**).

The purpose of the Severan Elliptical Building is as mysterious as its Flavian predecessor. The extent of post-Roman robbing and other disturbances coupled with the unsympathetic circumstances under which most of it was excavated meant that little of the interior of the chambers could be examined and so there is no information about decoration, fittings or contents to furnish clues. The absence, as before, of creature comforts such as hypocausts suggests it was not residential. Additional offices and/or a records archive are possibilities as perhaps is a *macellum*. Otherwise, one can only assume that, like the original building, it was intended as some form of commemorative structure celebrating Rome and its emperors. Possibly the approach of the 1000th anniversary of Rome's legendary foundation, to be celebrated in 248, was on the minds of those who decided to recreate this unusual building. The buildings which shared this *insula* (*XVII*) underwent extensive reconstruction at the same time.

The range of *tabernae* along the north edge of the plot was rebuilt. An unusual feature introduced at this time, one not seen on any other building in the fortress so far, was the

111 Statue base in east entrance of third-century Elliptical Building, Old Market Hall Site, Phase II, 1968

employment of square section pillars instead of round columns to support the veranda along its frontage. A new building, possibly a short range of *tabernae*, was erected at the south-west corner of the *insula*, while the neighbouring *balneum* was rebuilt from ground level. All the latter's hypocausts were renewed, as was its drainage system, while the *apodyterium*'s facilities were enhanced by the provision of a cold plunge-bath at its south end.

Stores compound

Paralleling developments on the Elliptical Building *insula*, that lying immediately to the north (*XXI*) was now fully occupied by buildings for the very first time. The *tabernae* along the eastern side of the plot were retained and rebuilt once more. The late second-century saw-pit, however, was filled in and henceforth the remainder of the *insula* was occupied by a single large building measuring 120pM (35.4m) east-west by 340pM (100.3m) north-south. Elements of the southern end of this were revealed by Newstead & Droop's Princess Street Excavation of 1939 but it was not until the Hunter Street/Princess Street Excavation of 1978-82 that the overall form of the building became clear. The southern and smaller half of the building consisted of a courtyard 75pM (22.1m) square surrounded on all four sides by 20pM (5.8m) deep ranges of accommodation. Access from the exterior seems to have been restricted to a single entrance centrally located in the south range. Directly opposite this in the centre of the north range was a second entrance passage, a little under 16ft (5m) wide, which gave access to the remainder of the building. The rooms to either side of this were entered up low flights of steps immediately inside the entrance passage, not directly from the courtyard as one might have supposed. Very small rooms here may in fact have housed stairwells giving access to an upper floor. Another much smaller court lay beyond with an inward facing room to each side; it was bounded on the north by a free-standing wall. Once again, access to the rooms was via a short upward flight of steps and it seems that the rooms were equipped with raised timber floors about 1ft 3in (40cm) higher than the exterior. In the centre of the north wall was another doorway leading into the northern and larger half of the building which took the form of a walled compound nearly 180ft (55m) long. The metalled surface of the courtyard to the south fanned out into this area in front of the entrance but then gave way to roughly laid sandstone brash. No evidence of industrial activity of any sort was found and the building has been tentatively interpreted as a stores-compound with accompanying offices. The presence of *LEG XXVV ANTO* tiles suggests this building was erected somewhat earlier than the rebuilt *principia* and the Elliptical Building.

The *praetorium* and senior officers' houses

As described above, very little of the *praetorium* has been explored and so the nature of the refurbishments which would undoubtedly have been carried out to the building at this time can only be imagined. The amenities partially revealed so far — hypocausts, bathing-chambers, and mosaic floors — all appear to have continued in use into the fourth century. Regarding the residences of the other senior officers, third-century walls together with a mosaic floor found in the area north of the north-east corner of the *thermae* could belong to one of these buildings. If so, however, it would mean that the tribunes' houses were larger and extended further south than hitherto imagined; possibly a rearrangement of the buildings in this area as part of the third-century reconstruction of the fortress created additional space into which the tribunes' accommodation could expand (for a reconstruction view up the *via praetoria* in this period *see* **colour plate 31**).

The *thermae*

This massive complex also underwent extensive renovation at this time. The entire hypocaust system in the *tepidarium* and *caldarium* was renewed, along obviously with the floors above, and the apsidal bay housing a hot plunge-bath at the west end of the latter seems likely to have been enlarged. Part of the wall running across the chord of the apse and supporting the front of the *alveus* was exposed in 1988 and was found to be more than 2m thick. The furnace at the east end of the *tepidarium* was demolished to make way for a new and additional heated chamber which in turn caused the drainage culverts serving the facilities in the neighbouring *frigidarium* to be re-routed. This entailed the removal of sections of the mosaic floor in the *frigidarium* which rather surprisingly was clumsily repaired with slabs of stone or slate. There was also a reversal of the previous bathing arrangements with the cold plunge-baths now located in the recesses at the south-east and south-west corners of the main part of the hall and the *labra* housed in the end-chambers (**112**). There can be little doubt that the hypocausts in the suite of dry-heat *sudatoria*

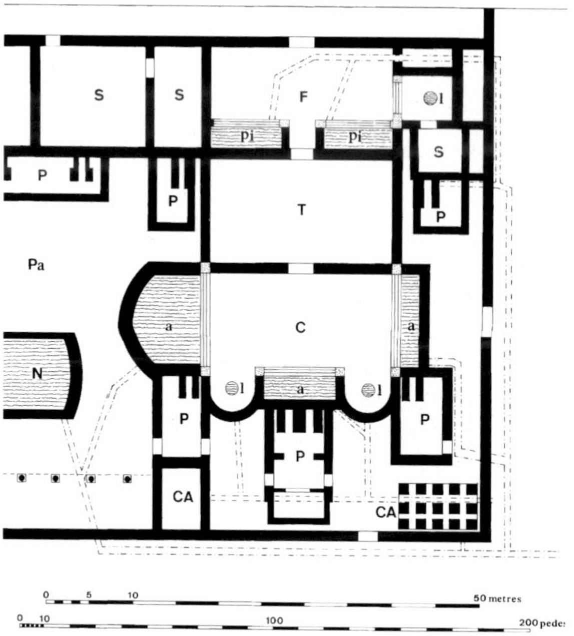

112 *Plan of main baths-suite in fortress baths, third century. Plunge-baths and large wash-basins shaded. C* = caldarium *(hot and steamy bathing-hall); CA* = castellum aquae *(water reservoir); F* = frigidarium *(bathing-hall of ambient temperature); N* = natatio *(swimming-bath); P* = praefurnium *(furnace-house); Pa* = palaestra *(exercise-yard); S* = sudatorium *(hot dry bathing chamber); T* = tepidarium *(bathing-hall of medium temperature); a* = alveus *(hot plunge-bath; l* = labrum *(large, raised shallow water-basin); pi* = piscina *(cold plunge-bath)*

attached to the south side of the basilica were also renewed on this occasion.

The renovation works of the early third century extended to the replacement of the concrete roofing-vaults over the main bathing suite. By an unusual and extremely fortunate set of circumstances, details of the vaults' construction were recovered during the hasty investigations conducted in 1964. A section across the east end of the *tepidarium* revealed the hypocaust and its *suspensura* still intact, including the latest flooring which utilised large slabs of slate. Covering the latter was a 1ft (30cm) thick deposit of fine earth. This, judging from the pieces of animal bone and charcoal within it, had accumulated as a consequence of squatter occupation during the centuries following the demise of the building as a functioning bath-house. It in turn was sealed by what at first sight seemed to be a jumbled mass of broken brick, tile and lumps of fine concrete, evidently the remains of the collapsed roof-vault. On closer examination, it soon became clear that distinct layers representing the component parts of the vault could still be discerned within this material. Obviously when the vault had finally failed and crashed to the ground the layer of earth covering the floor had cushioned the impact and prevented its components from being shattered into tiny pieces and dispersed over a wide area. At the base of the debris, above a thin layer of plaster render, lay the smashed remains of box-tiles (*tubuli*) which had formed an extension across the ceiling of the hollow wall-jacketing conveying heat from the hypocaust. Above this was the main body of the vault consisting of lightweight but dense concrete and above this again fragmented *tegulae* and *imbrices* belonging to the exterior weatherproof cladding of the vault. At one point within the lower part of the concrete layer were five or six lines of hollow, interlocking, syringe-shaped terracotta pipes bonded together with plaster (**113**). These are of a type known as *tubi fittili* which make their first appearance in vault construction in the North African provinces in the latter part

113 Remains of collapsed roof-vault of tepidarium *showing rib of terracotta 'tubes', Newgate/Pepper Street Site 1964*

of the second century. They also occur frequently in domes and vaults of the late fourth century in northern Italy. Normally, they were employed to construct a continuous formwork or lining for concrete vaults. In the Chester baths however they were used more sparingly, apparently to form 'ribs' within the body of the vault thus dividing it up into a form of cellular construction; presumably this made it easier to build and endowed it with added strength. There may well have been more substantial ribs of stone or brick voussoirs at more widely spaced intervals. In addition to carrying the vault these might also, by rising above the surface of the concrete, have provided supports for a timber superstructure to take the external tile cladding and thus lessen the loading on the vault.

Buildings west of the *thermae*

The area opposite the *thermae* on the west side of the *via praetoria* seems to have undergone a drastic reorganisation in the Severan scheme. Information is still limited about this area but small-scale excavations in recent years have clarified chance discoveries made in the nineteenth century. A new building was erected at the south end of *insula III* which ran the full width of the plot (300pM or 88.5m) and measured 140pM (41.3m) north-south. Its internal arrangements are unknown but it possessed colonnaded porticoes on its north and south frontages (and probably the east also as this gave onto the *via principalis*) with the columns set on stylobates formed of massive blocks of sandstone accompanied by equally robust eavesdrip gutters (**114**). A minor street about 12pM (3.55m) wide separated this building from its neighbour to the north. Like many other thoroughfares of the fortress its alignment persisted into and through the medieval period, eventually to become Pierpoint Lane. Commonhall Street, in reality itself little more than a lane, runs parallel with Pierpoint Lane some 130ft (40m) to its north and, because it lines up with the street which ran along the north side of the *thermae* opposite, it had always seemed likely also to perpetuate the line of a Roman predecessor. However, the excavations carried out at the rear of 30 Bridge Street in 1988 showed this not to be the case. As part of the Severan

114 Column bases and eavesdrip gutter of courtyard building west of Bridge Street, 1899

reconstruction, the second-century building which had stood here was completely demolished and its site levelled. In the new scheme the area became part of a large courtyard. A short section of stylobate for the colonnaded portico defining its easterly extent was exposed in the excavation together with its accompanying line of gutter blocks. This was in fact the continuation of an immediately adjoining section of the same feature revealed and photographed in 1899. Assuming a standard depth for the portico of about 13ft (4m) there would have been space for a range of accommodation about 30ft (9.1m) wide between it and the portico fronting onto the *via principalis*. The courtyard is known to have extended for at least 40ft (12m) in a westerly direction.

Sections of Roman masonry revealed by small-scale excavations both to the north and to the south of the 30 Bridge Street site suggest that the area was occupied by a single large building. It filled not only the remainder of *insula* III but also the whole of the shallow *insula* V to the north, giving it an overall size of 300 pM (88.5m) east-west by 240pM (70.8m) north-south. Its function is a matter for speculation although the legionary hospital seems a strong candidate in view of its location opposite the *thermae*.

Other buildings

The main workshops complex in *insula XVIII* was rebuilt in the Severan period, keeping very much to the second-century plan. The granaries too would undoubtedly have been refurbished at this time although the evidence of the 1950s excavations suggests this may have been restricted to re-roofing. Elsewhere, one or more buildings were now erected for the first time on the outer western *insula* (*XXVI*) in the shallow *scamnum* at the back of the *latera praetorii*. Excavations in 1982 exposed the end wall of a buttressed structure beside the *via sagularis*, tentatively identified as a granary. The results of further excavations conducted in 1996 to the east have however cast doubts upon this interpretation.

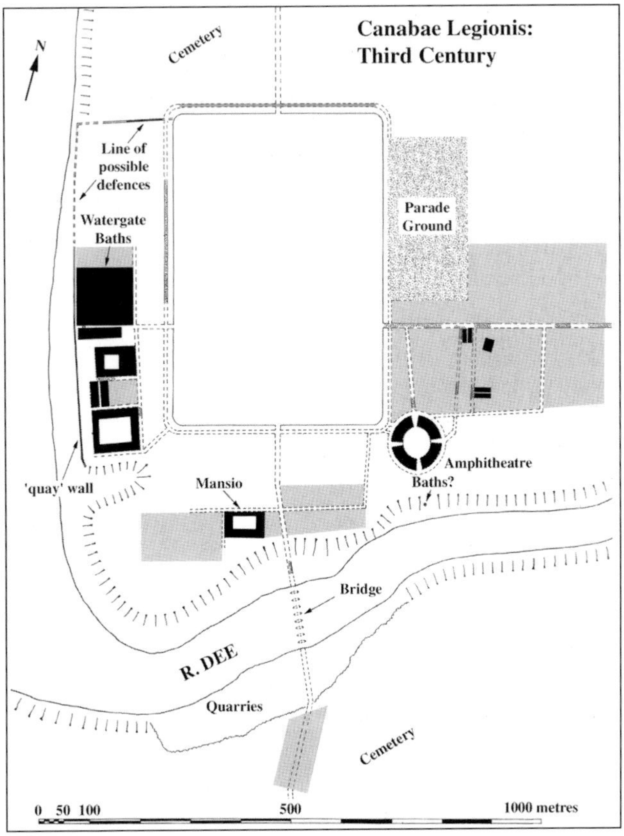

115 Plan of extramural settlement in the early third century showing line of possible defences. Solid black = excavated buildings; shading indicates general extent of built-up area

The *canabae legionis*

The return of the legion must have provided an enormous stimulus to the economy of the *canabae* — or perhaps it should now be termed the town — of *Deva* and evidence of intensified building activity has been found throughout the extramural settlement (**115**). In the main commercial part of the settlement lying east of the fortress, the examined buildings erected in the second century have nearly all produced evidence for continued occupation beyond 200. This includes those located on side-streets like the examples found at Priory Place. One of the more unusual features discovered in the area and probably belonging to this period of occupation takes the form of a very worn pavement composed of various coloured cobbles laid in a geometric pattern. Positioned beside the northern kerb of the main road just over 700ft (210m) out from the east gate, this may have been commissioned by an enterprising shopkeeper as a way of drawing attention to his premises, a device employed by modern retailers in the same area. It has been suggested that lengths of ditch of considerable size found at various locations formed part of a system of defences erected around the eastern suburbs in the late Roman period. Yet in no case has conclusive dating evidence been forthcoming and so this idea must be treated with great caution.

Dating of the later repairs and modifications carried out at the amphitheatre is a little

116 Altar to the 'Guiding Spirits of the Emperors' found in the mansio, *1976*

confused but it would be surprising if such an important facility had not been included in the programme of renovation. South-west of the amphitheatre, buildings of quality occupied the edge of the plateau overlooking the river. Only fragments have been seen but one building included an apsidal chamber equipped with a hypocaust. On the far side of the road leading down to the bridge, the *mansio* as planned in the Hadrianic period was finally completed. The rooms in the south wing were equipped with concrete floors and brightly coloured wall-paintings. Their occupants would also have enjoyed the excellent view of the river and the bridge across it from under the lee of the adjacent colonnaded portico. Also under the shelter of the portico were two wells whose fillings provided valuable information about the later history of the *mansio*. To anyone crossing the bridge below from the south this would have appeared a very imposing building indeed, stretching as it did for some 200ft (60m) along the edge of the plateau (**138**). An altar found reused in the base of a later wall probably derives from this phase of the *mansio* (**116**). It is dedicated to the *Numina Augustorum* or 'guiding spirits of the emperors' by a man named Commitus, a suitable dedication in a building whose purpose was to facilitate the smooth running of the courier system carrying imperial orders and correspondence.

As mentioned in chapter 9, other buildings existed to the south-west in the area now occupied by the Castle but nothing is known of them in detail. Building debris together with a plain altar (its dedication presumably painted on and long since faded) found about 330ft (100m) out from the south-west angle of the fortress suggests the possibility of a shrine. Other religious buildings may also have existed in the vicinity. For example, a sculpture in low relief of Cautopates, one of the attendant deities of Mithras, found built into the cellar wall of a house in White Friars just inside the south defences, suggests the possibility of a *Mithraeum* in an adjacent part of the extramural area. Chester may have had more than one *Mithraeum* as a second sculpture of Cautopates, this time executed in high relief about 3ft (90cm) tall, was discovered on the opposite bank of the river in Handbridge. This area also contains a religious structure whose location is in no doubt, namely the Shrine of Minerva. Immediately west of the road running through this suburb, which approximates to the line of its Roman predecessor, lies Edgar's Field and near the centre of this is a rock outcrop. Quarried out of this is a small, cave-like recess, now protected by iron railings, which formed the actual shrine and inside which stood a sculpted figure set in a gabled pediment carved in the rock face. Much eroded, descriptions by early antiquarians indicate the figure held a spear and shield with an owl perched on its shoulder. The owl is associated with the goddess Minerva. As she was regarded as patroness of artisans, the shrine is thought to have been constructed by the quarrymen and masons who toiled in the legionary quarries. The remarkable survival of the shrine is thought to have been due to the figure being mistaken for the Virgin in medieval times. It can still be inspected although the original carving has been removed for protection and replaced by a replica.

The masonry building erected closer to the road about 150 appears to have continued in use into the third century, while the discovery of a hypocaust *pila*, a Corinthian column capital and other occupation debris in the vicinity of St Mary's Church implies that civilian buildings had by this time spread even further south onto the higher ground above the quarries.

There were significant developments on the land west of the fortress in the third century (**117**). In the Greyfriars Court area the westernmost building overlooking the Roodee was demolished and its site covered by a bank of clay 3ft (90cm) high and at least 10ft (3.3m) wide. Its western side had been destroyed by a mixture of erosion and later activity so its full width could not be ascertained. Its purpose is unclear but may be connected with other developments along the shoreline shortly to be described. The two buildings aligned north-south immediately beside it to the east underwent minor refurbishment and alterations. To the north-east, in an area which had remained free of buildings since the early second century, a new building was erected around 200 which featured a recessed porch on its southern frontage. Further east and north-east again, excavations at Nicholas Street Mews in 1988 revealed the badly robbed remains of further structures including a number of rooms equipped with hypocausts. As yet, it is unclear if there are several separate buildings here or they are all part of one large courtyard complex. Further north, the Watergate Baths would undoubtedly have undergone major renovations and possibly alterations in the Severan period. A complex sequence of structural changes was seen in the Sedan House excavations of 1989 in the middle of its western side but a lack of dating evidence makes it impossible to attribute any particular works to this period (**118**).

Some of the civilian inhabitants of third-century Chester can be identified from tombstones. For example, there is Aurelius Timothaeus, who lived to see his 90th birthday, along with Gaius Valerius Victor and his wife Voconia Nigrina (**119**). Perhaps reflecting the increasingly urban character of Chester in this period there are a number of fine memorials belonging to wealthy women. Fesonia Severiana and Curatia Dionysia, who died aged 25 and 40 respectively, are two whose names have survived and there are quite a number of others whose tombstones have lost their inscriptions but which retain portraits of women (**120**). Of these, mention might be made of that depicting a wealthy woman with a richly braided coiffure, clad in a long tunic with long pointed sleeves,

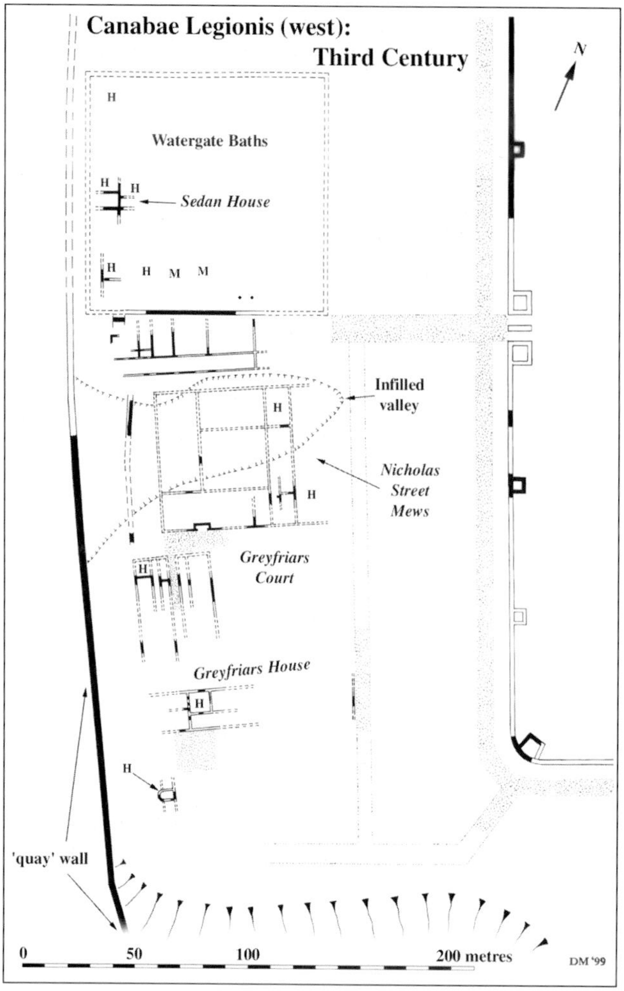

117 Plan of western sector of the extramural settlement in the early third century. H = hypocaust; M = mosaic

118 (below) Part of the Watergate Baths complex excavated at Sedan House1989 showing latest Roman concrete floor with underlying drain whose roof had collapsed. Note inverted roofing-tiles used to floor the drain and partially exposed earlier plunge-bath which it overran (see ***colour plate 19*** *for detail of this)*

119 Tombstone of Gaius Valerius Victor & Voconia Nigrina. The husband wears an ankle-length tunic with long tailed sleeves covered by a cloak. He holds a purse in his left hand and a scroll, probably his will, in the right. The wife wears a long robe with a wrap which hangs over her right shoulder. The round object, with a long straight handle and teeth, in her right hand is probably a weaving-comb. Found in the North Wall (west) 1890

accompanied by her little maidservant who carries a tray bearing a range of toilet articles and/or jewellery (**121**). On its discovery in 1887 this relief was thought to represent a medieval priest and acolyte and was for long known as the 'ecclesiastical stone'.

Most of the tombstones just mentioned, along with many other third-century examples and pieces of sculpture from funerary monuments, were recovered from the North Wall of the city and presumably originated from the cemeteries outside the *porta decumana*. Unfortunately, there have been no opportunities for the scientific examination of actual burials in this area. Occasionally one or more have been encountered by accident, such as the very battered example of a lead coffin uncovered by building work in the 1980s not far outside the Northgate. Some of the tombs in this area were clearly quite elaborate, taking the form of mausoleums rather than simple tombstones. One such had a fine pediment decorated with a carving of a Minerva mask conflated with the head of Neptune; the former a device for warding off evil and the latter referring to the voyage of the deceased to the Isles of the Blessed (**122**). Tritons and sea-centaurs, whose appearance in funerary reliefs also refers to this journey of the soul, occur on more than half-a-dozen examples including an arcuate window-lintel from an elaborate mausoleum (**123**). There are also depictions of Attys and Adonis, both examples of deities believed to be resurrected each Spring and symbolic of Life triumphing over Death, along with a scene of Hercules rescuing Hesione, indicating superhuman salvation. A partly preserved frieze has decoration in the form of a running acanthus scroll with rosette-like flowers in the centre of each spiral while the space between the top of each scroll is occupied by birds. If not from a mausoleum, this might have come from a temple or shrine, the birds possibly being the peacock, dove and owl associated with Juno, Venus and Minerva

respectively (**124**). Indeed, another stone from the east section of the North Wall, apparently from the arch-head of a building, refers to the construction of a temple and colonnade, so it is quite possible that there were several religious structures outside the *porta decumana*.

The other major cemetery of the fortress, that lying south of the river, also continued in use into the third century and beyond as coins running to the reign of Constantine testify. The majority of discoveries here have been accidental with varying degrees of detail recorded depending on the circumstances. Numerous cremation burials are recorded beside Eaton Road, lining it for over half a mile (1km) south of the river, while later inhumation burials occur further back from the road frontage over a wide area. Of the latter, mention should be made of a

120 Tombstone of Curatia Dinysia carved with a typical funerary banquet scene set in a round-headed niche above the inscription. The spandrels of the niche are decorated with Tritons blowing shell-trumpets, an allusion to the deceased's voyage to the Isles of the Blest. Found in North Wall (west) 1891

121 Tombstone depicting a lady with her maidservant. The lady, on the left, is clad in a long tunic with pointed sleeves, a wrap or scarf covering her shoulders. She holds a comb in her right hand and a mirror in the left. Her hair is richly braided. The little maidservant is carrying a toilet-box or tray covered with various indistinguishable objects. Found North Wall (east) 1891

122 Pediment from a tomb decorated with a bearded and moustachioed head from which sprout, Gorgon-wise, four snakes per side. The piece has a parallel in the so-called Bath Gorgon. Found in the North Wall (west)

123 Arcuate window-lintel decorated with carvings of sea-centaurs or Tritons

124 Carved frieze decorated with birds, possibly from a temple pediment. Found in North Wall (east) 1887

stone sarcophagus found in Queen's Park in 1852. Covered by a strong stone slab, within it lay a lead coffin containing the skeleton of a child. Unfortunately, as in this case, the memorials accompanying these burials rarely survive, having been removed long ago for reuse as building stone. An exception is the slate panel commemorating a *praefectus castrorum* of *legio XX*. His name is on the part that has gone missing but a plaque of this type must have come from a built tomb of some size and a mausoleum is what one would expect of a man of his position and wealth. It was common practice for the more elaborate tombs to be enclosed in a precinct defined by a low wall. The corner of such a tomb surround was in fact excavated east of Eaton Road in 1929. It took the form of a rectangular slab surmounted by a kerbing of semi-circular profile which at the angle became a flat plinth. On the latter at all four corners would have stood a sculpture, possibly either a pine-cone finial (symbolising life after death) or a figure of a lion (to fend off evil spirits or representing the suddenness of death), examples of both having been

125 Coping-stone from tomb surround decorated with a lion sculpture. From the cemetery which lined the road south to Heronbridge, 1848

found in the vicinity (**125**). Other examples of such kerb/coping blocks can be seen incorporated into the lower courses of the outer face of the North Wall west of the Northgate. They were found during the rebuilding works of 1890 together with another example, decorated with a wild beard and a stiff fringe of hair, possibly either Neptune or Jupiter (**51 & 52**). These stones presumably derive from a tomb precinct wall in the Northgate cemetery; alternatively they might be coping-stones from the fortress wall itself.

The harbour

The only visible Roman monument on the west side of the city is the so-called 'quay wall' which lies about 13ft (4m) in advance of the base of the medieval city wall and runs at a slight angle to it so that the two merge in the vicinity of the Watergate (**117**). It has been traced nearly as far as the latter but the only section now extant lies much further to the south opposite the end of Blackfriars Lane. Here a length of some 45m can be inspected, at the south end apparently turning into the mouth of the gully opposite the south-west angle of the fortress. The wall generally stands about 3ft (90cm) proud of the present Roodee surface but at one point, the scene of the only recorded investigation conducted in 1884, it rises to a height of *c.*10ft (3.3m) (**126**). This is the equivalent of *c.* +36ft (11m) OD while Roman ground surface as measured on the Greyfriars Court excavation some 70ft (21m) to the rear of the face of the 'quay wall' lay at *c.* +42ft (13m) OD. The wall is built of large blocks of sandstone up to 5ft (1.5m) long laid in courses varying from 14 to 18in (35 to 45cm) in height and bonded together with mortar. The present step-like appearance in places is due to robbing of the facing blocks. The investigation carried out in 1884 revealed that the wall was once far more impressive than it appears at present. Excavation traced it to a depth of just over 15ft (4.5m) below the existing ground level, at

126 The best preserved section of the 'quay wall' beside the Roodee racecourse

which point there was an offset course, and it obviously continued down for some distance beyond this but the ingress of water forced operations to be abandoned. In fact, in order to construct a secure foundation it would have had to have continued down to the solid ancient river bed which at this spot can be estimated to lie between +3 and 6ft (0.9-1.8m) OD, or *c.*5-8ft (1.5-2.5m) below the observed offset. Pilaster-like buttresses were found projecting out from the face and the wall itself was found to be 8ft (2.4m) thick reinforced with a 5ft (1.5m) thick backing of concrete.

Thus, rising a minimum of 9m from the river bed and running for a distance of at least 250m this wall was clearly a major engineering project. However, the traditional view that it functioned as a quay wall is open to question. At the time that the long series of debates about Chester's Walls took place in the 1880s and 1890s the position of the west wall of the fortress had not yet been determined and some suggested this may have been the function of the wall on the Roodee. Others thought it might belong to a circuit of defences erected around the civil settlement in the later Roman period while yet a third group viewed it as a quay. When confirmation finally came in 1945 that the western defences of the fortress followed an alignment roughly parallel with Nicholas Street the interpretation of the Roodee wall as a quay came to the fore and this is how it has since been described. Yet when one begins to investigate the practicalities of ships approaching and tying up alongside this structure, the flaws in the interpretation become very apparent. The top of the best preserved section of the wall lies at *c.*+36ft (11m) OD while the deck of an average sized and fully laden Roman merchant ship would, even allowing for a high tide level of *c.*+13ft (4m) OD and a generous height of deck above waterline of 10ft (3.3m), still be 13ft (4m) below it. In fact, it seems very likely that the 'quay wall' continued upwards for the remaining 7ft (2m) to attain the same level as the general interior ground surface. There is also the question of whether there would have been a depth of water immediately in front of the wall sufficient for ships to approach it.

Although not precisely known, the solid riverbed hereabouts lay between +3 and +6ft (0.9-1.8m) OD. However, it has been shown that a significant amount of silting had already taken place along the eastern side of the Roodee by the beginning of the Roman period; this is what one would expect given that this lay on the inside of the river bend where the current was slower and thus the rate of deposition higher. The evidence of the grave of Callimorphus and the tombstone found and then reburied beneath the Dee Stand implies that an area stretching out into the Roodee for at least 36ft (11m) had in fact silted up, to the point where it was to all intents and purposes dry land by the beginning of the Roman era. Most conclusive of all is the timber jetty (together with its possible masonry replacement) whose remains were found on the Gas Works site. Its construction can surely only be explained by the inability of ships to approach anywhere near the eastern shoreline of the Roodee, except possibly at its extreme north end. It might be suggested that there were further jetties and allied structures to the south running back to the 'quay wall', but this does not overcome the enormous change in levels. The idea of a system of cranes and/or enormous ramps simply fails to convince. Similarly, although there was a rise in sea level of perhaps as much as 5ft (1.5m) in the later Roman period this would have made little difference to the basic problem. The only other place where ships might have been able to tie up actually along the river's edge was immediately west of the bridge to the south of the fortress, although the space available here was quite restricted.

If not a quay then what was the purpose of the 'quay wall'? As a revetment to enable infilling behind and thus the creation of additional building space it makes little sense. For the effort of building a wall in size equivalent to roughly half the entire fortress curtain wall, the gain would have been a strip of land no more than 30ft (9.1m) wide; rather nonsensical given that there was plenty of building space south of the fortress. The only remaining option, first mooted during the discussions by Victorian antiquarians, is that it was a defensive structure erected to protect part of the civil settlement. As such, its position at the foot rather than at the crest of the slope might seem surprising; however, the rock there was covered by a thick mantle of clay which would not have provided a very secure base for a weighty structure such as this. Furthermore, it meant an attacker was faced with the daunting prospect of a sheer wall some 30ft (9.1m) or more in height rather than a sloping bank capped by a wall of less extravagant proportions. Also, the position of existing buildings might have been a determining factor. There are various possibilities as to the course taken by the remainder of this putative defensive circuit. At the south end of the extant section it turns in a south-easterly direction hinting that it perhaps followed the north side of the Nun's Field valley and joined up with the fortress defences somewhere in the vicinity of the south-west angle. To the north, it is possible that the 6ft (1.8m) thick wall found beneath Watergate Street in 1866 was not the southern perimeter wall of the baths after all but in fact an eastwards return of the 'quay wall' forming the north side of the defended enceinte. If so, it would have joined the fortress defences at the north tower of the *porta principalis dextra* and the enclosed area would have totalled *c.*12 acres (5ha). However, it seems very likely that an important building such as the Watergate Baths would have been included and, if so, the most probable route beyond the baths would be the line taken by the later city walls, thus linking up with the fortress at the north-west angle (**115**). Certainly there are signs of various phases of earlier masonry below the

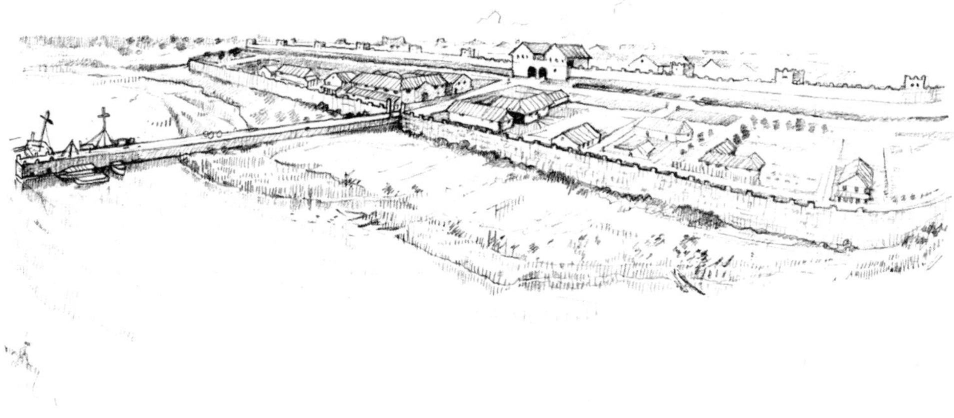

127 Sketch reconstruction of the harbour in the third century showing the 'quay wall' re-interpreted as a defensive wall around the western suburbs and with a stone jetty replacing the original timber pier

known medieval wall in the sector between the north-west angle and Bonewaldesthorne's Tower. There is circumstantial evidence too that there were defences here (built atop the collapsed remains of Roman fortifications?) as early as the beginning of the tenth century. In this case the enclosed area would have been around 27 acres (11.25ha) (**127**).

A third but far remoter possibility is that the southwards continuation of the 'quay wall' followed the shoreline of the Dee round to and beyond the bridge, eventually striking uphill and linking up with the fortress defences at the south-east angle; if this scenario were correct then the extension of the defended area usually attributed to the early medieval period would in fact have been a Roman development. On the analogy of similar developments at other fortresses, the section of the legionary defences to which the new civil fortifications were appended would have remained in commission.

The precise date of the wall's construction is unknown although it seems clear that it post-dates a number of late first-/early second-century burials in the area. Assuming that it was a defensive wall its most likely date of construction is the third century. This would parallel the provision of stone defences at many Romano-British towns and around sections of the other *canabae* settlements like those at *Mogontiacum*, *Aquincum* and *Novae*. Furthermore, the vast amount of building activity at Chester in this period makes it the most likely context for such a development. It would also fit with the apparent lack of projecting bastions, a defensive feature which became commonplace in the later third and fourth centuries. The nature of the works carried out behind the 'quay wall' in the early third century as evidenced by the Greyfriars Court site, entailing the demolition of the building closest to the shoreline and the formation of a substantial clay bank, could be viewed as supporting a construction date in this period.

The hinterland

The settlement at Heronbridge apparently continued to thrive throughout most of the third century and excavation has produced widespread evidence of continued occupation as well as rebuilding. Excavations in 1958 east of the main road at the north end of the settlement exposed the remains of an open-sided industrial building belonging to the late second/early third century. At its west end was a circular stone base which had presumably supported a metal water-tank, as a lead pipe led from it. It may be that lead was actually worked in this shed, for vitrified and distorted roof-tiles with traces of lead glaze on them were found in association with it. Further south on the opposite side of the road, pre-war investigations located several new buildings erected at the beginning of the third century and the general layout of the settlement seems to have been unaltered.

The reconstruction of the fortress in the opening decades of the third century involved an upsurge in brick and tile production at Holt as evidenced by examples bearing the abbreviated cognomen *ANTO*. How long production at Holt continued is unknown but tiles bearing the legionary stamp ending with the letters *DE* and others with a third *V* have been posited as the imperial cognomina *Deciana* and *Victoriniana* respectively, that is the reigns of the Emperors Trajan Decius (249-51) and Victorinus (268-70) (**101**). Neither expansion is certain, however, and some have interpreted the first of these as *Devana*, being derived from the placename.

Further out in the hinterland, the main period of occupation at Prestatyn appears to have ended by the late second century but at Pentre-Oakenholt the official residence underwent another phase of alterations in the early third century and lead-smelting operations apparently continued. The site at Ffrith also continued to be occupied throughout the third century.

12 Decline and resurgence (*c.*260-*c.*350)

Even as the rebuilding of the Chester fortress was progressing, events were taking place across the Channel which were to usher in a period that gradually progressed from unease and uncertainty to severe political and military instability and, for some parts of the Empire, outright catastrophe. For much of this period Britain escaped the worst effects of the storm and remained a tranquil backwater. There were repercussions, however, especially for the army. An invasion of Upper Germany and Raetia in 233 sparked off a war that lasted for three years and probably required troop reinforcements from Britain. Much of *II Augusta* was absent from its base at Caerleon after *c.*230, though elements did return after an interval as an inscription of 253-8 recording the rebuilding of the barracks of the seventh cohort demonstrates. The Twentieth is also likely to have furnished one or more vexillations for service abroad in the 230s; certainly both it and the Second *Augusta* did so slightly later, as is proven by an inscription dated to 255 recording their joint presence at Mainz. *Legio XX* also continued to supply specialist building expertise closer to home as an inscription recording its construction of facilities at Maryport during the reign of Gordian (238-44) attests. Unlike the men who spent time in Cumbria, however, those at Mainz are unlikely to have returned home. After settling scores with the Alamanni and Franks, Gallienus transferred them and the vexillation of *II Augusta* to *Sirmium* on the Danube *c.*260 to aid in the suppression of a revolt by the Pannonian army. In 260 Gallienus' general Caius Latinius Postumus rebelled and set up the secessionist empire of the '*Imperium Galliarum*' in the west. Consisting of Gaul, Spain and Britain, it lasted for 14 years until Aurelian reunited the Empire in 274.

Gallienus introduced a number of reforms, some of which, after its reunification with the Empire, would have affected the army in Britain. The first of these, as a response to the pressing need for more mobile forces to deal with the multiplying barbarian incursions, was to increase the number of cavalry units and the strength of the legionary cavalry, perhaps enlarging the latter from 120 to about 720, although the figures are far from certain. The second was the transfer of command of legions from senators to equestrians; senatorial *legati* were gradually replaced by equestrian *praefecti*. As *praefecti* were probably recruited from senior centurions and as ordinary soldiers could reach the centurionate this meant that, in theory at least, the way to legionary command was now open to the lowest ranks. This in turn had the effect of provincial governorships being held by equestrian rather than senatorial appointees.

Twelve years after Britain was rejoined to the Empire it was embroiled in the final separatist movement of the third century. In 285 the Emperor Diocletian appointed

Marcus Aurelius Valerius Maximianus as his deputy, with the title of 'Caesar' to Diocletian's 'Augustus', who was charged with responsibility for the defence of Italy and the western provinces. In addition to restoring order in the wake of the great Germanic invasion across the Rhine in 276, Maximian had to contend with swarms of Frankish and Saxon raiders who were attacking the coasts of Brittany and Gallia Belgica. To deal with the latter he appointed Marcus Aurelius Mausaeus Carausius to the position of Prefect of the British fleet. Carausius enjoyed considerable success but by the following year he was suspected of taking bribes and of not intercepting the raiders until they were returning home laden with booty which he then kept for himself. Maximian, by now elevated to the rank of co-Augustus, ordered his execution but Carausius was forewarned, declared himself emperor and seized the provinces of Britain. He could not have done this without the support of the British legions; it seems likely that the reputation for military prowess which had got him the job of Prefect of the Fleet was gained in Britain, perhaps during the successful campaign which led Diocletian to take the title of *Britannicus Maximus* in 285. Carausius also seems to have been supported by the landed gentry of Britain and northern Gaul, eager to have the defence of their interests in the hands of a competent and local general. He initiated or accelerated the construction of the so-called Saxon Shore forts along the south-east coast. There is evidence for increased military activity in Wales too during the last quarter of the third century. The forts at Loughor and Neath were reoccupied, a new walled compound was built on the shore next to the fort at Caernarfon, and a new fort of Saxon-Shore type with thick walls and projecting bastions was constructed at Cardiff. Sea-raiders were becoming a problem in the Irish Sea as well as the Channel.

In 293, Constantius Caesar, the new junior emperor in the West, retook the Gaulish part of Carausius' empire. Confidence in Carausius was dented and he was murdered by his finance minister Allectus, who now took control. Three years later a massive fleet transported Constantius' forces across the Channel. The rebels were defeated and Allectus was killed in a great battle somewhere in south-central Britain. Constantius returned to Gaul the following year and the army in Britain was put to restoring and renovating its installations throughout the North. Some of these, like the *praetorium* at Birdoswald, had 'fallen into ruin' through a lack of maintenance. A number of large new forts, such as those at Elslack, Newton Kyme and Piercebridge were also built around this time and work also probably continued on the construction of Saxon Shore forts in the south-east. To strengthen coastal defences on the west, another Saxon Shore-type fort was built at Lancaster some time after 326. The number of milestones surviving from the early fourth century points to the implementation of a major programme of road repairs alongside these other works. Constantius returned to Britain in 306 in his recently acquired capacity as the senior Augustus — Diocletian and Maximian having retired the previous year — to lead a campaign against the Highland tribes of Scotland (henceforth referred to as the Picts). Shortly after victory was won, Constantius died at his headquarters in York. His son Constantine was proclaimed Augustus, eventually becoming sole emperor in 324.

In the early years of the fourth century Diocletian's reform of the administrative structure of the Empire was extended to Britain. The overall intention was the separation of military and civil administration. This led ultimately to provincial governors, often now referred to as *praeses* or rector, becoming purely civil officials and the command of armies in their provinces being taken over by officers whose duties were solely military. The Severan subdivision of provinces was also taken further and Britain was now split into four provinces. These were Britannia Prima, Britannia Secunda, Flavia Caesariensis and Maxima Caesariensis and their respective capitals are thought to have been Cirencester, York, Lincoln and London. Chester most probably lay in Britannia Prima as this consisted of Wales and the west of England. The multiplication of provinces resulted in the introduction of a new tier of administration. A number of provinces were grouped together to form a diocese headed by a *vicarius*. He in turn was responsible to a praetorian prefect, deputy to one of the senior or junior *Augusti*, who was in charge of a prefecture consisting of a number of dioceses. London was the capital of the entire diocese of Britain which in turn formed part of the Prefecture of the Gauls.

The latest evidence we have for *legio XX Valeria Victrix* is the reference to it on coins issued by Carausius. It is not mentioned in the late Roman inventory of military forces known as the *Notitia Dignitatum* compiled *c.*395, appearing to have been lost or disbanded by that date. However, the fact that *II Augusta* is mentioned in the same document, although split into a number of vexillations stationed in Britain and on the Continent, shows that it was not cashiered for its part in the Carausian episode; the same was presumably true of the Twentieth. While there is no certainty that it was still based at Chester the contrasting situations at the *Isca* and *Deva* fortresses suggest this was indeed the case. At Caerleon, many of the major buildings were dismantled *c.*300. Although there is evidence for a subsequent military presence, the force involved was clearly much smaller than a full legion. At Chester, by contrast, all of the major buildings examined so far together with a considerable proportion of the barrack accommodation not only continued in use for many decades after this date but were also properly maintained and, in the case of the former, subjected to periodic and extensive alterations. In the absence of conclusive proof of an ongoing military role there remains an outside chance that the fortress was handed over to a civil authority in the fourth century. However, the large scale of the building works implemented around AD 300 and the lack of any major changes to the layout of the fortress argue strongly in favour of the army still being in control.

As the fourth century wore on and the need for mobile field-armies grew, it became commonplace for vexillations originally detached from legions for specific campaigns to be separated permanently from their parent units and formally constituted as legions in their own right. Thus these new legions belonging to the *comitatenses* had only a fraction of the strength of the old imperial legions, often with a complement of just 1,000 or 500 men. At the same time of course, the legions in the forces of the frontier provinces (*limitanei*) were also reduced in size by the loss of these vexillations.

In view of these empire-wide developments it would be surprising if the strength of the garrison at Chester had not been reduced in the fourth century, perhaps by the successive and permanent detachment of vexillations. There may well have been other changes. The army accepted increasing responsibility for a soldier's immediate dependants, including them in the rations allowance and providing transport for them when units had to be transferred to other postings. The wives of centurions had been living in the fortress with their husbands since the beginning of the third century, if not earlier; this privilege might have been extended to the ordinary legionary after *c*.300 with the barracks, or some of them, in effect becoming married quarters. Such a change should be detectable in the archaeology of the barracks themselves and this is something that ought to be borne in mind should the opportunity ever arise in the future to examine a significant proportion of one of these buildings.

The fortress

Beginning with the buildings other than barracks, in the *latera praetorii* both the *principia* and the large (?)store building behind it have produced evidence for refurbishment works at the beginning of the fourth century. In the former, new floors were laid in the range of rooms along the back of the *basilica*. New floors were also inserted in the rooms of the outer ranges of the building behind, those in the west range composed of sandstone rubble which included a number of reused architectural fragments. The wide doorways of these chambers opening on to the internal courtyard were narrowed further, in one case being blocked up completely, and direct communication with the exterior was provided for the first time by the insertion of a doorway in the outer wall of one room (**87**). Hearths were also now provided in these rooms, suggesting the possibility of conversion to residential use. New paving was laid in the outer courtyard at the same time, one of the stones employed being the discarded altar dedicated to Aesculapius, Hygeia and Panacea by the Greek doctor Antiochus (**128**).

Nearby, the southern half of the range along the eastern frontage of the Elliptical Building was modified by the insertion of a new longitudinal wall. The most significant change here, however, was the refurbishment of the neighbouring bath-building and the addition of a new chamber which encroached upon the south-east corner of the Elliptical Building. The whole hypocaust system was rebuilt for the second time in its history, including as before the provision of new basal floors. The *frigidarium* was converted to a

128 *Two altars dedicated by Greek doctors. On the left is the lower portion of an altar dedicated to the 'Mighty Saviour Gods' by Hermogenes. That on the right is dedicated to 'Asklepius of the gentle hands, Hygeia and Panakeia' by Antiochus. Both found within the curtilage of the large building behind the* principia, *the first in 1851, the second in 1968*

heated room by the lowering of its floor and the insertion of a hypocaust, and an entirely new heated chamber was built against the north wall of the former *frigidarium*, served by its own separate furnace (**129**). The stores compound in *insula XXI* was also modified in the early fourth century. The ranges around the courtyard at the south end of the building underwent refurbishment which included the insertion of several new partition walls and the courtyard itself was re-paved. The character of the large walled compound to the north was radically altered by the construction of an east-west wall against which timber lean-to structures were erected. In most of the buildings mentioned so far, as in many others throughout the fortress, there was a change in the material used for roof coverings, the terracotta *tegulae* and *imbrices* of earlier periods giving way to hexagonal flags of micaceous sandstone or North Welsh slate. That brick and tile manufacture was no longer practised, or at least not on any significant scale, is further indicated by the use in hypocausts from now on of monolithic *pilae* of local stone instead of the earlier brick-stack variety. This appears to have been a fairly widespread phenomenon as stone *pilae* were also used in a contemporary reconstruction of the Eaton by Tarporley villa. Portions of hypocaust incorporating stone *pilae* found immediately east of Lower Northgate Street indicate the continuing use of the *praetorium* into the fourth century.

129 North apse of caldarium *(hot room) in Elliptical Building baths*

In the *praetentura*, little is known of developments concerning the senior officers' houses but the larger of the two buildings directly opposite the *thermae* had its courtyard resurfaced on at least two occasions during the course of the fourth century. The *thermae*, however, underwent extensive modifications soon after the beginning of the fourth century (**130**). As in the Severan period, and like the *balneum* beside the Elliptical Building, the hypocaust systems throughout the entire complex were renewed. In the range of dry-heat chambers along the south side of the *basilica* the old brick-stack *pilae* were removed and replaced with stone pillars. Similarly, in the main bathing suite of steam baths, the hypocausts of both *tepidarium* and *caldarium* were reconstructed although using a different technique for each. In the *tepidarium* the *suspensura* was removed but the brick *pilae* were left in position and rubble laid down around their feet to reduce the height of the cavity; presumably this was an attempt to achieve the same temperatures with a reduced amount of fuel. The *pilae* were

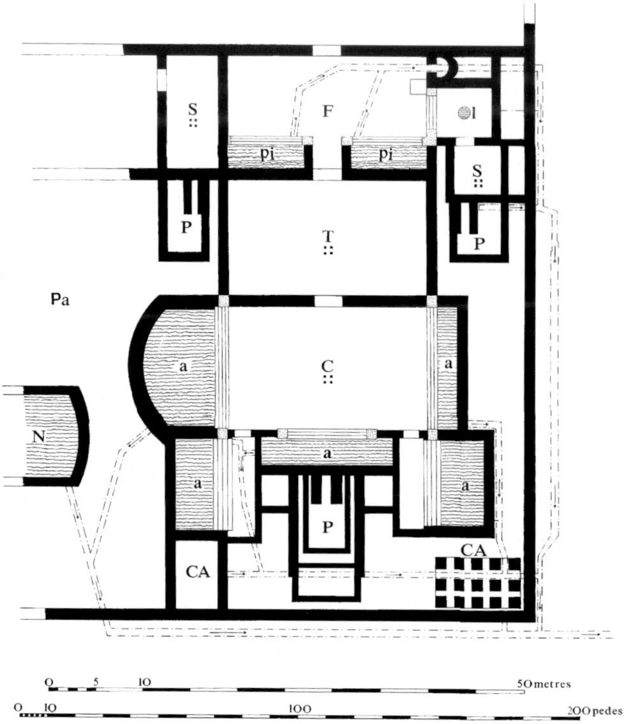

130 *Main baths-suite of fortress baths showing early fourth-century alterations. Plunge-baths and large wash-basins shown shaded.* C = caldarium *(hot and steamy bathing-hall); CA* = castellum aquae *(water reservoir); F* = frigidarium *(bathing-hall of ambient temperature); N* = natatio *(swimming-bath)*; *P* = praefurnium *(furnace-house); Pa* = palaestra *(exercise-yard); S* = sudatorium *(hot dry bathing chamber); T* = tepidarium *(bathing-hall of medium temperature); a* = alveus *(hot plunge-bath; l* = labrum *(large, raised shallow water-basin); pi* = piscina *(cold plunge-bath)*

then rebuilt and a new *suspensura* laid on top. In the *caldarium* on the other hand the brick *pilae* were removed completely before a layer of rubble derived from the demolition of the previous hypocaust and from other works shortly to be described was laid down. This was sealed with a thin layer of concrete to form the new basal floor on which stone *pilae* were placed to support the new *suspensura*. Because of the appalling circumstances under which this part of the building was examined in the 1960s it is unclear whether or not mosaics were a feature of these two halls in their ultimate form. What is clear, however, is that in its final years the *tepidarium* was floored with large slabs of slate. There were also major changes to the facilities along the south side of the *caldarium*. The apsidal *labra* recesses were demolished and in their place were created extensions to the neighbouring auxiliary furnace-chambers which were now converted into additional (cold) plunge-baths or *piscinae*. At the same time the opportunity was taken to enlarge the hot plunge-bath or *alveus* previously located between the two apses. These modifications of course required quite drastic changes to the layout of the drainage system.

With regard to the granaries, limited excavation in the 1950s disclosed the presence both in the alleyways between them and in the gaps between their internal sleeper-walls of a thick layer of broken roof tile which included six examples of the *LEG XX VV DE* stamp. There was no trace of the floor slabs which had once sat atop the sleeper-walls and so this material was taken to indicate the wholesale demolition of the granaries at some time in the last quarter of the third century. However, at no point did this material seal any of the walls; it is possible that, alternatively, it derived from a reconstruction operation in which the floor slabs had been removed and then put back at a higher level, to be robbed at some subsequent stage. A collection of rodent (mice, shrews and water vole) and bird (sparrows and pigeons) bones was found at one spot within the tile layer and a group of herring bones at another, presumably the residue from meals by birds nesting among the granary rafters. When it comes to the barrack accommodation it is hardly surprising, given the known secondment of detachments on duty elsewhere, that individual cohort groups have differing structural histories.

One point that must be clarified immediately however concerns the notion put forward some years ago that many barracks were demolished in the late third century and their sites paved over. This idea grew out of the discovery that the top of the surviving masonry of the barracks was frequently found to be level with late Roman paving. Subsequent and more detailed scrutiny of the evidence has shown however that the paving is the latest internal surfacing of the barracks and the coincidence in levels is due to post-Roman robbing of the walls down to the same horizon as the paving. That said, the life of some barracks definitely did come to an end long before the demise of the fortress. For example, on the evidence of the Northgate Brewery excavation of 1974/5 those in the right (west) half of the *retentura* (*XXVIII*) were demolished towards the close of the third century and were never rebuilt. Further south, the cohort group of barracks next to the *fabrica* in *insula XXII* were allowed to fall into a state of severe disrepair in the second half of the third century and their site was still derelict *c*.350. By contrast, the barracks in the sinistral half of the *retentura* (*XXVII*) continued to be occupied right down to the end of the Roman period, if those examined during the 1975-8 Abbey Green excavation are typical. So too did those of the first cohort and those in the cohort group next to the *thermae* (*I*). On this evidence it would appear that at least half of the legion was still present in the opening years of the fourth century.

There remains the vexed question of the fortress defences in this period. The date of certain sections of Chester's Walls has been a topic of great debate ever since large sections of the north wall were taken down and rebuilt in the late nineteenth century, when they were found to contain numerous examples of Roman tombstones and items of architectural sculpture. Some of the tombstones commemorate serving legionaries who were married and are thus probably third-century. Another is the memorial of Gabinius Felix, a soldier of *legio II Augusta*. His legion is given the title *Antoniniana* (current 213-22) and his tombstone is very weathered, facts which together indicate a date no earlier than the late third century for its reuse. Discussions centred on the date at which the wall containing this material was erected (Roman, Saxon or medieval?) and its implications for the date of those sections of the walls which were assumed to consist largely of surviving Roman masonry. Successive archaeological investigations in the twentieth century, culminating in a programme of research instigated as a consequence of extensive stabilisation works in the period 1978-90, have produced much additional information about the Roman and later defences and clarified some aspects of their development.

Investigations have shown that the primary fortress wall was executed in *opus quadratum* style and have confirmed that the upstanding sections of wall replete with projecting cornice east of the Northgate do, as long suspected, belong to this wall. The

131 Core of North Wall (east) showing material re-used from Roman buildings and tombs 1887

pronounced 'batter' of these sections, which caused some to doubt their Roman origin in the past, is not a design feature but is in fact due to the wall collapsing backwards. The length of wall between the north-east angle-tower and the first interval tower to its west underwent extensive repairs in the late nineteenth century. On being dismantled it was found to consist of masonry 10ft (3.3m) thick built of courses of large blocks, many reused, running through to the rear face and was clearly a reconstruction (**131**). The programme of Victorian rebuilding also encompassed nearly the entire section of wall running from the Northgate to the vicinity of the north-west angle and this too produced a wealth of tombstones and architectural fragments. Here however, as the recent investigations have shown, the fortress wall had been rebuilt keeping to the original width of 5ft (1.5m). It featured new facing blocks rather taller than those in the original *opus quadratum* wall at 1ft 3in vs 1ft (45 vs 30cm) and a crude attempt had been made to imitate the chamfered plinth at the base by the use of roughly squared blocks (**132, 133 & 134**). The style of the Roman masonry revealed when the city wall was breached to allow the passage of the new inner ring-road in 1964 suggests this reconstruction extended all the way to the north-west angle.

On the west side of the fortress, as on the south, only the lowest courses of the fortress wall survive owing to the removal of the superstructure in the medieval period when the defences were extended. Little examination of the southern defences has occurred, but on the west excavations have produced evidence for rebuilding of the fortress wall. A section through the defences a short distance south of the west gate in the 1950s revealed the base of a wall of standard width; included in its lowest course however was a reused cornice block, suggesting a reconstruction similar to that of the western section of the north wall. An excavation in the 1960s, this time north of the west gate, found that the wall here had been rebuilt on a base 10ft (3.3m) wide consisting of large slabs of stone including the upper portion of a tombstone with a carving of a funerary banquet scene (**135 & 136**). This rebuilding appears to have affected only that stretch of wall from the west gate as far as the first interval tower to the north.

On the east, as on the north, the medieval wall sits atop and slightly back from the Roman wall. In the sector from the Eastgate to the north-east angle (the Roman corner tower being overlain by King Charles' Tower) the massive masonry of the Roman wall is visible for long stretches rising up from the bank of earth at the foot of the walls which

132 North-west angle showing fortress wall exposed by demolition of city wall, 1964

133 (below) North Wall (west) showing external face of late Roman masonry c.*1892*

obscures its lower courses. The reason for the medieval wall being set further back is plain from the way in which the Roman wall leans outwards at a considerable angle. An excavation at Frodsham Street car park in 1966 afforded a section across the ditch system of the fortress defences and also exposed the face of the fortress wall. This was composed of blocks of the usual size and the chamfered plinth at the base of the wall was well preserved. Running up to the face, and sealing the drip-eroded channel on the projecting plinth course beneath, was a layer of compacted sandstone rubble which at the time was interpreted as the latest surfacing of the narrow berm area in front of the wall. The lower portion of this layer and a deposit of brown sand beneath it produced a few sherds of pottery no earlier than the mid-third century together with a much eroded coin of *c*.270 or later. This approximated to the same level as the top of the wall foundation which, unusually, was covered with a thin layer of dark sandy soil, a coincidence suggestive of a reconstruction of the wall itself.

South of the Eastgate the relationship between the two walls changes. The line of the medieval wall diverges rearwards from that of its Roman predecessor, increasingly towards the south; the latter is only visible near the south-east angle. An excavation on the site of

134 Close-up of late Roman masonry in facing of fortress wall at north-west angle, 1964

135 Broad foundation of rebuilt fortress wall north of west gate, 1963

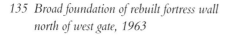

the Old Public Library in St John Street in 1988/9 revealed the reason for this situation. When the stump of the fortress wall was exposed several metres in advance of the medieval wall all of the facing blocks were found to be severely damaged, not merely cracked and fractured but actually missing sizeable portions which had split off under pressure and fallen away. Damage such as this can only have been caused by the wall falling forwards and outwards. A thick layer of debris in front of the wall, containing both intact and fragmented examples of wall facing-blocks, showed that the tilt had eventually become so great that the wall had suffered a total and cataclysmic collapse. The debris had eventually combined with the collapsed and weathered rampart behind to form a low mound. There was evidence for a subsequent refortification, possibly associated with the foundation of the Anglo-Saxon *burh c.*907, prior to the construction of the medieval wall on the existing alignment and accompanied by a massive ditch probably at some time in the later twelfth century. This sequence was much as anticipated in the light of the tilting sections of fortress wall further north. Obviously the outwards lean had occurred more rapidly in this section resulting in total collapse, the obscuration of the exact line of the wall, and the erection of its replacement on firmer ground a few metres to the rear. What came as a complete surprise, however, was the discovery that this was not the first time that the fortress wall had collapsed.

Beneath the debris formed by the fallen wall was a surfacing of sandstone brash up to 1ft (30cm) thick. Like that encountered at Frodsham Street this ran up to the face of the fortress wall and sealed the water-worn concavity on the surface of the basal plinth. Fortunately the medieval ditch was positioned further out than at Frodsham Street thus

136 Tombstone found reused in base of rebuilt fortress wall north of west gate, 1964

preserving a greater proportion of the Roman stratigraphy in the ditch area. It was clear that this material had not simply been a surfacing of the berm but had in fact extended much further out completely sealing the fortress ditch. The nature of the fill in the latter consisted of a homogeneous deposit of brown sandy soil without tip-lines of any sort, indicating that the ditch had been allowed to fill up gradually over a long period through a lack of maintenance and cleaning-out rather than being deliberately backfilled on a single occasion. That the ditch had been allowed to fill up completely to ground level is demonstrated by the fact that the brown sandy soil also covered the drip-gully on the basal plinth (**colour plate 36**). Examination of the fortress wall showed that it had been rebuilt from the level of the fourth course above the chamfered plinth. This was indicated by a change in the backing material from mortar to clay at this level and also by the presence in the uppermost surviving course of a block with mouldings imported from elsewhere as building material. Further examples of *spolia* recovered from the debris in front of the wall presumably derive from higher courses. The rebuilding of the wall and the laying down of a substantial new surfacing in front of it would seem to go together as elements of a thorough overhaul of this sector of the defences. In this overhaul either a ditch was no longer deemed necessary or a new one was provided further out from the wall, although there is no evidence for the latter. The small amount of pottery from the surfacing suggests a date in the first quarter of the fourth century.

The reason why the wall needed rebuilding was revealed by the ditch fills. Immediately below the sandstone brash surfacing and intruding into the soft fill beneath was a mass of heavy rubble which included damaged facing-blocks from the fortress wall. This could be interpreted as an underpinning for the sandstone brash surface to counteract subsidence into the soft and presumably boggy fill of the ditch. Yet the presence of facing-blocks in this material, the lengthy period of neglect which preceded the refurbishment, and the weakness of this sector as evidenced by its structural failure later, all tend to suggest that the jumbled rubble in the ditch was derived from a collapse of the fortress wall. This may have been the event which prompted the rebuilding; alternatively, the collapse might have happened during the early stages of the remedial work, either accidentally or as deliberate demolition to make it safe. Either way, the

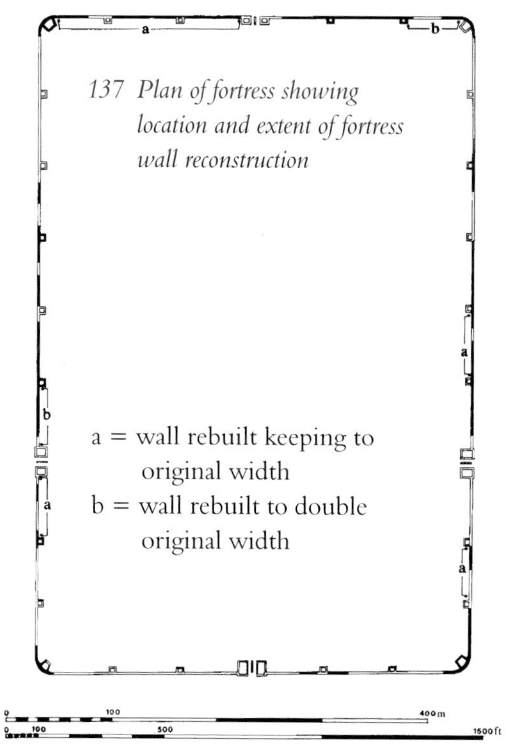

137 Plan of fortress showing location and extent of fortress wall reconstruction

a = wall rebuilt keeping to original width
b = wall rebuilt to double original width

defences had obviously been allowed to fall into a very poor state of repair. The apparent instability of this and perhaps other sections of the wall may simply have been due to the age of the structure; it had after all been standing for at least 200 years by this time. In addition, the Severan re-cutting of the ditch in front of the wall had all but removed any berm. It was certainly noticeable at St John Street how slippage of the clay lining on the inner side of the ditch had exposed the foundation beneath the basal plinth course. The visible sections of masonry north of the Eastgate demonstrate that the tendency of the fortress wall to fall outwards is not restricted to the stretch south of the Eastgate. Indeed, the very same phenomenon was found during the recent work to have affected the sole surviving length of original wall in the sector west of the Northgate. It may explain why this part of the circuit, but not that east of the Northgate which has generally tended to fall inwards, was subjected to such a fundamental reconstruction. Unfortunately, corroborative evidence of the type recovered from the fortress ditch at St John Street is unavailable as those sections of the ditch which have survived the digging of the canal in the eighteenth century remain unexplored. However, it is worth noting in passing that concentrations of heavy rubble have been seen in sections across the fortress ditch on both the west and south sides.

Thus, to summarise, there appear to have been two quite distinct phases of reconstruction of the fortress wall; one adhering to the original thickness which encompassed very extensive portions of the circuit, and a second where the wall was doubled in thickness, at least at the base, which was confined to limited stretches (**137**). Both made extensive use of tombstones, other funerary monuments and pieces of architectural sculpture. On the basis of constructional technique the second would seem to be the later and could possibly be post-Roman, even perhaps as late as the tenth century.

A coin of Constantius II as Caesar (324-37) was found in amongst the stones of the thicker rebuild east of the Northgate in 1887 but this means little in isolation. On the evidence presently available the narrower and far more extensive rebuild would appear to have been carried out at some time in the first half of the fourth century and probably closer to 300 than 350. The renewal of Chester's curtain wall is probably best understood in the context of the general overhaul of the infrastructure and defences of Britain instigated by Constantius and Constantine.

The town and its suburbs

Examination of buildings along the road heading east from the fortress has always been difficult owing to the intense commercial use of this area in modern times. It was also the scene of industrial activity, especially tanning, in the medieval period and so much of the later Roman stratigraphy has been damaged or removed. Nevertheless excavation has yielded some insights into the nature of its late Roman occupation. The strip-buildings fronting onto the side street encountered on Priory Place site were occupied throughout the third century and possibly longer. To the north, on the west corner of the junction of this street with the main road, excavations in the early 1960s showed that the stone shops erected in the early second century had been demolished at some time in the following century and replaced by a new building *c.*280 which remained in use until *c.*350. No traces of later Roman occupation were found. It has been suggested that lengths of large size ditch found at various locations in this area might belong to a system of late Roman defences erected around the eastern *canabae* but this is pure speculation.

South of the fortress what little has been seen of the more impressive buildings situated along the edge of the river cliff (**138**) suggests they were occupied until quite late in the Roman period. West of the road down to the bridge there were dramatic developments at the *mansio* towards the close of the third century. Fire destroyed a large part of the building and a number of the inhabitants perished in the flames. That there were fatalities is proven by the discovery of human bone amongst debris from the destroyed building which had been dumped into one of the wells on the site in the subsequent tidying-up operation (**139 & 140**). There was sufficient skeletal material from one individual to show that the victim was a young man in his early 20s. Any attempt he may have made to escape the burning building could have been hampered by the fact that he walked badly owing to a poorly mended fracture sustained earlier in his youth. A pot recovered from the same debris carried a scratched *graffito* which included the names of two men — Dexter and Egnatius — who appear to have been drinking friends. Perhaps one of these was the unfortunate youth. The fill also yielded nearly complete examples of samian and glass vessels (**colour plates 32 & 33**). The *mansio* was subsequently rebuilt,

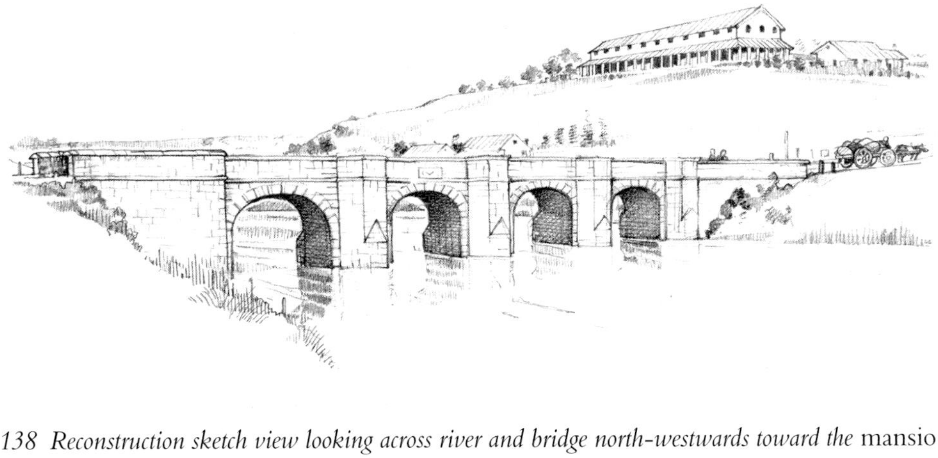

138 Reconstruction sketch view looking across river and bridge north-westwards toward the mansio

139 Top of well located in colonnaded portico along south side of mansio, *Castle Street 1976*

though now lacking a colonnaded portico along its southern frontage, and continued to be used and modified down to *c*.350 when part or all of it was demolished and the site vacated.

Ceramic and numismatic evidence indicate continued occupation of the more upmarket buildings lying west of the fortress down to at least the middle of the fourth century, their ruins still being detectable as sources of building stone for the various religious houses established in the area in the medieval period. The Watergate Baths was certainly still functioning in the fourth century and in one of the rooms examined on the Sedan House site in 1989 a new brick floor in herringbone pattern was laid down in this period (**118**).

There was a gradual rise in sea level in the late Roman period, perhaps by as much as 1m. How this might have affected the harbour at Chester is unknown. It would presumably have made it easier for ships to reach and use the port although it might also have required modifications to the actual facilities. One definite disadvantage is that it might well have facilitated access up river estuaries by the seaborne raiding parties whose activities increased during the fourth century. It is tempting to see the fire at the *mansio* as an early example of the sort of sneak attack which they carried out, but it is far more likely that this was an accidental conflagration. Nonetheless, the threat was a very real one as both the reinforcement of the western coastal defences and events later in the century demonstrate. There would very probably have been increased naval activity at Chester itself in the fourth century. No new coastal forts were built within 60 miles of it and so presumably it continued as the principal naval base for the Liverpool Bay area. To counteract the small, swift ships of the raiders new tactics had to be adopted. Small scouting vessels were used to spot the enemy, either intercepting them directly or signalling the enemy's position to larger ships which then took up the pursuit. The historian Vegetius has left us a graphic description of these vessels:

Associated with the larger vessels are scouting skiffs, which have around twenty oars on each side, and which the Britons call *Picati*. These are intended to locate and at times intercept the passage of enemy ships and to discover by observation their arrival or plans. However, to prevent these scout vessels being easily visible through the brightness of their appearance, their sails and rigging are dyed the colour of the sea, and even the pitch with which the ships are ordinarily daubed is made that colour. The sailors and marines wear sea-green clothing so that as they go about their scouting they may escape detection the more easily not only by night but also by day.

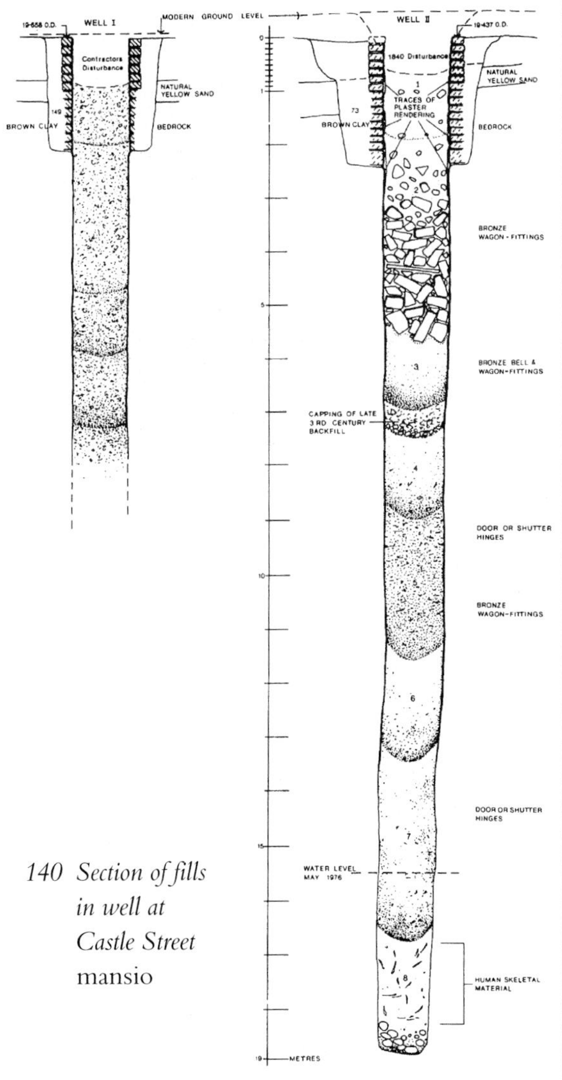

140 Section of fills in well at Castle Street mansio

At the outlying settlement of Saltney the pottery recovered points to occupation continuing into the fourth century. Heronbridge presents a similar picture. While some buildings east of the main road appear to have become obsolete by *c.*300, with their sites remaining vacant thereafter, coins and pottery from the area generally indicate occupation lasting until at least the middle of the fourth century. More substantial evidence comes from the west side of the road where several new buildings were constructed at the beginning of the fourth century including one with rooms equipped with hypocausts. This general picture of prosperity and continued investment in property, typical of Britain as a whole in the first half of the fourth century, is also reflected further out in the countryside by the villa at Eaton by Tarporley which was completely rebuilt and improved around 300 and continued to be occupied beyond *c.*370.

13 Twilight and transformation: from *Deva Victrix* to *Legacaestir* (*c*.350-*c*.650)

In 350 there was an uprising against the unpopular Constans, emperor in the West, and his throne was seized by an officer named Magnentius. The following year hostilities broke out with Constantius II, emperor in the East, which culminated in a battle near *Mursa Major* in Lower Pannonia. Magnentius was defeated and his forces reportedly lost 24,000 men. The victorious side in fact lost even more than this with 30,000 dead. Many of the recruits to Magnentius' cause came from Gaul, but vexillations from Britain are also likely to have been involved. The losses could not be replaced, at least in the short term, and there is numismatic evidence for the final withdrawal of garrisons from a number of Welsh forts at this time. Indeed, it may have been now rather than under the later usurper Magnus Maximus that the *Seguntienses*, the former garrison of *Segontium* (Caernarfon) were transferred to the Continent where they appear in the *Notitia Dignitatum* listed under regiments of the *auxilia palatina*. The legion at Chester is unlikely to have remained unaffected by these events. Magnentius survived for another two years but eventually committed suicide and with Constantius' regain of control over the West there came savage reprisals against his supporters in Britain.

The 360s saw increasingly successful attacks by Picts, Scots and Attacotti — the last two based in Ireland — on the frontier region of Hadrian's Wall and along the western seaboard, suggesting that army numbers in Britain had still not been made good after the losses at *Mursa*. These culminated in the *barbarica conspiratio* of late 367 when a concerted attack overran or by-passed Hadrian's Wall. The Count of the Saxon Shore, the *Comes Litoris Saxonici*, was killed and the *Dux Britanniarum*, the Duke or general in charge of the British provinces' frontier forces, was besieged or captured. It took two years to retrieve the situation during which time bands of raiders, along with large numbers of Roman deserters, roamed the countryside looking for plunder before returning home. Several commanders were sent by the western emperor Valentinian (364-75) but real success was not achieved until the elder Theodosius, whose son was to become the Emperor Theodosius I (379-95), was despatched to Britain in 369 accompanied by four regiments of *comitatenses*. Order was restored, the northern frontier reconstructed and there is a hint of punitive raids far into enemy territory. Closer to home, attention was paid to the defences of north-west Wales. The fort at Caerhun was brought back into commission for a time, *Segontium* continued to be held and it was probably now that the late Roman fort at Caer Gybi (Holyhead) was constructed, along with a stone watch-tower on Holyhead Mountain. The occurrence of late Roman material at hilltop sites along the North Wales

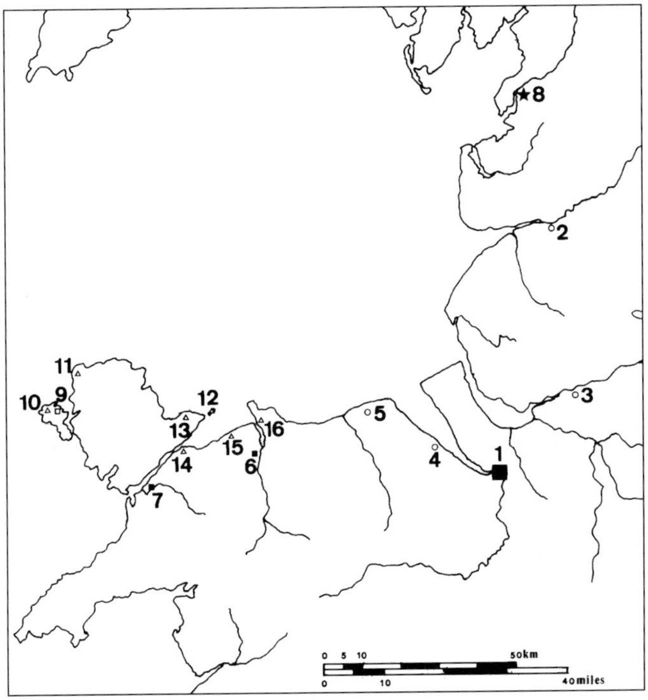

141 Map of putative late Roman coastal defence system for Liverpool Bay and Morecambe Bay area. Legionary fortress: *1 Chester.* Existing civil ports: *2 Walton le Dale, 3 Wilderspool, 4 Pentre, 5 Prestatyn.* Existing forts with harbours: *6 Caerhun, 7 Caernarfon* New 'Saxon Shore' style forts with bastions: *8 Lancaster.* New walled compounds: *9 Caer Gybi.* New lookout posts/signal towers: *10 Holyhead Mountain, 11 Pen Bryn yr Eglwys (Carmel Head), 12 Ynys Seriol, 13 Din Silwy, 14 Bangor, 15 Braich yr Ddinas, 16 Deganwy Castle*

coast hints at the possibility of the creation of a more extensive signalling system designed to warn of the approach of sea-raiders (**141**). As will be seen shortly, there is also evidence of renewed activity at Chester in this period.

In 383, Magnus Maximus, who probably held the post of *Dux Britanniarum*, launched a bid for the purple and crossed to Gaul with his forces apparently enhanced by many volunteers. With the murder of Gratian, emperor in the West, Maximus gained control of Gaul and Spain and set up his capital at Trier. His rule came to an end five years later when he attempted to invade Italy and was defeated and killed by the forces of Theodosius I. The army in Britain was depleted further by these events and attacks by the Picts, Scots and Saxons continued. Stilicho, the Vandal general who was the power behind the throne of the young emperor Honorius (395-423), sent an expedition to Britain *c*.396 and the fight was carried to the enemy by means which included naval action in the Irish Sea. Security was achieved but only a few years later, in 402 (and perhaps again in 405/6), Stilicho was forced to withdraw further troops from Britain for the defence of Italy.

Late in 406, hordes of Alans, Sueves and Vandals crossed the frozen Rhine and invaded Gaul. The Roman forces were too weak to resist and the army in Britain — as the historian Zosimus tells us — became alarmed lest the barbarians should cross the Channel. Stilicho was too busy to send any help and the situation could only be saved by intervention from Britain. Some were of the opinion that the defence of Britain should come first but others realised that its defence was inseparable from that of Gaul. The latter group won the day and the choice of leader fell on Constantine III. By the end of 407 the Rhine frontier was being restored and Gaul was under the control of Constantine after forces loyal to Honorius had been defeated. The following year Spain too came under his sway. In 408, however, Britain was subjected to serious attack by Saxons and others. The enemy were repulsed but, fed up with having their security compromised by adventurous usurpers, the civic authorities acted together to expel Constantine's officials and appointed their own. Contact appears to have been made with Honorius in 410 which resulted in the famous 'Rescript' telling the cities of Britain to look to their own defence. By the following year Honorius' forces had regained the initiative and before the year was over, Constantine's life had been ended by his own hand. However, Roman forces never crossed the Channel again and to all intents and purposes Britain had ceased to be part of the Roman Empire.

While we still have much to learn about events at Chester in the second half of the fourth century, certain facts are clear. Most of the major buildings were still standing and being maintained well after 350. Refloorings and resurfacings continued to be effected in the large store building behind the *principia* for long after the refurbishment works of *c*.300. In the *principia* itself the rooms at the rear of the *basilica* were refloored on a number of occasions in the fourth century, and that next to the *aedes* on the west was at some stage converted into a secondary shrine. Upon excavation in 1969 it was found that at least five column capitals and bases had been reused as altar bases by turning them upside down (**142**). The Elliptical Building and adjacent baths also underwent further modification later on in the fourth century and here the dating evidence was capable of greater accuracy. A new partition wall was inserted into the southern half of the street range along the eastern frontage of the Elliptical Building while the changes to the baths were more extensive. The colonnaded portico down the east side of the baths was now enclosed and became an ante-chamber to the *apodyterium*. A new doorway giving access to the latter was inserted at the north end of its east wall and from the mortar bedding for its timber door sill came no fewer than 24 coins dating to the joint reign of the Emperors Valens and Valentinian I (364-75). Whether the result of an accidental loss or some form of deliberate votive offering is unclear. Other alterations most likely instituted at the same time included yet another rebuild of the hypocaust system throughout the *tepidarium* and *caldarium*, part of the *suspensura* in the latter found still intact when excavated in 1969, the provision of a new furnace for the *frigidarium* converted into a heated chamber half a century earlier, and the erection of structures of unknown form across part of the yard west of the furnace-house. In the walled compound at the north end of the building in *insula XXI* evidence for specialised metal-working was found during the 1978-82 excavations in the form of gold-working crucibles. This perhaps included the melting down of gold coinage as a gold *solidus* of the Emperor Magnentius was found nearby (**colour plate 37**). In the *praetentura*, the *thermae* underwent a further round of alterations

142 Column capitals reused as altar/statue bases in headquarters building, Old Market Hall Site, Phase V, 1969

in the later fourth century. The extra plunge-baths previously inserted along the south side of the *caldarium* were now abolished and filled in. The large building opposite the *thermae* continued to have its courtyard repaired and resurfaced throughout the fourth century, while sections of the colonnaded portico around it were enclosed by the insertion of new masonry.

As to the barracks, most if not all of those occupied in the early fourth century appear to have continued in use after 350 though, for reasons already described, it is impossible to know how many men each accommodated. Like all the other buildings in the fortress, the barracks were not demolished but were ultimately simply abandoned and left to decay.

In view of the coin evidence from the baths next to the Elliptical Building, the latest detectable programme of building works in the fortress can probably be attributed to the overhaul of army installations implemented by the elder Theodosius *c.*370. This could additionally have included the rebuilding to double the original width of localised sections of the curtain wall. The strength of the garrison must have been depleted as a consequence of the Magnentius episode and the events leading up to Theodosius' expedition presumably also had an effect. Assuming that it was still based at Chester, *legio XX* is likely to have made a significant contribution to the forces which Magnus Maximus took to the Continent in 383/4. Coins of Theodosius I (379-95) and of Arcadius (395-408) occur both within and outside the fortress but issues of Honorius are absent, suggesting that there was still a garrison here in the years immediately following the end of Maximus' empire but not beyond *c.*400. The *Notitia Dignitatum*, compiled *c.*395, is of no help in determining if this was a remnant of the Twentieth or some other unit as it lists no garrison for Chester. The *Notitia* in fact fails to mention any military units for the whole of Wales. Either all garrisons had been withdrawn and the defence of these areas placed in the hands of local militias or the document is incomplete. If the former, then the end of *Deva* as an outpost of the Roman Army came in the early-mid 390s.

What exactly was happening at Chester during the period of 200 years which saw its transition from Roman *Deva Victrix* to Anglo-Saxon *Legacaestir* is still very much a mystery.

The removal of the remaining garrison and their families, followed by the breakdown of the monetary economy by *c*.425 and gradually that of the other strands of the provincial infrastructure, no doubt had its effects upon *Deva* and its inhabitants, but the population certainly did not simply disperse into the surrounding countryside overnight. It probably possessed a residual importance as a commercial centre and, equipped with serviceable fortifications which only a modest defence force could still make effective, would have continued to provide a place of safety and security. Indeed, it may well have persisted as the principal military and administrative centre of the region, perhaps eventually becoming the capital of one of the sub-kingdoms of which the kingdom of Powys was comprised. For a while, everyday life probably went on much the same.

There are hints that Chester may have become an ecclesiastical centre of some importance in this period. Christianity was already well established throughout much of Britain by the late fourth century and even as early as 314 each of the four British provinces had been able to send representatives to the Council of Arles. It was the belief of medieval chroniclers that the Church of Saints Peter and Paul, which was already of high antiquity when the relics of St Werburgh were transferred to it in 874 and was later to become the site of the cathedral, was a Roman foundation. There is no proof of this but the possibility is strengthened, as is that of Chester's continued existence as a place of some considerable importance throughout the 'Dark Ages', by its being chosen as the location for a synod of the British church *c*.601. Called to discuss Augustine of Canterbury's proposals for the reform of the British church, this was attended by no fewer than seven bishops and was chaired by Dinoot, abbot of the monastery at Bangor-on-Dee. The sizeable retinues which undoubtedly accompanied the delegates and the statement in the sources that the event was attended by 'many very learned men, who came mainly from the most famous monastery which the English call *Bancornaburg* (Bangor-on-Dee)' implies that the community in Chester was still capable of organising and providing the requisite facilities for such an important conference.

Another indication of the survival of a British Christian community throughout this period is the place-name Eccleston, derived from the Latin *ecclesia* — a 'congregation' or 'church' — via Primitive Welsh *egles* (Modern Welsh *eglwys*) and Old English *tun* — a 'settlement'. The village in question lies less than 1km south of the Roman site at Heronbridge and might perhaps have originated as a result of the latter's population relocating at some time in the fifth century. Heronbridge itself possesses two features which have often been linked with this general period. The best known, because it still forms a prominent landmark today, is a crescent-shaped earthwork overlying that portion of the Roman settlement situated between the main road and the Dee. Enclosing an area of about 14 acres (6ha) the earthwork has been proved to be defensive in nature, consisting originally of a rampart about 20ft (6m) wide accompanied by a ditch approximately 23ft (7m) wide and 10ft (3.3m) deep. Although undated, it has been tentatively interpreted as a bridgehead fort established by Aethelfrith of Northumbria following his defeat of the forces of the British kingdoms of Powys and Gwynedd at the Battle of Chester *c*.613. As Bede relates it, this battle was fought at '*civitas Legionum* ('City of the Legions') which the English call *Legacaestir* but which the British more correctly call *Carlegion*'. Inspiration for this suggestion came partly from the second feature, a cemetery containing exclusively

143 Cattle jaw-bones lying on courtyard paving in building west of Bridge Street, 30 Bridge Street 1987

male burials with many of the skeletons exhibiting obvious signs of a violent death. The burials, clearly post-dating the Roman settlement and many actually overlain by the earthwork, were seen as casualties from this battle. Alternatively, they might derive from the legendary ninth battle fought by Arthur *c*.485 at a place described as '*in urbe Legionis*' which could just as easily be Chester as Caerleon.

The stratigraphic evidence relating to this transitional period in Chester's development is limited in its usefulness, providing information about the eventual demise of the Roman buildings but nothing at all about any new building activity. There is of course the additional problem in this period of a paucity of artefacts as both coinage and pottery ceased to be used soon after 400. Timber buildings discovered on many sites throughout the fortress during excavations in the 1970s and '80s and tentatively assigned to the late fourth or fifth century are now, in the light of further work, seen actually to belong to the Anglo-Scandinavian town of the tenth and eleventh centuries. Additionally, subsequent large-scale excavations in the centre of the fortress have shown that there was no extensive complex of sub-Roman timber buildings like those found at Wroxeter or, if there were, then it was not in this part of the fortress. In both the compound building north of the Elliptical Building and the larger of the two buildings opposite the *thermae*, the courtyards gradually became covered with earth containing large amounts of animal bone. In the latter, this included complete cattle jaw and leg bones suggesting the possibility that carcasses were actually being butchered on the spot (**143**). Overlying the latest Roman surfaces on a number of sites and sealed by the first recognisable Anglo-Saxon occupation is a deposit up to 1ft 6in (45cm) thick referred to as the 'dark earth' layer, a phenomenon encountered at many urban centres, not just Chester. Although its generation has been ascribed to activities varying in detail there is general agreement that they are all in some way connected with agricultural, horticultural or pastoral farming activities. In some cases soil may have been imported from surrounding areas, in others the dark earth seems to have been formed by the working over of debris from Roman buildings and their accompanying occupation deposits. Whichever, its existence implies occupation, albeit probably of a low density.

144 Fortress baths showing sub-Roman 'dark earth' layer over tepidarium *floor, Newgate/Pepper Street Site 1964*

As mentioned above, in the *tepidarium* of the *thermae* a 1ft (30cm) thick layer of earth containing charcoal and fragmented animal bone accumulated over its floor, implying that parts of this massive building were now turned over to residential purposes (**144**). Parts of other fortress buildings also probably continued in use for many decades until they were no longer required or the skills to repair and maintain them vanished. What interval passed before the roofing vaults of the *thermae* failed is unknown but certainly large portions of this building survived above ground well into the medieval period and so could, in theory at least, have continued in use for several centuries. This would also have been true of the *principia* and it is tempting to see it as the venue for the synod of 601. In both the *principia* and the *thermae* the columns of the *basilica* were found lying where they had fallen. This might indicate a final structural collapse after long neglect or it may be that they were toppled as part of the demolition process in the early medieval period and left where they fell because the stone-robbers had no use for them. By contrast, smaller columns were sometimes reused, as happened at the cathedral where examples can be seen incorporated into the upper part of the north transept of the original Norman church.

Gradual, piecemeal collapse would have been the inevitable fate of many fortress buildings, alongside the eventual breakdown of the water-supply and drainage systems, due to a lack of maintenance and the disappearance of the knowledge of how to repair them. It is sobering indeed to reflect that it was to be another 1,500 years before Chester again enjoyed the benefits of proper sanitation, let alone any form of central heating. Apart from the odd section of the fortress wall that collapsed, like that south of the east gate (**145**), the defences appear to have survived substantially intact, eventually undergoing minor repairs with the creation of a fortified *burh* in 907. Because of their extremely robust construction some buildings, such as the *thermae*, would have remained prominent features of the townscape for a very long time. As the Mercian *burh* developed into the Anglo-Scandinavian town, the frontages of the major Roman streets were cleared of ruins for, being a community whose existence depended largely on trade, these areas contained the most commercially desirable building plots. The further development of Chester in the century or so after the Conquest saw the building of the castle, the extension and refurbishment of the city walls, the expansion in the number and size of churches and

145 *Face of fortress wall fractured by post-Roman outwards collapse, St John Street 1989*

monasteries, and the erection of many impressive merchants' houses — works which in combination engendered a vast upsurge in demand for building stone. It was now that the final elements of Roman buildings remaining above ground were demolished and the rubble gone through for reusable stone, like the bones of a noble beast being picked over by scavengers. Much of the stone from the central buildings was incorporated into the fabric of the cathedral and its outbuildings, material from the Watergate Baths and superior residences of the western suburb was recycled into the series of medieval religious houses built over their remains, and a large proportion of the amphitheatre's masonry was transformed into the superstructure of St John's Church and that of the neighbouring monastery of St Mary. Thus were the works of Imperial Rome appropriated by the Church of Rome. Of the monuments erected by those who followed the eagle, the east gate was one of very few that continued to stand for centuries to come, the tramp of legionaries' feet and the shrill clangour of trumpets to which its arches had once resounded surviving only as a faint echo embedded deep in the grain of its stones.

14 *Deva* past and Chester future

The large number of excavations carried out over the last 40 years has produced a vast amount of information which has revolutionised our knowledge, understanding and perceptions of Roman Chester. That the investigations undertaken at the beginning of that period should have been far better resourced, and the consideration given to the preservation of remains *in situ* far greater, is undeniable. However, when the wholesale destruction of archaeological remains without any record whatsoever that occurred in other historic towns and cities both in the 1960s and also far more recently is considered, Chester is perhaps less deserving of criticism than many.

On both the national and the local scene recent years have seen the pendulum swing in the opposite direction, with the widespread adoption of the 'leave it undisturbed if at all possible' approach enshrined in PPG 16. In general terms, this is the correct policy as archaeological deposits are of course finite and irreplaceable and should not be disturbed, even in the quest for greater knowledge, without full and proper assessment of all the considerations involved. Yet, just like many other forms of 'resource' or asset, part has to be put to use for the benefit of the whole and in the case of archaeology that means active investigation. This should be done not just for academic research, worthy and justifiable though that is, but also to maintain and stimulate public interest and support. This is something that has become increasingly difficult over the last decade as research excavation has been squeezed out by the pressures of commercially financed archaeology to enable development on the one hand and the withdrawal of central government funding for archaeology on the other. Yet without the new information produced by active and targeted research our understanding of the past will simply stagnate and the capability for rigorous intellectual analysis will atrophy. Deprived of the excitement generated by new discoveries other than those unearthed as a consequence of commercial television programmes, public interest will decline, their understanding and support will diminish, and then it is but a short step to protective legislation for a neglected resource being quietly repealed.

It used to be the case that the general public were denied access to the physical remains of their past because they were simply destroyed as fast as they were uncovered. Now they are prevented because there are no funds for research investigation. Developer-funded excavations are carried out under commercial contract stipulations of maximum speed (and sometimes secrecy) as well as planning conditions, restricting investigation to 'key-hole' archaeology, a mechanical and unrewarding operation for those involved, with results impossible to interpret in any wider sense. For the health of the discipline (I prefer this term to profession), those involved in it, and society in general, the means of carrying out research excavations must be found. Perhaps, as the evidence from a number of places including Chester suggests, the long-established local archaeological societies still have a substantive contribution to make in this direction, mounting projects conducted by informed lay people with the aid of academic expertise which bridge the gap between amateur and professional. Similarly, those involved in implementing the policies set out in PPG 16 should, as far as possible, take a more flexible and broader view of the archaeological requirements, including research questions to be addressed, when formulating briefs for investigations undertaken as a requirement of planning permission. There is in addition a pressing need for the ever-growing mass of data produced in a piecemeal fashion in recent years to be collated and analysed so that its value is not wasted. It is also sadly still the case that there are many local authorities who have yet to appreciate the value of the contribution which their archaeological heritage can make, not only to the cultural life of their community but also to its economic vitality.

Returning to the specific case of Roman Chester, there are many questions still to be resolved. Those of a general nature will and can only be answered by the acquisition, necessarily gradual, of information from various parts of the settlement. Although, barring disaster, there are many parts of the historic core of the city which will never become available for excavation owing to the presence of historic buildings, there are others where information could be recovered by targeted research projects if the necessary permissions and resources were to become available. A selection is offered below.

i) Barrack-blocks are the basic source of information about the intensity of military occupation and the everyday life of the ordinary legionary. Since Newstead & Droop's excavation of those in the sinistral half of the *retentura* in the 1920s, only restricted portions of others have been examined. Many have been destroyed but those assumed to occupy *insula* IV in the south-west corner of the *praetentura*, largely unencumbered by modern buildings, afford a potential opportunity.

ii) Information about the harbour, its associated installations and river levels is desperately needed. Given the depth of accumulated deposits and the problems of deep excavation this might best be obtained by sediment core sampling along with a ground penetrating radar survey.

iii) In many ways inseparable from the previous item is the date and true purpose of the so-called 'quay wall'. Here, excavation is the only solution for determining whether this was a harbour facility or a defensive structure. Improved conservation and display is also urgently needed.

iv) Heronbridge is one of the few examples of the outer of the two civil settlements found in close proximity to legionary fortresses which is not buried beneath modern settlement. It thus has the potential, should it prove possible to undertake a medium to long-term research project, to make a significant contribution to the study and understanding of this dual-settlement phenomenon. In addition to elucidating the history, extent and character of the settlement, such a project might answer the question of whether or not there was a river crossing at this location.

An excavation which not only produces information but also enables the placing on permanent display of archaeological remains obviously possesses enormous additional benefits in educational, tourism and cultural terms. There are three such potential opportunities as far as Roman Chester is concerned, all of which however would be contentious to a greater or lesser degree.

i) The first and most obvious is the exposure of the unexcavated half of the amphitheatre. This is something which the City Council recently committed itself to trying to achieve at some point, although the situation is complicated by the fact that the building which overlies part of it — Dee House — has Grade II listed status. Permission for demolition of the latter was actually granted in 1990 to facilitate the excavation of the amphitheatre and the construction of a new Roman Centre, but the businessman behind the scheme could not find the necessary financial guarantors. When British Telecom sold the site a few years later the older portion of Dee House was bought by the City Council and a 1930s extension to the rear was purchased by a property developer. The latter obtained planning permission for an office block, eventually modified to allow the building of a county court which was erected despite great public opposition. It is much to be hoped that one day this travesty will be rectified and the entire amphitheatre exposed so that this most public of public buildings can be restored to the people.

ii) The second concerns the only surviving substantial portion of the fortress baths. This is contained in the plot of land on the north side of Feathers Lane and to the rear of the Bridge Street Row properties. Evaluation excavations in 1988 revealed masonry still standing to a height of at least 10ft (3.3m) with the possibility in addition of intact portions of hypocaust. A development proposal which would have seen these remains excavated and placed on permanent display in a purpose-built basement was in the planning stages but the scheme had to be abandoned when some nineteenth-century buildings standing on part of the area were listed. Should views on the value of the latter change, resulting in their de-listing, then this would make a superb project.

iii) The third possibility, one thankfully that would not require the demolition of listed buildings, involves the barracks in the north-east corner of the fortress excavated in the early decades of the twentieth century. Those investigations and the landscaping carried out afterwards to form a playing field may well have removed all but the lowest deposits and features. However, the objective here would not primarily be research excavation but the reconstruction on their actual site of one or more pairs of barrack blocks using evidence recovered from barracks throughout the fortress. This would enable the public to walk around full-size replicas of the living quarters of the ordinary legionary and the centurion, while the location — beside the Walls on one of the most heavily used 'tourist trails' — is ideal for attracting a large number of visitors.

Further reading

Roman Chester and Cheshire

Much of the new information on which this account is based is contained in the archives of Chester Archaeology and includes many draft reports awaiting publication. Interim reports on many excavations of the last 30 years, as well as articles on specific aspects of Roman Chester, have appeared in volumes of the *Journal of the Chester Archaeological Society* where also, in earlier volumes, can be found full accounts of the investigations carried out by Newstead and his successors. The report on the excavation of the amphitheatre can be found in Volume 105 of *Archaeologia*, a journal published by the Society of Antiquaries of London. Excavation reports on Roman and related topics already published by Chester Archaeology are as follows:

LeQuesne, C. 1999: *Excavations at Chester. The Roman and Later Defences Part 1*
Mason, D.J.P. 2001: *The Roman Elliptical Building at Chester: An Image of the Roman World*
Mason, D.J.P. 1980: *Excavations at Chester. 11-15 Castle Street and Neighbouring Sites 1974-8: A Possible Roman Posting-House (Mansio)*
Ward, S. 1988: *Excavations at Chester. 12 Watergate Street 1985: Roman Headquarters Building to Medieval Row*
Ward, S. & Strickland, T.J. 1978: *Chester Excavations. Northgate Brewery 1974-5: A Roman Centurion's Quarters & Barrack*
Thompson, F.H. 1965: *Roman Cheshire*
Watkin, W.T. 1974: *Roman Cheshire* (reprint)

The Roman Army and its Fortresses

Bidwell, P.T. 1979: *The Legionary Bath-house and Basilica and Forum at Exeter*
Bohec, le Y. 1994: *The Roman Imperial Army*
Boon, G.C. 1987: *The Legionary Fortress of Caerleon — Isca*
Brewer, R.J. (ed) 2000: *Roman Fortresses and Their Legions*
Davies, R. 1989: *Service in the Roman Army* (eds. Breeze, D. & Maxwell, V.)
Dixon, K.R. & Southern, P. 1992: *The Roman Cavalry*
Johnson, A. 1983: *Roman Forts*
Keppie, L. 1984: *The Making of the Roman Army*
Marsden, E.W. 1969: *Greek and Roman Artillery*
Ottaway, P. 1993: *Roman York*
Parker, H.M.D. 1980: *The Roman Legions* (reprint)
Peddie, J. 1994: *The Roman War Machine*
Pitts, L.F. & St Joseph, J.K. 1985: *Inchtuthil. The Roman Legionary Fortress*
Roth, P.R. 1999: *The Logistics of the Roman Army at War*
Shirley, E.A.M. 2000: *The Construction of the Roman Legionary Fortress at Inchtuthil*
Southern, P. & Dixon, K.R. 1996: *The Late Roman Army*
Watson, G.R. 1969: *The Roman Soldier*
Webster, G. 1985: *The Roman Imperial Army of the First and Second Centuries A.D*
Zienkiewicz, J.D. 1986: *The Legionary Fortress Baths at Caerleon* (2 vols)

The Roman Navy and the *Classis Britannica*

Johnson, S. 1976: *The Roman Forts of the Saxon Shore*
Philp, B. 1981: *The Excavation of the Roman Forts of the Classis Britannica at Dover*
Starr, C.G. 1993: *The Roman Imperial Navy 31 BC-AD 324* (reprint)

Roman Britain

Esmonde Cleary, A.S. 1989: *The Ending of Roman Britain*
Frere, S.S. 1987: *Britannia. A History of Roman Britain* (revised edition)
Hanson, W.S. 1987: *Agricola and the Conquest of the North*

Henig, M. 1984: *Religion in Roman Britain*
Johnson, S. 1980: *Later Roman Britain*
Jones, B. & Mattingly, D. 1990: *An Atlas of Roman Britain*
Salway, P. 1981: *Roman Britain*
Webster, G. (ed) 1988: *Fortress into City: The Consolidation of Roman Britain, First Century AD*
White, R. & Barker, P. 1998: *Wroxeter. The Life and Death of a Roman City*

Other

Hodge, A.T. 1992: *Roman Aqueducts and Water Supply*
Levick, B. 1999: *Vespasian*
Luttwak, E. 1976: *The Grand Strategy of the Roman Empire*
Mocsy, A. 1974: *Pannonia and Upper Moesia*
Nicolet, C. 1991: *Space, Geography and Politics in the Early Roman Empire*
Wellesley, K. 2000: *The Year of the Four Emperors* (3rd ed.)
Whittaker, C.R. 1994: *Frontiers of the Roman Empire.*

Index

PEOPLE OF ROMAN CHESTER MENTIONED IN THE TEXT